THE RISE OF THE STYLIST

THE RISE OF THE STYLIST

Subculture, Style and the Fashion Image in London 1980–1990

Philip Clarke

BLOOMSBURY VISUAL ARTS
LONDON • NEW YORK • OXFORD • NEW DELHI • SYDNEY

BLOOMSBURY VISUAL ARTS
Bloomsbury Publishing Plc
50 Bedford Square, London, WC1B 3DP, UK
1385 Broadway, New York, NY 10018, USA
29 Earlsfort Terrace, Dublin 2, Ireland

BLOOMSBURY, BLOOMSBURY VISUAL ARTS and the Diana logo are
trademarks of Bloomsbury Publishing Plc
First published in Great Britain 2024

Cover design by Adriana Brioso
Cover image © Peter Paul Hartnett, The Hartnett Archive/Camera Press

A catalogue record for this book is available from the British Library.

A catalog record for this book is available from the Library of Congress.

ISBN: HB: 978-1-3503-0166-5
ePDF: 978-1-3503-0167-2
eBook: 978-1-3503-0168-9

Typeset by RefineCatch Limited, Bungay, Suffolk
Printed and bound in Great Britain

To find out more about our authors and books visit www.bloomsbury.com
and sign up for our newsletters.

CONTENTS

PLATES

ACKNOWLEDGEMENTS

Many people have assisted in the research, development and writing of this book. I would particularly like to thank Alistair O'Neill and Anne Burke for their support throughout the project, and Anne Massey and Paolo Volonté for their contribution in its early stages. I'd like to thank my interviewees, both for taking the time to speak to me, and for checking quotes and adding details when the book was being finalized. Mitzi Lorenz and Caryn Franklin were especially generous in sharing contacts and providing introductions to participants. Thanks also to the Research Degrees team at Middlesex University and the Fashion Programme at Central Saint Martins, for academic and financial support at various stages, to Liam Leslie for photographing the magazine pages, and to Marketa Uhlirova for her scrutiny and encouragement in the final few months.

PREFACE

When I first started teaching fashion courses, I was surprised to find a relative dearth of academic literature on the stylist as a cultural producer. This seemed all the more striking when compared with the profusion of texts on the fashion designer. The terms 'styling' or 'fashion styling' were cropping up in the titles of many degree-level courses in the United Kingdom and overseas, and an element of styling was being included in many fashion curricula – from the Instituto Marangoni to Middlesex University, De Montfort University and London College of Fashion. This book grows out of my personal experience in the field, as well as my academic interests. I worked for several years as a freelance stylist and writer after graduating from art college and, although I had done mainly interior styling work, in 2008 I was encouraged to apply for a teaching role on a new suite of fashion and styling courses at Solent University in Southampton. In 2013 I joined Middlesex University as the programme leader of BA Fashion Communication and Styling, and in the same year submitted a proposal for a doctoral research project, which aimed to address this lack of theoretical consideration of fashion styling.

In 2019 I became the Course Leader of BA Fashion Communication at Central Saint Martins, overseeing three pathways covering journalism, history and theory, and visual communication. The original Fashion Communication and Promotion (FCP) pathway, introduced in 1974, was one of the first courses to acknowledge fashion media as a valid career specialism. The curriculum has retained a broad, collaborative focus, enabling students to explore a range of media and roles through practice-based projects, underpinned with a common core of cultural studies and fashion history. The course has evolved and expanded significantly, very much in line with the development of a more diverse range of fashion communication roles in the fashion industry and beyond. Although it was introduced at a time when styling was a relatively unknown occupation, the course has since been responsible for launching the careers of high-profile stylists as well as others who have fulfilled more discreet, in-house roles within fashion businesses. However, much like those I interviewed for this book, there are also many contemporary fashion stylists who come from fashion design backgrounds. This is often reflected in certain styling practices but also in the way stylists are perceived and how they view their own creative practice and occupation.

Since I started my PhD in 2013, the range of literature discussing styling has expanded and I acknowledge, and respond to, new research in this field throughout this book. Largely for practical reasons, the parameters of my doctoral project were limited to British publishing between January 1980 and December 1985. In this book, I have extended the range to incorporate a further five years of fashion editorial. Having identified that a specific type of stylist emerged during the first half of the decade, it is during the late 1980s that many of the customs that continue today were established. I have retained a focus on London as a centre for cultural activity, and for fashion (and style) publishing; I reference styling in a broader historical and geographic span only occasionally. In doing this, I am in no way claiming that publishing in the United Kingdom has greater influence or relevance than that in other places, nor am I claiming that the stylist is a uniquely British phenomenon. I am merely noting that this period of social and cultural history in London contributed to a blossoming of freelance styling as an occupation, to the development of certain practices, processes and cultural themes in fashion and lifestyle publishing, and to a wider acknowledgement of the role.

INTRODUCTION

In February 1986, *Honey* magazine ran an editorial feature on the emergence of a new role in fashion image-making (see Fig. 1). Written by Maggie Alderson, 'The Stylistics' set about explaining to the magazine's readers how the stylist, a previously invisible, behind-the-scenes occupation, had quickly become a visible, sought-after and well-paid career choice (1986: 42). Three London stylists – Caroline Baker, Iain [R.] Webb and Mitzi Lorenz – were asked to discuss their views on fashion and give an insight into the working habits of their freelance existence. Each represented a different type of styling work and had differing career experiences. Baker had been a fashion editor for *Nova* magazine in the late 1960s and had worked for several fashion and women's publications, including *Vogue* and *Cosmopolitan*. Webb and Lorenz were relative novices but had already achieved success through an association with a new wave of young, independent style magazines, known as the 'style press' or 'style bibles', that launched in the early 1980s. It was these newly emerging titles – *The Face*, *i-D* and *Blitz* – that provided Lorenz, Webb and other up-and-coming image-makers with their first experiences of editorial work. Representing a radically new form of youth publishing, they challenged established modes of presenting editorial content, having more in common with self-published, DIY 'fanzines' than with mainstream fashion publications. Produced by teams of largely inexperienced journalists, photographers and editors, they targeted young people while legitimizing new expressions of taste.

Astonishingly, Lorenz herself was only eighteen in 1986 but she had already been styling for a few years, both independently and as part of the Buffalo collective, a group of London-based creatives founded by the stylist Ray Petri in the mid-1980s. Webb had established himself as fashion editor for *Blitz*, but moved on to paid roles as an editor and journalist for the *Evening Standard* and *Harpers & Queen*. The *Honey* feature likened the stylist's job to that of a film director, listing the qualities considered necessary to successfully embody the role. Organization skills, charisma and a developed social network featured prominently, emphasizing that styling as an occupation involved more than merely 'a love of clothes' (a quality that was also listed). Rising into prominence through her involvement in *Nova*, Baker is habitually cited as an influential figure in fashion media and as a precursor to the 1980s stylist (see, for example, Beard 2013; Webb 2021). The way she selected, combined and manipulated not only clothing but also other objects in fashion images represented a new form of disruptive dressing. In her features, rainbow-coloured curtain trims were wrapped around a model's calves to create layered legwear; oversized men's shirts worn loose, braless, cinched at the waist and with a striped satin tie; cream-lined rubber wellingtons turned inside out to create cuffed boots; strings of beaded leather straps pulled across bare breasts, repurposed as Amazonian armour. Though Baker's creative and playful attitude towards constructing looks very much anticipated that of the stylist, she was never credited as such at *Nova* – at that point she was always known as a fashion editor. She insists that the term 'stylist' was introduced into the context of fashion image-making only later, arguing that Michael Roberts (another name to have received an 'honourable mention' in the *Honey* feature) was the first to label himself as such at *Tatler*. And yet, Baker is often thought of as a stylist because her images did the job of drawing attention not only to her artful clothing assemblages but also, crucially, to the person behind these creations – their author.

The Remit of the Book

This book considers the fashion stylist as an author and cultural intermediary, asking how a new wave of British freelance stylists came to be viewed and how they perceived themselves. If the stylists' collective identity drew on earlier styling roles in the fashion publishing establishment, their social circles, education and freelance status, paired with an association with the youthful style press, led to entirely new circumstances, in which the stylist came to be regarded as an artist and creative visionary, more so than merely an interpreter of commercial trends.

The book's aim is to document the stylist's growing recognition in British fashion publishing at a certain moment in time, the 1980s. It was during this period that freelance stylists started to be recognized – and much more regularly credited – for their contribution to magazine photography. The book debates how the apparent rise of the freelance stylist at that time relates to social histories, of London especially but also more broadly; to shifting practices in fashion and subcultures; and to changes in attitudes to labour and cultural production. The style press played a pivotal role in this shift. These were decisively unisex magazines, anchored in the realization that teenage boys and young men were equally valid consumers of fashion as their female counterparts. They produced a heady, hitherto unprecedented editorial mix of both menswear and womenswear, and coverage of subjects that appealed to all genders. The establishment of the stylist as a key role in fashion image-making was also strengthened as they appeared in more mainstream magazines later in the decade, notably *Elle* and *Arena*. Other magazines rebranded their editorial roles with titles such as 'style editor' or 'style correspondent' – a powerful testament to the rising currency of the word 'style' as a counterpoint, or at least an alternative, to fashion.

Who is the Fashion Stylist?

In the 1980s, 'stylist' became a fashionable term for a fashionable occupation, but it was by no means the first time that the term was used as a job description – stylists had previously worked in other fields, some related to the sale and manufacture of clothing, others in altogether different sectors of the arts and industry. In many parts of Europe, the profession of the *styliste* (in French) or *stilista* (Italian) has been associated with industrial fashion. Although the role is also closely linked with the postwar boom of consumer culture and mass manufacture in the US, the use of the term in fashion typically differentiated those who designed or marketed prêt-à-porter fashions from the couturiers who created high-end, artisanal clothing (Grumbach 1993; Volonté 2023). The rise of the fashion stylist coincided with the increased credibility of ready-to-wear but can also, as this book documents, be linked to the growing recognition of subcultural or street styles as fashion.

In magazine publishing, the occupation of the fashion stylist existed prior to the 1980s but was labelled instead as 'fashion editor'[1] and, in simple terms, the stylist is a freelance version of the latter, which would have been a permanent position. It could be argued that there is no clear distinction between these two roles. The image-making of major stylists emerging during the 1980s, such as Ray Petri and Simon Foxton, is now discussed in direct comparison with Caroline Baker's work as a fashion editor from the late 1960s or early 1970s (Webb 2021). To be sure, fashion editors have traditionally been involved in the styling of fashion stories, or features, and increasingly, as freelance culture and flexible working have become more commonplace, stylists began to work as fashion editors while simultaneously also working independently on various projects. It should be noted that practices differ in other countries, where self-employment is more strictly regulated or taxed more heavily than in the United Kingdom, and so freelancing may be less common than being salaried.

Styling is an inherently collaborative practice. The characteristics of a fashion image represent the combined input of a complex network of complementary roles. Fashion image-making is the result of a process of negotiation, involving interaction with a host of creative and organizational roles: the editor or fashion editor, art director, PR agents or designers, the stylist, their assistants, the photographer, the photographer's assistants, the photographer's agent, the model, the model agency, a make-up artist, and a hair stylist. This book concentrates on the fashion stylist's contribution to the production of editorial and advertising photography. Nevertheless, contemporary fashion stylists are likely to work across a broader range of platforms: aside from contributing to photography and increasingly moving image, they may also assist in the process of fashion design or be employed by personal (sometimes celebrity) clients, who pay them to advise on clothing choices for self-promotional activities. Defining the practices of stylists and fashion editors in more abstract terms, Paolo Volonté argues that stylists are style creators and, indeed, 'gatekeepers', as well as consumer educators. In his view, they work as intermediaries: like journalists or critics, they are informed decision-makers in the communication of fashion to the consumer, selecting from a range of available 'vestimentary possibilities' to define contemporary tastes (2020: 201–2). For example, in an editorial environment, in image production for a magazine or digital platform, they construct an outfit or scene that communicates a fashionable style to an audience of consumers. They suggest clothing items that the reader may consider buying. For the 1980s style press, less concerned with selling clothes than with showcasing new attitudes, stylists affirmed a lifestyle, affiliation to a subcultural tribe, or choice of individual identity. In choosing and combining clothing and accessories, casting particular models, and dressing them in particular ways, the fashion stylist was involved in identity construction and the development of a 'style narrative', essentially telling a story with clothing (Tulloch 2016: 4). The range of the fashion stylist's responsibilities links to those in wardrobe design in the film industries, and in the latter there is a clear objective to align the clothing choices for the characters with the narrative.

This book focuses predominantly on the processes of styling fashion but acknowledges that there are areas of overlap with similar roles in related fields, such as interior decoration or food and drink. There is also overlap between the commercial fashion stylist's role in advertising photography and those working in the film industry, which means that many key resources are shared, such as studio rental services, location scouts or prop-hire companies. For example, set building for advertising shoots, and the sourcing or making of the props, accessories and furnishings that dress the set, are practices that developed in tandem with set design for film and television.

In fashion image production, the degree of creative responsibility and range of tasks conferred to a stylist can vary, but the stylist is always actively involved in identifying, sourcing and assembling the visual ingredients of a photographed scenario. In the initial stages, styling involves the research and development of the concept or visual theme of a shoot, in collaboration with a magazine's art director and editors, or, in a commercial setting, representatives of the product manufacturer. While the common perception of the stylist is someone who selects and combines clothes, in reality they typically do much more than that. A stylist can be responsible for finding appropriate locations and casting models, and even for booking the photographer and make-up artists or hairdressers. Indeed, as Frank Mort (1996: 55) notes, the stylist can be seen as the 'director' of the shoot – a claim that calls into question the photographer's assumed primacy in the creation of the fashion image.

Still, the fundamental role of the stylist remains dressing the model for a shoot and the decision-making on the clothing to be used. This involves gathering the garments and accessories, though the collection and return of these may be delegated to an assistant. The practice of designers, brands and shops loaning clothing to magazines to be photographed and tagged with a printed credit predates the involvement of the freelance stylist. The public relations agent of a designer or brand remains the primary intermediary in acquiring clothing for photography. This was already an established feature of editorial content and it was previously the fashion editor's responsibility to liaise with the clothing supplier or their representative to negotiate the acquisition of items to feature in fashion stories. The freelancers working as emerging stylists in the early 1980s often didn't have access to the same resources as the fashion editors working in-house for magazines or have the same relationships with designers (Lifter 2018). Despite this, there was a desire, frequently motivated by their mistrust of the mainstream, to engage with new designers, small-scale fashion retailers and second-hand stores to source material for photographic shoots. For example, Barrie Sharpe, who was interviewed for this book, first met Ray Petri because he came into his store, Duffer of St George, to borrow clothes (2017), as did Michael Costiff, who ran the boutique World in central London (2022). Simon Foxton says that when he started styling, he went around shops begging for clothes. Yet he also recalls that as a graduate he was contacted by *i-D* magazine who wanted to borrow his degree collection for a shoot (2017).

Following the preparatory stages of sourcing clothing and casting, the final stage of the image-styling process involves working alongside the photographer in the studio or on location, assembling the clothing on the model and creating the 'look'. Caroline Baker claims that as a stylist, one must see through the eyes of other people: of the photographer, the editor, and of the magazine. She says that in the studio she would stand behind the photographer and watch the process closely (2017). Her description of the stylist is of someone with an overview of production, but also acting as a conduit for the ideas of a team of creative or commercial stakeholders and the needs of the audience or customer.

Literature on Styling

The stylist has so far received little academic attention, though there are several texts that provide an important foundation for the study of the subject. Didier Grumbach (1993) was among the first to treat the *styliste* as an influential designer figure in the creation and merchandising of French fashion from the 1960s onwards. Exploring the Italian context during a similar period, Paolo Volonté focused on the *stilista* as both a clothing designer and, later, a creative involved in image-making and industrial design (2008, 2022, 2023). However, stylists have existed outside the clothing industries and are not solely a postwar phenomenon. As Cesare Silla (2018) notes, the advertiser E. E. Calkin referenced the role's place in American industrial design in the 1920s. His article 'Why the Stylist?' was published in the US as early as 1929, and he went on to publish 'Stylists Interpret Consumer Demand' and 'The Place of the Stylist in Modern Merchandising', each drawing attention to an aspect of this emerging occupation.

Reference to the fashion stylist in image-making coincided with an increase of interest in fashion photography or magazines from the 1980s onwards. Dick Hebdige described a 'fetishization of style' in 1980s Britain, though, curiously, he failed to mention the stylist as an important corollary of this (1988: 10). The cultural and media historians Frank Mort and Sean Nixon (both 1996) considered the role in their studies of masculinity in 1980s fashion journalism and advertising. Mort discussed styling as an emerging 'art form', naming Mitzi Lorenz and Judy

Blame, but mainly focusing on the career of Ray Petri and his collaboration with the Buffalo collective (56). Nixon, again focusing mainly on Petri's work with Buffalo, hailed the 'ascendency of stylists', analysing some of the images they produced as evidence of their creative flair (180–5). Later, other critics and curators – namely, Val Williams, Paul Jobling and Charlotte Cotton (1999, 1999 and 2000 respectively) – drew attention to the significance of the stylist in British fashion photography, examining how contemporary fashion imagery was created and presented in magazines. Significantly, Jobling chose 1980 as the starting point for his analysis because, he claims, British publishing became more 'diverse and diffuse' at that moment in time (1999: 17). Yet despite listing all the stylists responsible for the fashion spreads he analyses, his evaluation of their contribution is minimal.

In 2000, Lorenz published a posthumous book on Petri and Buffalo, the first monograph dedicated to a stylist. Almost a decade later, Penny Martin highlighted the importance of Foxton's contribution to fashion photography in an exhibition at London's Photographer's Gallery (2009). Titled 'When You're a Boy', after a line in the David Bowie song 'Boys Keep Swinging', the exhibition was unique in that it foregrounded the creative authorship of the stylist over that of the photographer in the image-making process. Based around the theme of collaboration, Martin's exhibition explored Foxton's working relationship with three photographers. In 2013, Baker's styling was appraised in Alice Beard's book *Fun with Pins and Rope: How Caroline Baker Styled the Seventies* and has since been celebrated in a book by Iain R. Webb, produced in collaboration with Baker herself (*Rebel Stylist* in 2021). Judy Blame's retrospective at the Institute of Contemporary Arts in 2016 again brought to light the influence of the stylist in contemporary fashion editorial and advertising. The most comprehensive scholarly treatment of the stylist to date is Ane Lynge-Jorlen's edited anthology *Fashion Stylists: History, Meaning and Practice* (2020), which incorporated historical and contemporary case studies, as well as interviews with practising stylists. Of all the contributions in *Fashion Stylists*, Shaun Cole's chapter on the work of Petri is the most relevant to the period covered in this book. In addition, some academic papers have been presented at fashion-themed conferences, primarily by those who teach on related courses, including myself (Anyan and Clarke 2011; Volonté 2013; Markham 2012; Clarke 2014, 2015).

A growing interest in the creative output of stylists has also prompted the publication of several lavishly illustrated hardback books (Mower and Martinez 2007; Baron 2013). These are chiefly picture books, although the text accompanying the images often describes the work of stylists and includes first-hand accounts by the stylists themselves, or those working in associated fields of fashion media. Yet more publications have catered for students of styling currently enrolled on styling or fashion promotion courses within the UK (Dingemans 1999; Buckley and McAssey 2011; Griffiths 2016). These books draw attention to the creative process and output of the stylist, showing them as having different roles, be they contributor, collaborator or creative director, the initiator of concepts or the manager of the image-production process. They provide invaluable insights into individual stylists' careers and education backgrounds, their motivations and interests, their routines and working life, while also showcasing the sheer breadth of fields in which the stylist can apply their expertise, and the fundamentally collaborative and networked nature of this role. Crucially, they also reveal the position the stylist occupies within the fashion industry's inherent hierarchy.

More recently, stylists have become globally recognized celebrities, with the American stylist Rachel Zoe being a prime example. As of 2023, she has almost four million followers on Instagram and has also appeared in her own reality TV show, *The Rachel Zoe Project*. There are others, like Mel Ottenberg, Nicola Formichetti and William Baker, who have gained considerable status primarily through their association with successful music acts and celebrities – with Rihanna, Lady Gaga and Kyle Minogue respectively. An unmistakable indicator of the stylist's growing recognition was the introduction of the British Fashion Award category for 'Stylist' in 1999, first awarded to Lucinda Chambers, followed by Alexander McQueen's collaborator Katy England in 2000, Chambers again in 2001[2] and the stylist and editor Katie Grand in 2003. Relatively short-lived, the category was replaced by the more loosely defined 'Fashion Creator' award in the years that followed and given to the make-up artist Pat McGrath.

When, in 2013, *The Business of Fashion* website launched their 'BoF500' listing of the most influential figures active in the fashion industry, as many as ten stylists were featured. Their profiles, as published by the BoF, provide a telling insight into the varied nature of their role while also demonstrating how the profession is now recognized globally – in Russia and India as much as in France. The profiles also show how the remit of a stylist, or indeed their career path, can differ depending on the availability of opportunities. For example, Anaita Shroff Adjania, now the fashion editor of *Vogue India*, is credited as 'fashion stylist and costumer' and described as running her own 'personal styling consultancy' as well as masterclasses at wedding shows (*Business of Fashion* 2013). The current editor-in-chief of British *Vogue*, Edward Enninful, is of course a distinguished stylist, one who was awarded an OBE in 2014.

The stylist has now entered the realm of popular culture, with literary, television and film coverage testifying to their new notoriety. In the reality TV series *Style the Nation* (2011), for example, a group of contestants competed to win a 'dream job' as a stylist for the high-street fashion retailer New Look, spurred on by designer Giles Deacon and the store's creative director, Barbara Horspool. Elsewhere, in the *Hunger Games* novels (2008–10) and their screen adaptations (2012–15), the character of the stylist played a vital role in creating the media profile of the 'reality' game show contestants, achieving the kind of celebrity status of their real-world counterparts. And there have even been children's books: *Hello Kitty Fashion Stylist* and *Hello Kitty: Be a Super Stylist* have targeted the 8+ market, encouraging aspiring young stylists to 'design, create and style [their] own fabulous fashions' (2010, 2013).

The Structure of the Book

To understand how and why perceptions and practices of styling changed in the 1980s, I examined printed editorial content in the style press from between January

1980 and December 1989, while also drawing on oral history interviews conducted with stylists, other image-makers and their social circle. The former demonstrates how the stylist became increasingly recognized, showing how changes in styling practice may have led to this increase in prominence. To identify markers of their status or hierarchy within fashion shoots, I documented the frequency of their credits in print, and the ways that the stylist was listed in relation to other creative roles. Although the book focuses largely on the style press, other key British magazines are examined, including traditional society titles with fashion content (*Tatler*, *Harpers & Queen*), lifestyle publications targeting a uniquely female or male readership (*Nova*, *Cosmopolitan*, *Elle*, *GQ*, *FHM* and *Arena*) and newspaper supplements (*Observer* and *Sunday Times*).

The book's first chapter defines style and styling, and provides histories of previous iterations of the stylist, both in fashion and in other professional and social spheres. Chapter 2 discusses the social and cultural context of 1980s London, while also considering the political and economic climate as crucial factors contributing to the changes in fashion media and independent publishing. Chapters 3 and 5 are structured around the findings of a detailed editorial analysis. This is presented in two sections, the first covering the period between 1980 and 1985, the second examining the rest of the decade up until 1990. Chapter 4 defines the practices and aesthetic references of the new generation of stylists, considering how their styling reflected the political themes of the time and how the visual statements they made drew attention to their work. Chapter 6 distinguishes the type of work that came to constitute styling as an occupation and its legitimation within the hierarchies of fashion image-making. It considers the stylist's occupational remit and status.

Overall, the book assesses how the stylist operated in both the style press and established fashion and women's titles, comparing how their structures and hierarchies were navigated differently. It demonstrates that the style press was influential in raising wider awareness of the stylist while at the same time cementing certain practices as styling. I analyse the stylist's work across multiple areas, drawing on oral history interviews for invaluable insights into the stylist's wide-ranging working practices and their ways of negotiating London's social and cultural milieu. Angela McRobbie's sociological study of the fashion designer (1998) has been an important reference point for me, as a blueprint for how to analyse a fashion industry role. Unlike McRobbie's study, however, I chose not to anonymize interviewees because their identities seem vital in telling this little-known history. Besides, they have also regularly referenced each other by name. For this book, I conducted eighteen interviews over a six-year period (see appendix) with stylists and fashion editors (Caroline Baker, David Bradshaw, Simon Foxton, Caryn Franklin, Paul Frecker, Mitzi Lorenz, Debbi Mason, Sarah Miller, Zee Shore and Iain R. Webb), photographers (Roger Charity and Jamie Morgan), art directors (Robin Derrick), designers (Stephen Jones and Barrie Sharpe), agents (Ziggi Golding) and artists (Michael Costiff and Jeffrey Hinton) who have enjoyed considerable prominence in the industry.

Interviewees were largely selected through a review of editorial content or by recommendation. Of all the leading stylists to emerge in the 1980s, Ray Petri, Judy

Blame and Simon Foxton remain essential to the understanding of the profession and its status within the fashion industry. Sadly, I wasn't able to interview Petri or Blame, both of whom died before I began my research. Petri died in 1989 but there are many sources discussing his contribution (Lorenz 2000; Tulloch 2011; Cole 2022). I was able to build on these by interviewing Petri's close friends and collaborators Roger Charity, Mitzi Lorenz and Jamie Morgan, all of whom cited his influence on their own creative practice. Blame died in 2018, although the material generated for his ICA exhibition has provided sufficient insight into his career, predominantly a recorded conversation with the exhibition curator Gregor Muir from 2016.

This book argues that the rise of the stylist occurred within specific social, political and economic conditions of 1980s London. It explores these plural contexts, zeroing in on the factors that contributed to the changes in editorial practices within the fashion media at the time as well as the (sub)cultural activities from which new the new creative roles and publishing formats evolved. Furthermore, the book discusses what styling looked like and how it was practised at that moment in time. It shows how it reflected broader youth culture, especially punk and the New Romantics, which themselves drew attention to the acts of creation and disruption by means of dressing up. The legacy of the British stylists of the 1980s, who built a reputation for themselves as well as their profession, is considered in the concluding part of this book. These stylists neither invented style, nor the role of the stylist, but they fundamentally changed the industry's – and indeed the public's – perception of this singular creative role.

Notes

1 The term 'sittings editor' was also used in magazine publishing.

2 There was no award ceremony in 2002.

Chapter 1

HISTORIES OF STYLING: CONNOISSEURSHIP, CONSUMPTION AND SUBCULTURE

Before turning to the stylist as a particular kind of cultural producer, which emerged from a specific context in 1980s London, it seems necessary to understand how distinct it was from earlier professions with similar remit, and how prior uses of the term stylist may not have intersected with these professions. The work responsibilities that were recognized as fashion styling in British magazine publishing from the 1980s onwards can be traced to earlier professional roles. Perhaps most obviously, it is the fashion editor, a well-established role in publishing. But there are other, less often evoked professions which have performed similar sets of duties to the fashion stylist. These include the costume designer or costume supervisor in the film or television industries, or design consultant in industrial manufacture and fashion (Silla 2018).

This chapter focuses on genealogies and histories. It starts by explaining the origins of style, the stylist's field of interest, and considers the role of the connoisseur as a forerunner to the stylist. The opinions of connoisseurs and critics became essential to the production of art and design; their opinions were necessary in defining contemporary tastes. As industrialization made it possible to manufacture products in a broad range of styles, stylists were employed to ensure that these styles mapped with the tastes of customers. Stylists were professionalized connoisseurs who understood how aesthetic informed sales. However, the stylist has also existed in a non-professional environment. In postwar Britain, young stylists formed subcultural groups, as a form of resistance, and developed collective identities through the ways they dressed. Although seemingly disconnected, each of these historical versions of the stylist informed the way that a new wave of fashion stylists practised and were perceived in London in the 1980s.

Connoisseurship and Style

> No stylistic characterization of a work of art is possible without presupposing at least implicit reference to the possible alternatives, whether simultaneous – to distinguish it from its contemporaries – or successive – to contrast it with earlier

> or later works by the same or a different artist. Exhibitions devoted to an artist's whole oeuvre or to a genre are the objective realization of the field of interchangeable stylistic possibilities which is brought into play when one 'recognizes' the singularities of the characteristic style of a work of art.[1]

The notion of 'style' in European visual arts became more apparent in the eighteenth century, as the field of art criticism was developing. The stylistic qualities of art forms were noted and debated. Differences were highlighted between the attributes of works of art. Art forms were classified according to the person, or group of people, who created them or the time or place in which they were made. In art criticism, a distinction was being drawn between broader, general styles and individual styles. A general style could be bound to a specific period; for example, the Rococo style, where common characteristics were seen in forms of ornamentation across Europe. A general style could be shared by a school, a movement or a group of artists with similar education and values. It could also be a cultural phenomenon, where certain commonalities were seen in decorative motifs in one specific culture or group of cultures (Wollheim 1987; Bourdieu 2010).

The idea of individual style, though, became something associated with artists, in some way connected to their personality. How someone chose to create art was seen as representative of how they wanted to be viewed, of their aspirations or ideals. Social setting and education are obviously factors. To develop a personal style the artist still needs to be aware of available resources, to identify the set of rules they will adopt to use those resources and be able to access and manipulate the resources. The resulting style of a work is dependent on the selection process, on the specific way an artist has chosen to work, and both the choice of resources and the technique they have used. These ideas became key to the way some modern artists were perceived, with a distinct style that they had cultivated, and which influenced their peers. Although its relevance has been questioned,[2] this definition of individual style would later inform the way that stylists perceived their practice and how they wanted to be seen (Robinson 1985; Bourdieu 2010; Riggle 2015).

In most of the spheres listed in this chapter, the stylist was a cipher for fashionable tastes or styles. This could be in a professional capacity or as a lifestyle choice. The contribution of experts in the construction of taste traces back to the 'connoisseur' of the arts in eighteenth-century European society. Connoisseurs became known in conjunction with more critical approaches to the appreciation of art (Mount 2006). A culture was developing around continental art, initially French and Italian. Connoisseurship elevated criticism of painting beyond a simple respect for technical skill and artisanship. Academic writing on art already existed; however, starting with the Salons at the Louvre in Paris in the late seventeenth century, art was progressively exposed to a wider audience and it became a topic of public debate. Writers like Diderot (1713–84) were among the first to combine the role of connoisseur with that of the art writer, generating art criticism that was discursive and related to public taste. Commercial and cultural value was being accorded to art. Connoisseurship was associated with the acquisition of cultural capital, and connoisseurs were the patrons of the arts, positioning themselves in society but also affecting the reputation of the artists themselves. Appreciation of the arts became a defining characteristic of the upper classes in eighteenth-century England.

The collection of 'curiosities' had become a popular pursuit among wealthy members of society in the previous century. They were keen to demonstrate their discerning, eclectic taste. As evidenced in early auction catalogues, seventeenth-century collectors accumulated art pieces but also historical objects and natural treasures, such as exotic shells, stones or gems (Brewer 2013: 204). The connoisseur developed from someone who demonstrated their own personal and aesthetic style, to a role that also involved passing comment on the artistic styles of others. Connoisseurs were not without their own critics. For example, in England the painter Joshua Reynolds was an artist who also wrote art criticism, under the pseudonym 'The Idler'. He was disapproving of the role of connoisseurs. He saw them as blaggers who namedropped artists and talked louder than their peers but lacked any artistic ability or valid art education. The establishment of the Royal Academy in 1768, as an association that represented artists and tasked itself with defining art, represented a threat to the influence of the connoisseur. Competition developed between 'those who produced and those who collected art' (2013: 223).

There were similar patterns in the development of taste in dress, which relied on opinions disseminated by etiquette writers and journalists, and on individuals who used their status and style to influence public opinion. The French periodical *Le Mercure Galant*, originally published in 1672, is widely considered to be the first fashion magazine. It featured reports on society life and the arts, and listed the addresses of fashion merchants. In London, *The Lady's Magazine* began publication in 1770 and included fashion plates, coloured engravings produced by artists. Although not considered a fashion magazine, it covered the latest dress trends in more detail than previous women's magazines.

Fashion magazines did more than capture taste – they prescribed it (Miller 2013). But there were other sources of fashion influence. In the early nineteenth century, the West End became a hub for fashionable people, as retail and social spaces emerged in this newly developed part of London. Notorious figures like the dandy George (Beau) Brummell became a reference point for style, but existed as a counterpoint for uniform, prescribed fashions. Brummell represented individual style, in the items he chose to wear and how he chose to wear them. The dandy's devotion to detail in dress and lifestyle was a forerunner to that later displayed by members of London's subcultures; it was 'an entire way of being and furthermore, one composed entirely of nuances' (Evans and Vaccari 2020). Peter Wollen likens Brummell to an artist. Significantly, he even calls him a precursor of the contemporary stylist. Brummell treated his own dress as an art form; the items he selected for each outfit and the ways he chose to wear them were meticulously considered. Each outfit reflected his own personal tastes and identity and communicated his status as an arbiter of taste (1999). Brummell's own sartorial choices also existed as a form of critique of contemporary tastes.

Personal style is described by Elizabeth Wilson as the 'elegance and essence' of a woman. Style became a quality that fashion media historically encouraged a woman to develop and maintain, regardless of changes in fashionable trends. This definition of style reflected a certain individualism, where someone has made choices on the characteristics of their clothing, make-up, haircut, perfume – or any other aspects of their lifestyle – that remain constant and are relatively unaffected by trend-led changes in popular style (2009). The term 'stylist' was first associated with literature. In the eighteenth century, a stylist was 'a writer who is skilled in or cultivates the art of literary style' (Taylor 1795). Stylists were later acknowledged in sport and music. Someone who 'plays with style' was classed as a stylist. Collins currently lists a stylist as someone who pays 'a lot of attention to the way that they write, say, or do, something so that it is attractive and elegant'. In a specifically British context, a stylist is 'a person who performs, writes, or acts with attention to style'. Suggesting that a stylist could also be a specialist in the visual arts, *The Stylist* magazine (1905) presented an alternative iteration. A publication produced at the turn of the twentieth century, it devoted its pages to communicating 'new designs and styles'. The title catered for a readership of consumers of current trends in clothing and home décor. *The Stylist* reflected societal awareness of consumption as a mode of social distinction and communicated appropriate lifestyle choices to those who needed to know. The reader of the magazine was someone who wanted to educate themselves in contemporary tastes and show how their own stylistic choices reflected this (Bourdieu 2010).

Couture fashion and modern art developed in tandem. In modern art, it was expected that one style or movement would supersede the last. The fashion system was reliant on the promotion of general styles and operated with an understanding that the popularity of a style would result in its obsolescence and the introduction of a subsequent, usually equally short-lived, popular style. Modern notions of style, in both art and fashion, were overturned in consumer-driven, late twentieth-century society by the possibility that one could consider many different fashions simultaneously. Paul Greenhalgh refers to the period from 1970 to 1990 as the last true style debate. He claims that style, in the senses that we understood it, will be forever associated with a certain version of modernity. What differed between modern and postmodern versions of the style debate is that modernism presented a universal style and noted any shift in this style across Western society as a whole. This could be a change in fashionable dress or popular music, or a new movement in art or design. The postmodern debate acknowledges that multiple styles can coexist, that each has a value (Hebdige 1988). However, says Wilson, there is still room for the cultivation of a personal style in a postmodern context. The adoption of a fixed, distinctive style of dress provides an opportunity to demonstrate individuality and a sense of self in a society that has become subsumed by fashion. For Wilson, if someone claims a particular style as their own it serves as a means of self-affirmation in a society that offers a relentless plurality of styles (2009: 124). As we discuss in Chapter 3, both perspectives on style fed into the style culture of 1980s London and the working habits of the stylist.

In the 1970s, the English writer and socialite Quentin Crisp presented himself as a stylist. He considered himself a contemporary version of the connoisseur or dandy. In *How to Have a Lifestyle*, which was first published in 1975, he offered his perspective on style, on how to behave, shop and conduct one's life with style. Throughout the book, which is peppered with anecdotes from his colourful life, he discussed what attributes one would need to be a stylist. Crisp differentiates between style and stylishness. Stylishness, he argues, is not necessarily linked to an individual's personality and is not a constant, maintained state; rather, it is 'something snatched out of the air to shock the neighbours' (1975: 8). In line with Wilson's definition, Crisp's stylist is aware of fashion but chooses not to be influenced by it.

The Stylist as Consumption Engineer

The technological revolution of the late nineteenth and early twentieth century made it possible for manufacturers to make large quantities of products. Because they were making so many, it was important to ensure beforehand that the products appealed to their customer. In America the term styling started to be used to describe the process of rebranding conventional merchandise. A new profession, the stylist, was a middleman who mediated between 'the manufacturers' need for standardization and consumers' desire for individualization' (Silla 2018: 584). Indeed, the most widely referenced examples of the stylist throughout the twentieth century related to the design and manufacture of products, and to the display and promotion of these products. The advertiser E. E. Calkins called these middlemen 'consumption engineers' (Silla 2018: 584), and Bourdieu has since used the term cultural intermediary to describe this type of role (2010).

The occupation of the stylist is described as comparable to, or even interchangeable with, that of the industrial designer. The importance of a distinct aesthetic in the marketing of products was acknowledged by manufacturers. The evolution of styling was closely linked to advances in manufacturing processes. The pressing of steel in vehicle production allowed new shapes to be created quickly and effortlessly. Producers could now respond to increasing demand for differentiation and novelty (Hebdige 1988; Silla 2018). In the car industry, the automobile stylist's job was to adapt the design of mechanically identical, mass-produced cars to create individualized products. They could generate successions of desirable shapes that appealed to a new audience of style-conscious consumers. General Motors and Ford were the biggest global competitors. Stylists were initially employed by the former to gain the upper hand over Ford, who continued to favour function over decoration. General Motors' Art and Colour section was founded in the mid-to-late 1920s, and the team became officially known as the Styling Staff (Gartman 1994). Promotional material produced by General Motors pinpoints 1927 as the 'beginning of modern automotive styling as we know it', the LaSalle model of car being the first 'professionally styled' car to achieve commercial success (General Motors 1955: 37).

There is evidence to suggest that stylists became as well known in the United Kingdom as in the US. Ford eventually also employed them to consult on appropriate design decisions, opening a new styling section at Dearborn, in England (Gurr 1955). These departments were multifaceted in terms of personnel and roles. The Styling Buildings at the General Motors Technical Center in Warren, Michigan comprised an administration building, studio-shop and a viewing auditorium, for consultants to monitor the production lines (Wayt 2015). Within this facility, 150 designers, engineers and specialists in 'glass, plastics, paint, colors, and clay models' collaborated to realize every aspect of the car design. In marketing brochures, General Motors made a point of highlighting the commercial awareness of the stylist and their knowledge of contemporary taste. They compared them with the artist or writer, and suggested they possessed the skills to communicate with the 'minds and emotions of the viewer' (General Motors 1955: 6). Despite this, the stylists were not always popular with the engineers, who felt that their contribution to the design process was unnecessary and unjustified (Gartman 1994). A hierarchy existed within design teams, and despite being an important role in the manufacturing process, the stylists were not seen to have the authority or knowledge to make the final decision on the models being built by the company (General Motors 1955: 61).

Styling was seen in other fields of product design as well, beyond the car industry. For example, the industrial John Vassos worked with the styling team of the radio manufacturer RCA. Before Vassos' arrival the team were only involved at the end of the design process, after the engineering department had made key decisions. He was keen to ensure that his team collaborated from the outset and that styling was considered intrinsic to the functional aspects of radio design (Shapiro 2016: 83). Documentation of the role in other fields of American design can be found in newspapers. For example, the *New York Times* reported in 1954 that the 'stylist for ships' Harry Neafie was being retained by the Matson Navigation Company to work on the interior design of two new passenger ships (21 November 1954: 11). A further feature, in 1957, unfortunately reporting Neafie's premature death, described his role in the 'interior layout, décor and exterior styling' of liners, suggesting similarities with the occupation of the automobile stylist (*New York Times*, 25 May 1957: 16).

The importance of aesthetic in reaching a wider audience began to become more widely understood. These kinds of roles were found in many other areas, for instance the cosmetics industry. The roles expanded to include overview of the design of retail environments, packaging and advertising. Beauty manufacturers, for example, were faced with the challenge of selling unattractive or bland creams. Paying more attention to the styling, manufacturers started displaying lotions or liquids in sculpted jars or bottles, elevating them to desirable, luxury items. Industrial designers were commissioned to oversee the styling of products and their advertising. The work of the artist and designer Reco Capey for Yardley was seen as a contributing factor in the commercial success of that brand. New technologies in metalworking had enabled the styling of a broader range of product shapes in the automobile industries, and the development of plastic moulding techniques also allowed the packaging of cosmetics to be developed into more sophisticated forms. Capey was best known for his moulded foundation cream jars, which were shaped with a symmetrical honeybee motif on the lid. His remit extended beyond the packaging to the design of instore displays and advertising artwork. In other sources, Capey was listed as the 'Director of design'. The RIBA website credits him as being the architect/designer of the filigree entrance door of the Yardley store in Old Bond Street in London. His remit extended beyond that of the stylist in automobile design; he was employed to consult on the overall visual identity of the brand, but also appears to have been actively involved in the design process.

An example of the term stylist being used to describe a very similar role to the contemporary fashion stylist is that of Tobé (or Taubé) Coller-Davis. A 1937 article in the US publication *Delineator* claimed that Coller-Davis was the first person within the fashion industry to label herself as a stylist. Her expertise was defined as 'someone who knows from experience, better than anyone else, what styles you are going to like best and what will be most useful to you' (*Delineator* 1937: 24). She was referenced consistently in the *New York Times* from the 1930s to her death in the early 1960s and – in addition to her capacity as retail consultant – was the founder of the Tobé-Coburn fashion school. Coller-Davis operated predominantly as a brand consultant, or style influencer, and also organized promotional events. Veronique Pouillard sees her as an early example of a fashion forecaster. Couturiers, such as Charles-Frederick Worth, were the 'style leaders' in France. However, the US adopted a consumer-influenced model of production much earlier than its European counterparts, and the promotional industries developed in tandem with mass manufacture. In the 1920s, Coller-Davis had already started to produce weekly fashion reports. As a wealthy socialite, she spent time in Paris during the fashion show seasons and sent back a Tobé Report with sketches of garment silhouettes and details of colours, fabrics and patterns. Other fashion consultants started to offer similar services. Amos Parrish, for example, offered a biannual Fashion Merchandising Clinic in New York from the 1920s to the mid-1950s (Pouillard 2013: 165).

Consultants became more commonly used in France, as department stores started to sell ready-to-wear fashion. They advised department stores on what ranges to stock, in accordance with the perceived tastes of the customers. Galeries Lafayette employed the socialite Ghislaine de Polignac in 1952. She has been called France's 'first fashion stylist', although Grumach says the term wasn't used until the 1960s (1993: 202). Several years later, Printemps employed the former editor of both *Femina* and *Elle* magazines as the head of the store's 'style office'. Stylists became increasingly influential in the late 1960s. French *stylistes* fulfilled a slightly different role to American stylists. A *styliste* was more like a fashion designer, and the terms were often used interchangeably. They were, however, seen as beholden to the manufacturer. The term 'créateurs de mode' was introduced later as a preferable, blanket term for all fashion designers or creators of fashion (Grumbach 1993: 290). Grumbach names Alain Lalonde, Christiane Bailly and Emanuelle Khanh (Emma-Christie), Michèle Rosier, Daniel Hechter, Sonia Rykiel and Jacques

Delahaye as the first *stylistes.*

In Italy, says Paolo Volonté, the role of the stylist (or *stilista*) also became more prominent in the early 1960s. Giorgio Armani, for example, worked for the department store La Rinascente as creative director. He was responsible for window displays and then became a consultant stylist for the store's buyers. Cerruti later hired him to help refresh his collections and he was actively promoted as *stilista* by the designer. In the early 1970s, other Italian manufacturers followed suit, employing style consultants. Versace worked in this capacity for Callaghan and Genny, and Gianfranco Ferré. Volonté explains what the *stilista*'s remit would be, in comparison with that of the couturier. He stresses that they would not be expected to have tailoring skills but would work between 'the creative idea (the style, the concept, the mood, the semantic content of the garment) and its industrial viability (technical drawings, budgets, marketing, saleability)' (2023: 265). Volonté credits the stylists of the 1980s for introducing a wider range of social groups to the language of fashion. The brand identity was gradually replacing the product itself as the main selling point.

This book nonetheless focuses on the photographic image. The first instance I found of a stylist being credited for their role in dressing an image was for the front and back cover of *Living Arts*, a 1963 ICA (Institute of Contemporary Arts) publication. It was photographed by Robert Freeman, arranged by the British artist Richard Hamilton and listed Betsey Scherman as 'stylist' in a fourteen-item list of props and crew. In editorial fashion, the role can also be found credited in in Andy Warhol's magazine *Interview* as early as January 1977, with stylists Peter Lester and Richard Bernstein named for portrait shots of Jodie Foster and Grace Jones. First launched as a publication for film critics, *Interview*'s focus gradually shifted to incorporate a degree of fashion content. From 1977 onwards, it continued to credit the stylist, also using the terms 'styled by' and 'styling'. What is unclear is the role that Bernstein and Lester played in constructing the image. Lester was an editor and Bernstein an illustrator, responsible for the airbrushed portraits that became synonymous with *Interview*'s visual identity. I note elsewhere that the art director Jean-Paul Goude was credited for the 'photo-styling' of a heavily manipulated image. It is possible that Lester and Bernstein have also been acknowledged for a similar role – for their treatment of the photograph rather than dressing the model.

For this book, the remit of the stylist has been limited to work that involves dressing for the fashion image. As noted, the role of the stylist in image-making has parallels with that of the fashion editor in magazines. The stylist in a commercial context, for advertising photography or moving image, has antecedents in other film industry roles. The film and television industries typically require larger teams, and a more structured and hierarchic system of designating creative roles existed much earlier here than in photography for advertising, or indeed fashion. An article about H. M. K. Smith, the costume director of Paramount Studios, appeared in the *New York Times* in 1923 (2 December 1923: 147). A 1926 issue of the same newspaper described the tasks and responsibilities of the costume team. They were involved in both shopping for clothing and commissioning tailors to create anything that could not be found. The feature claimed that for 'purely modern' pictures the costume team operated in a similar way to contemporary fashion stylists, sourcing and purchasing clothing rather than designing and manufacturing. Only items for period costume dramas were made, because the clothing necessary for these features could not be found in stores (*New York Times* 10 January 1926).

The responsibilities for the dressing of characters in films was the remit of a large team of related roles, including the costume designer and costume supervisor. It is the costume designer's role to research and design each of the actors' costumes. The costume supervisor maintains an organizational role, overseeing the shopping or sourcing of clothing, the transportation of materials and the budgets. There are further parallels between the costume-related roles in film and the stylist or fashion editor in fashion photography. Deborah Nadoolman Landis suggests that, like the stylist, the costume designer's role is overlooked and misunderstood. She attributes this to 'nefarious gender bias' in an industry that often overlooks the contribution of women. As recently as 2012 the Director's Guild of America magazine continued to omit the costume designer in the production credits of a film, which include the production designer, cinematographer and editor. More significantly, the rates of pay for costume designer are lower than those for these other, typically male, film roles (Nadoolman Landis 2012: 11).

Stylists are now credited for film and TV work. Nonetheless, there is also evidence of stigmatization of this role, and prejudice often comes from established costume designers. It is perhaps to be expected. The costume departments had already experienced cuts, and the previous decade had seen a move away from large, expensive studio-owned costume departments. There was also freelance competition among costume, make-up and hair designers. The appearance of stylists in film and television production in the 1980s and 1990s was attributed to the prominence of the music video and to big-budget TV commercials, both no doubt linked to the increased success of the music cable channel MTV. It was, rather sneeringly, claimed that production companies hired 'anyone who could do the job' (La Motte 2001: 4). As will be discussed in Chapter 5, many of the self-defined stylists working for new, style press magazines were grateful of any opportunity of paid work that music videos and advertising campaigns provided.

Subcultural Stylists

The third factor to inform the rise of the stylist in British publishing in the 1980s was the increasing debate around subcultural style. It informed the way stylists worked but also their choice of occupational label. British subculture became the subject of academic study in the second half of the twentieth century, as cultural criticism expanded to consider popular culture beyond established, traditional art forms. Ethnographic studies of urban youth culture had been conducted before, both in the UK and US. However, in the 1960s and 1970s the focus became dress, and the origin and meaning of style (Irwin 1977; Cohen 1997). Subcultural theory was concerned with assessing the value of style among young people, as a mark of affiliation and status. In a subcultural context, the adoption of a common style creates allegiances, and it usually exists in opposition to the dominant fashion in a particular culture during a particular period. The form of subcultural styles is agreed at a local level among groups of young people. As well as consensus on the ways that members of the group should dress, there is often agreement on other aspects of lifestyle, from the types of music they listen to or play, the art they produce, or even the make and model of their motorbikes and cars.

Although Peter York has suggested that it became a fashionable term in the 1970s, style certainly became more of a buzz word in the 1980s (York 1980). It is no doubt awareness of subcultural debate that prompted its wider usage. John Clarke's essay 'Style' was first published in 1975 and was one of several texts discussing dress in Stuart Hall's subcultural anthology *Resistance Through Rituals* (1976). Dick Hebdige's *Subculture: The Meaning of Style* (1979) offered further definitions of the origins and form of British subcultural dress. It also helped to cement the association of the term style, as an alternative word for fashion or dress, with youth cultural dress and identity. The assertion that style is anti-fashion, which was the ethos of the style press publications when they were first introduced, correlates with the way that style was framed in subcultural studies. Style was a demonstration of countercultural values. But despite the opinion among its members that their activities sit outside of fashion, subcultural dress is a by-product of the fashion system. Subcultural groups retain the principles of fashion but operate in their own microcosm, in a way that counters or subverts how clothing is being worn in dominant society (Hebdige 1979).

Subculture tends to respond to specific societal conditions. Phil Cohen was among the first to observe subculture, in the 1950s. He focused on East End, working-class boys. For him, participants in subcultural activity demonstrated a desire to remain autonomous and distinct from their parents, while retaining a connection with traditional values. For example, the teds (teddy boys, Edwardians) are said to have developed a distinct, dressed-up style in response to postwar austerity in working-class areas of Britain. Writing in 1904, though, Georg Simmel had already noted a tendency for irrational behaviour among young people, manifesting as personal modes of dress prompted by 'individual demand for differentiation' (Simmel 1957: 554). The concept of countercultural dress can be traced even further back. As mentioned, the dandies of eighteenth-century London represented a form of subversive dress, an elite that formed in opposition to mainstream fashion, but that ultimately fed into it. Christopher Breward also classes the rational dress movement, which developed towards the end of the nineteenth century, as a precursor to the subcultural activity of the 1940s, 1960s and 1970s. Pockets of activity centred on specific areas. Kensington and Bedford Park were home to the communities of 'artistic, upper middle class' Londoners, who were attracted to the exotic styles of Liberty's and the freedoms of aesthetic dress (Breward, Ehrman and Evans 2004: 59). The idea that the consumption of clothing could be a leisure activity is fundamental in definitions of subculture. The youth culture that emerged in postwar Western societies was a result of the working classes having more disposable income, with an increase in the number of educated, middle-class 'affluent workers'. More young people now had the time and financial means to engage in activities outside the workplace.

The new, independent publications of the 1980s wrote their manifestos with awareness of definitions of style in both popular culture and subculture. The original aim of *i-D* magazine was to document style: it was intent on displaying the diversity of identities (or IDs) being explored by the individuals operating within various British subcultural groups. *The Face* started by reporting on the music scenes of the time but was equally concerned with the ways that musical phenomena were represented in dress and in all aspects of youth lifestyle.

Moreover, the term stylist has been used explicitly within some subcultures. From the 1950s onwards the term appeared within mod subculture, differentiating a certain type of mod (Paul Gorman personal communication, 8 March 2018). By the 1960s the mod subculture was established enough to have developed many subgroups. The stylists, as well as the individualists and tickets, are examples of these. Stylists were a more fashion-conscious alternative to the purist mod and were more interested in popular music and dress. The Beatles are an example of stylists being referenced in mainstream youth culture. In the mid-1960s, *Mod's Monthly* used Paul McCartney as an example of this less authentic version of the mod (Wickham 1964). The term continued to be used. In the early 1980s, *The New Stylist* became the name of a bimonthly, independently published 'zine for mods in the north of England (Paddison 1983). Paolo Hewitt referred to the mod phenomenon as 'soul stylism' which, he says, was an attempt by British mods to emulate the clothes and lifestyles of Black, American musicians (2000: 16).

As I will go on to discuss, the way that the stylists of the 1980s presented themselves incorporated aspects of each of the social figures discussed in this chapter. They were simultaneously connoisseurs, consumption engineers and subcultural stylists. They were aware of the currency of 'style' and this was reflected by their choice of job title. Style was used by subcultural writers to define anti-fashion. Yet mainstream culture was also obsessed with style, not just one fashionable style but all styles. The practice of styling and the work of the stylist became popularized but also in many ways redefined in the 1980s through its association with British style publishing. Superficially, the new wave of stylists working in independent style press magazines adopted the modus operandi of the subcultural stylist. The countercultural approach to editorial styling seen at that time would seem contrary to the expectations of the role of a professional stylist, which had traditionally aligned with mass manufacture and consumerism. However, the role evolved to incorporate both. The following chapters offer a more detailed exploration of a period of British social history that saw styling, and the work of the freelance fashion stylist, become more clearly delineated as a form of cultural production, and more embedded in both publishing and advertising.

Notes

1 P. Bourdieu (2010), *Distinction: A Social Critique of the Judgement of Taste* (Abingdon: Routledge Classics).

2 The postmodern perspective on authorship, in the latter part of the twentieth century, rejected the idea that the author's personality is the sole source of the work. It favoured a view of cultural products being collectively owned by those who participate in its interpretation (Barthes 1977).

Chapter 2

STYLE CULTURE AND THE LONDON SCENE

London's youth culture of the late 1970s and early 1980s has been well recorded and heavily mythologized. It continues to feature in books, films, television series and magazine articles, and is regularly referenced and recycled in contemporary fashion image-making. This social scene and club culture, and the media that reported on their activities, are often referred to holistically as 'style culture'. They are also where the freelance stylists would find their platform (Mort 1996). To understand the development of this style culture, it is first necessary to briefly examine a range of contexts that informed it. The style culture of the 1980s was in some ways a product of, and reaction to, the broader political and economic situation in Britain. However, it largely represented a continuation of London's history as a site of unique youth culture and social scenes, and as a source of street fashion. This chapter discusses geography and subculture, the ways that each affected the other and the way that external factors, such as political change, may have influenced local histories and interactions.

The stylists making a name for themselves in the early part of the 1980s, when the occupation – at least in the field of fashion image – was loosely formed and misunderstood, drew on a range of influences from their background and environment to inform their practice. The subcultural and social spaces of punk and New Romantic fed into the ways they dressed themselves and others. Art school education informed their views of creative practice. The collaborative opportunities afforded by belonging to social networks gave them work experiences and insight into both the fashion and publishing industries. The majority of those interviewed for this book were part of interconnected communities in disparate areas of London. These were private and creative communities that often overlapped and which shared a desire to create an alternative lifestyle, one that was disruptive and countercultural, and did not conform to societal expectations. The stylist Judy Blame described the culture within the city at the time as 'cliquey'. Certain scenes were associated with certain areas. Peripheral areas of the city became relevant, but by the early 1980s, the bulk of social and creative activity occurred in parts of central London – in Soho and Covent Garden – or in clusters of illegal squats around Euston station and Warren Street.

I have drawn on subcultural theory and historical studies to support oral history accounts of cultural practices in the city at this time, providing context to the development of these creative communities and to the practices, ideologies and aesthetic reference points that were shared by those who became the first recognized British fashion stylists.

London Fashion, Street Style and Social Space

London has a reputation for the cultivation and promotion of unique subcultural styles and singular, eccentric fashion that predates the 1980s. Caroline Evans attributes the 'triumph' of subcultural style in London to the democratization of fashion that occurred from the late 1950s, with the emergence of the youth market and the evolution of social spaces catering for new scenes (2004: 118). After a period of postwar austerity, the 1960s marked a period of renewed success for British fashion. Photography, modelling, magazine publishing and advertising were businesses that benefitted from international interest in the city's youth culture (Porter 1994). For the first time, youth fashion was being generated by young people, who understood and were often a part of the same social scene as their customers. Subcultural, or street, style filtered into the fashions being made by young designers, and vice versa. Many of the themes discussed in this book in relation to the practices of the stylist also have their origins in this evolving London youth culture. As the 1960s unfolded, the focus shifted away from modern to nostalgic styles, a progressive blurring of the boundaries between art and fashion, and an acceptance of street style as fashion. These themes informed the more experimental fashion editors of the late 1960s and fed into later definitions of styling.

From the mid-1960s, independent boutiques such as Biba, Glass and Black, Clobber, Hung on You, Granny Takes a Trip and Bus Stop were important in assisting the development and notoriety of British fashion (O'Byrne 2009). The location of fashion stores also contributed to the formation of local social scenes, and young people formed communities of similar tastes and styles. The fashion designer Mary Quant opened her first store on the King's Road in southwest London in 1964 and although it was still mainly a residential area, it had started to become home to an alternative youth scene, as coffee shops and bars opened. It was at the far end of this street, in the shop that had previously housed Hung on You, that Vivienne Westwood opened the first iteration of her fashion business (Evans 2004).[1]

By the beginning of the 1970s, many of the most successful boutiques of the previous decade had closed down. An increase in shoplifting and running costs were factors in their closure, but also the lack of business knowledge of their owners (Evans 2004). Although through the 1970s and 1980s a series of organizations were set up to provide support for designers, the British fashion industry lacked a centralized system for the promotion of British design compared to their French and Italian peers. Additionally, they had no fixed venue for show events. It is perhaps not unexpected that the influence of street style, and subsequently that of the style press and freelance stylist, evolved from a fashion system that was less clearly defined and centrally governed than some of its European counterparts. It was the synergy of social life, street style and small businesses that defined London fashion.

Into the 1970s, the relationship between London's street and club style, between social scene and fashion business, continued in various formats. Less well documented than the boutique culture of the 1960s or the punk activity that arrived several years later, a clique developed in the early part of the 1970s that Peter York labelled Them. It was a scene which formed a bridge between the two and fed into the glam rock styles that became popular in the early 1970s. Them was a crowd of art-school educated designers and artists. York described the phenomenon in an article in *Harpers & Queen* in 1976. He related their style to the wider influence of pop art and to the increasingly blurred distinction between art, fashion and other forms of popular culture (York 1980). Included in the list of young creatives who represented and were influenced by this ironic celebration of 'bad taste' were the artists Andrew Logan and Derek Jarman, fashion designers Zandra Rhodes and Anthony Price, and the (at the time) fashion editor Michael Roberts. This social circle was less centred on a part of London, or on a specific shopping district, because, said York, they got their clothes from second-hand shops or made their own. However, he listed Swanky Modes in Camden, shoe designer Manolo Blahnik's Zapata, Vivienne Westwood's SEX and the second-hand store Acme Attractions as places they might shop, the latter of which linked this scene to punk. Along with Westwood's boutique at the far end of the King's Road, Acme Attractions was a social centre (both Caroline Baker and Iain R. Webb mention borrowing clothes from here), and the street remained a hang-out for young people looking for others with similar tastes and interests. Above all, it became a destination for young, aspiring punks, as Judy Blame explained:

> If you weren't in Covent Garden at the time, as a dressed-up youngster, you'd parade down the King's Road still. There'd be all the markets, and Vivienne's shop was always the full-stop of the King's Road.[2]

The area around Covent Garden market was the location of PX, another clothing store, and Radar Records. It was also the location of the Blitz club, which was to become an important venue in the evolution of the New Romantic (or 'The Cult with No Name') style that followed punk, as those involved in the original scene became frustrated with its increasing homogeneity and uniformity. PX was a clothing store run by Helen Robinson and Stephane Raynor. Raynor had been a co-owner of Acme Attractions. The choice of locations for his stores is indicative of the drift of subcultural activity between Kings Road and Covent Garden (he also founded BOY, another boutique on the Kings Road that gained notoriety in the 1980s). The staff in PX were DJs and club promoters in the local scene; the designer Stephen Jones opened his first hat shop in its basement, and the types of clothing made and sold by Robinson would come to typify New Romantic fashion. This clustering of subcultures, networked with other central London stores, clubs and squats, would become key to the evolution of 1980s style culture. As I discuss in this chapter, this tight community of artists, clubbers and young designers, all with a highly competitive attitude to dressing up and a simultaneous mistrust of and obsession with fashion, contributed to the way that stylists were dressing themselves and the looks they were constructing for style magazines.

This local activity reflected a much broader shift in Western fashion – in tandem with the advent of ready-to-wear – from 'top down' couture-led fashion to a model that accepted the influence of 'bottom up' sources. Yet the established gatekeepers of British fashion were reluctant to consider street style's relevance. There remained a degree of snobbery amongst mainstream fashion publications regarding designers who were seen to have originated 'on the street'. As Stephen Jones explained:

> Street fashion was sort of anything for the under-25s. A label like BodyMap was termed 'street fashion' because 'real fashion' was Dior or Chanel, or Caroline Charles. And the magazines hated street fashion because it really threatened their supremacy and their links to advertising.[3]

Jones stressed that designers who are now considered credible by all the fashion press were not originally seen as legitimate:

> For example, Vivienne Westwood was never featured in *Vogue* because they thought she was street fashion, not real fashion. They were two very, very separate things, two very separate worlds. And it was really Terry Jones, when he started *i-D*, the reason he did that was because there was so much going on and absolutely nobody was featuring it. So, what they did was pictures of people walking down the street, putting their own looks together.[4]

Threaded through this book are various definitions of style and fashion. One that is revisited more than once is this subcultural definition of style as a form of 'anti-fashion'. The 1980s style culture in London was a further manifestation of this dialogue between street style and mainstream fashion. Postwar subcultures in Britain had – although the relationship between the two is more complex and mutually dependent – developed to oppose mainstream fashion. Valerie Steele also attributes the apparent anti-fashion sentiment in the 1970s to the countercultural activity and protests of the late 1960s, particularly feminism (1991: 280). Caroline Baker has, from the outset, maintained that her primary interest and source of inspiration was street fashion, and she was motivated by similar feminist principles. As I will go on to discuss in later chapters, this conversation between subculture and mainstream, or authenticity and commercialism, is key to the ways that the style press – especially *The Face* – addressed their audiences and is central to the way that the freelance fashion stylist evolved in the 1980s.

London Punk

Although it preceded the period covered in this book, the relatively short-lived subcultural genre of punk is fundamental to the development of the style press and the specific form of fashion styling that evolved from it. It represents a precursor to a shared approach to creative practice in music, dress and other forms of cultural production. It is cited by Simon Foxton and Iain R. Webb as a motivating factor in their decision to move to the city as teenagers. For many, it was a frame of reference for their countercultural, anti-establishment standpoint and experimental ways of working and dressing. British punk is commonly defined as arriving in London in the summer of 1976, although the ingredients that contributed to its style and ethos can be traced back to earlier moments in the 1970s, or the previous decade. Many of my interviewees were born at the tail end of the 1950s or at the very beginning of the 1960s, and were in their mid-teens when punk arrived, so it is perhaps not surprising that it figured as an important moment in their formation.

The year 1976 was an especially difficult one for the British economy. In March, the pound fell below two dollars for the first time ever. A fortnight later the prime minister, Harold Wilson, resigned, and the pound continued to lose value. By the end of September, Chancellor of the Exchequer Dennis Healey was forced to ask the International Monetary Fund for a $3.9 billion support package, an amount which, at the time, was the largest ever to have been offered by the fund. From the outset, the 1970s had been a time of economic insecurity in Britain. The early 1970s had marked a global tide-change that had, in part, been reliant on the financial and industrial success of the United States. A series of economic difficulties, notably the collapse of fixed exchange rates in 1971, followed by an Arab oil embargo in 1973 that targeted Israeli sympathizers, ended in a recession that affected most Western economies. The decline is often attributed to the left-wing government of the mid-1970s. However, the relative lack of success of the Conservative prime minister Edward Heath's tenure prior to this is also considered to be a factor. The social discontent of the 1970s is said to have contributed to the emergence of punk as a subcultural phenomenon and, although its roots can be traced further back, the nihilism of British punk is considered a dramatization of the political unrest in the country at the time (Hebdige 1979).

The origins and scope of British punk are commonly contested. Hebdige defines it as an amalgam of influences. It merged glam rock and David Bowie with American proto-punk (the Ramones, the Heartbreakers, Richard Hell) and mod, northern soul and reggae. Glam and Bowie, Hebdige says, contributed 'narcissism, nihilism and gender confusion', but also some stylistic reference points (1979: 25). Although the political climate provided a convenient excuse for the anger of punk, the aggression was also a symptom of its members' distaste for the hippies of the late 1960s, whose 'peace and love' principles now felt irrelevant and deeply unfashionable. The cult around Bowie that morphed into punk, and into the post-punk London club culture that followed, differed from previous subcultures because it dealt with gender issues rather than class-related problems.

In the mid- to late 1970s, the punk scene in London had been concentrated on certain clubs in the West End of London. The Roxy in Neal Street, Covent Garden, is often cited as the primary hub for the emerging punk scene, evolving from its previous incarnation as Chaguarama to a venue for punk music acts (Savage 2005). The lesbian club Louise's, in Poland Street in Soho, is also considered central to the scene, as is Crackers, another gay club whose Bowie night in 1975 was already attracting punks. Louise's had a reputation for its exclusive entry policy, which was partly motivated by its limited capacity as a venue. It forced its patrons to consider dress in a competitive way, to ensure that they looked interesting or unique enough to be let in (Miles 2010; Jones 2021).

Vivienne Westwood and her entrepreneur boyfriend Malcom McLaren are frequently referred to as the originators of punk. This was perpetuated by McLaren's role as the manager of the band The Sex Pistols, who were seen as the embodiment of punk style and music. Those interviewed for this book put forward varied perspectives on the origins and form of punk. Barrie Sharpe pointed out that, although many of the stereotypical stylistic references that we now associate with punk were generated by McLaren, punk as a subcultural phenomenon occurred before their intervention and in other parts of London:

> Punk didn't start as a musical movement in England. It started in a club called the Lacy Lady, in Seven Kings [in Ilford, Greater London], one of the trendiest clubs in England at the time; people came from all over the country to go there. It was a fun club. You had these girls, they wore bin liners and cat suits. Cutting cats ears into their hair and wearing safety pins as earrings. You know, the whole Malcolm McLaren thing was . . . they cashed into it after. It was already happening on the street. In the shops, they were a different sort of punk. Real punks, they wore second-hand suits and stuff. They might have had spiky hair but not Mohicans, none of that crap.[5]

Judy Blame refers to punk as 'the age of character' (2016), and initially punk was centred on the idea that everyone should have their own individual 'look' and dress as creatively as possible, often with very few available resources. Unlike previous postwar British subcultures, punk didn't have a unifying style. It borrowed motifs, themes and items of dress from other subcultures, but also from film costume, uniform and fetish wear. Caroline Baker says that although the constituents for punk style already existed, McLaren 'got hold of it and stirred it up'. As someone who was already in her thirties and had already worked for over a decade as a fashion editor and stylist when she collaborated with Westwood in the 1980s, Baker's perspective on punk as a cultural phenomenon would not be the same as those, like Sharpe, who experienced it in their formative years (Baker 2017). Westwood herself was already thirty-five in 1976 and McLaren was thirty. They had reinvented their store on the King's Road several times: from Let it Rock, it became Too Fast to Live Too Young to Die in 1972, dealing in biker rock items; in 1974 it became SEX, then Seditionaries in 1977. The store, despite being a social space and subcultural reference point, was run as a business and intended to make money. The clothing styles that were sold in the Seditionaries store were relatively expensive, with bondage trousers selling for £50 (equivalent to around £260 in 2024) and a parachute shirt for £30 (around £170).

According to the well-trodden principles of subcultural development, a subculture loses its authenticity when it is eventually recuperated into dominant, mainstream culture. This is often caused by overexposure in the media, which rationalizes or ridicules its behaviours, or as its styles of dress or music become mimicked or commodified. Nevertheless, Angela McRobbie is critical of those who suggest that subculture remains genuine until it is exploited by those who sell it to a mass market. She sees punk as an example of a seemingly countercultural form that understood and 'flirted with' the process of recuperation, being aware of its own subcultural status and capitalizing on its position (1994: 3). McRobbie claims that punks used mass media to gain publicity and to sell the artwork and merchandise they generated and considers McLaren and Westwood as central to this activity. She also suggests that they were integral to the formation of punk subculture, rather than merely operating as 'hustlers who push their way into the subculture from outside' (1994: 161). Their readiness to generate hype and publicity around punk was almost certainly directly linked to their desire for financial gain.

The legacy of punk, regardless of its origins, is central to the outlook of those involved in the creative scene in London in the early 1980s. Iain R. Webb claims that punk also inspired the way that he wrote, stating that Bowie, punk and St Martin's art college were his 'troika of style'. For Webb, the flamboyance and individualism that were key to punk, via glam rock and Bowie, shaped the way that he worked and his attitude to creative process throughout his career (Webb 2017). This mentality also had an influence on the attitudes of clubbers in the early 1980s and on the spirit and collective identity of Buffalo. Punk situated itself in 'the widening gap between artist and audience' (Hebdige 1979: 63), and the moral belief that 'anyone can do it' was key to the mindset of the young emerging freelance stylists, many of whom had no prior experience of, and limited access to, fashion.

The Now Crowd, New Romantic, or The Cult with No Name

Nightclubbing in London has always been important to the British fashion, music and publishing industries. Above all, it was London's nightlife that proved vital to the development of style culture. In the mid- to late 1970s, the punk scene in London had been focused on certain clubs. The entry policy of Louise's epitomized the spirit of the first British punks, who had prioritized ingenuity and the construction of a unique identity, or look, over loyalty to a tribal style. This tenet was retained by subsequent iterations of club culture in central London. Entry into venues was often restricted, with great importance placed on stylistic and aesthetic originality and innovative use of materials or themes (Elms 1980; Smith 2011; Stanfill 2013). The elitism propagated by these subcultural communities was a motivating force that encouraged a highly competitive approach to outfit construction. Evans and Thornton refer to this as a 'new aristocracy of dress display' (1989).

Street and club style was being documented by photographers, such as Steve Johnston, and was included in the pages of the style press when they launched. A feature in the July 1980 issue of *The Face*, entitled 'You're Not Going Out Dressed Like That (Again)', described the ambience, music and dress codes at Studio 21, a Saturday club night in a venue next to Tottenham Court Road tube station.[6] The photographs accompanying the written piece showed the breadth of sartorial styles among young clubbers. A later article in the same magazine by the then-young journalist Robert Elms (November 1980) announced the emergence of 'The Cult with No Name', a scene that had started with a David Bowie themed night in Billy's, a tiny club in a basement in Dean Street. Crackers had already hosted a Bowie night in 1975, and the singer's inventive use of make-up and costume to create various on-stage personas was an obvious influence on the eclecticism and 'conscious stylization' of clubbers attending these nights. Elms classes the environment as 'a mutual admiration society for budding narcissists, a creative and competitive environment where individualism was stressed, and change was vital' (1980: 23). The scene he describes is often more widely referred to as New Romantic but was also called 'the Now Crowd' at the time. Despite its legacy, Billy's was relatively short-lived, only lasting a few months. Its organizers opened a new event at Blitz, a wine bar in Great Queen Street in Covent Garden. New styles were being introduced amongst the clients of the club at a rapid pace. Looks included 'rockabillies, New Psychedelia, Regency fops, bobtails (artificial dreadlocks woven into hair and bound with rags), zoot suits, flat tops, African prints [and] 1960s pastiche (beehives and winklepickers)' (Evans and Thornton 1989: 37). A willingness to pillage the history of dress and to reappropriate and customize second-hand clothing was very evident amongst clubbers. Versions of these looks were being seen in the fashion images being created by young stylists, many of whom were regulars at the clubs. A sale of redundant stock at a London costume house was a contributing factor to some of the flamboyant looks being displayed at the more exclusive clubs. Local fashion businesses, such as PX, or second-hand stores, like Acme Attractions or Flip, provided further ingredients.

The term New Romantic, although often applied to this scene, is in many ways limiting. It refers to one style that existed for a short space of time before becoming a mainstream commodity when bands like Spandau Ballet (regulars at Blitz) achieved success and appeared in magazines and on television. It can mainly be attributed to the ruffled shirts sold by Robinson in PX, but elements of billowing romanticism can be seen in the styling of Caroline Baker, Westwood and also, notably, in the first collection of the young designer John Galliano a few years later. However, for the crowds patronizing Billy's, Blitz and the other nights that followed, there was no common style. Nobody wanted to look the same as everybody else.

Despite being highly elitist, there was tolerance and acceptance of a broader range of sexualities and genders in Billy's and Blitz, and in the later clubs in London that attracted similar crowds. The campness and extreme costumes worn by the clubbers meant that they would also not have been admitted to the more conservative gay clubs in London. In many gay venues, men still wore identical, hyper-masculine 'clone' looks. Stylists like Simon Foxton, Iain R. Webb, Judy Blame and Ray Petri were attracted to clubs like Blitz, Billy's or Cha Cha's for several reasons, partly because they welcomed gay men, but also because they tolerated, even celebrated, forms of dress that would have been ridiculed or aggressed in other social spaces. It was not only homosexual men who felt more comfortable in queer social spaces. Mitzi Lorenz said that she started going to gay clubs when she was fourteen, partly because her mother thought she would be safer among gay men than in straight clubs:

> I was already going out to clubs and hanging out with loads of famous people. [Record producer and DJ] Mark Moore was a friend of mine, he lived down the road. Mark was good because my mum allowed me to go with him. She didn't mind if I went to gay clubs. Because it was four girls, in a kind of rough neighbourhood, she used to always say 'Oh, we don't want any unwanted children in this house', but if I was going out to a gay club it was fine. Mark was so nice and polite, and he made sure I got home in a cab. So long as I went with him and I was going to be brought home by him, it was fine.[7]

The photographer's agent Ziggi Golding said that it never occurred to her that Taboo, which came later, in 1985, would be classed as a gay club. For her it was 'just another form of expression'. This club scene was, she says, not only accepting of sexuality but also of racial difference (Golding 2017). Taboo attracted, in addition to a crowd of young clubbers, what Barry Miles describes as 'the old glamour crowd', and what York had previously labelled Them. What these two scenes shared was a sense of camp and theatricality (Miles 2010; York 1980: 48). There was a common interest among these artists and clubbers in celebrating the artifice of popular culture in an ironic, knowing way. Taboo, which ran from 1985 to 1987, has been considered so influential that it has since been developed into a West End musical, loosely based on the lives of Boy George, Steve Strange and Leigh Bowery (although the timeline and plot incorporate various aspects of 1970s and 1980s club culture).

The late 1970s and early 1980s witnessed a proliferation of London club scenes, each catering for a different type of clientele and styles. The September 1986 issue of *The Face* featured a diagram that mapped the evolution of club nights starting with Billy's and Mayhem Studios, a warehouse event which also started in 1978. From these starting points, the diagram tracks 135 different club events over a ten-year period. It is colour-coded so the reader can identify the lineage of each scene. For example, it shows that Rusty Egan and Steve Strange, who hosted Billy's and Blitz went on to run Hell, Cha Cha's and Flicks in 1980, then Club for Heroes, The People's Palace, the Sterling Club and The Venue in 1981. There was a constant shift in relevance or status from club to club, or from night to night. Word-of-mouth was the primary mode of communication; young people shared the details about new events by picking up flyers in pubs or shops or going to areas, such as the Kings Road, where they knew they would meet people with similar tastes or interests. However, the style press also played a part in publicizing, or critiquing, the most important events of the London club scene. 'BPM/AM' in the February

1986 issue of *i-D* (see Fig. 2) is an example of the coverage of nightlife that continued to feature in the style press. It describes the environment within a range of new club nights but also serves to publicize future events. It lists what they are drinking, how they are behaving and what they are wearing, but also what they do for a living. Caryn Franklin describes the club culture in London as 'live social networking', comparing the experience of clubbing in the 1980s to contemporary social media (Franklin 2017). Robin Derrick, who appears in this feature, said that he would also go to clubs with the photographer Steve Johnston just to capture the looks of the clubbers, adding that he went to a club every single night between the ages of twenty and twenty-nine (Derrick 2017).

Clubbing was seen as a necessary way of ensuring currency, being seen and demonstrating belonging. Aside from the creative communities being developed in the art colleges and housing collectives of central London, the clubs provided an environment to share ideas, through talking to each other but also by observing and absorbing. Webb recalled that while clubbing, his peers were mostly 'talking about plans, making films, doing collections'. He says they were 'dreaming up ideas and creating' (Webb 2017). Mitzi Lorenz explained how clubs were an environment for fashion experimentation, for trialling looks that were translated into the fashion images that featured in magazines:

> Our mornings, our evenings, our nights, we would sort of live and breathe image-making. And talk about it. Our social lives were very much about going out to clubs and having a look for the night, and a different look every time we went out. So basically, what we were doing in the nightclubs, what I would be experimenting with in terms of looks and finding interesting, different things to make an outfit we just started doing in the studio on people.[8]

For Ziggi Golding, the club she ran was an extension of her business (Golding 2017). There was no boundary between the work of her creative agency and the events she facilitated, which were a promotional opportunity and a chance to demonstrate affiliation with a scene. As she explains:

> I remember, my agency, we took over the Tabernacle, which was then just a community centre, and we did this thing. So, [photographer and filmmaker] Dick Jewell did all the films, we'd project all the films up there. Rachel Auburn was one of our DJs. We had lots of DJs: Jeremy Healy, Rachel, the W11 Express. In the 1980s, I had the agency first and then I met someone, and we started a record company, and we were the early days of hip-hop so we would hijack hip hoppers coming in to go to our club. I mean, we had Slick Rick, Doug E Fresh, we had KRS-One. We were all part of a scene. So, while you had Taboo and all of that, you had all these kinds of things going on, so music, fashion, film and art were all in one place.[9]

The London club scene became known further afield. The city became a magnet for international designers coming from Paris, but also Tokyo and New York. Both ready-to-wear and couture designers from overseas were attracted to the nightlife and to the street style as a source of fashion, particularly clubs like the Mud Club and Taboo (Golding 2017). Conversely, international club culture was providing a platform for young designers connected to the London scene. For example, BodyMap, with the patronage of New York club promoter Suzanne Bartsch, gained commercial success in the United States and was subsequently stocked by the fashion retailers Joseph and Whistles. This had further benefit for the creatives within their own network. The designers Stevie Stewart and David Holah drew on the connections they had made in London, such as the dancer Michael Clark, for whom they later made stage costumes, or well-known clubbers like Leigh Bowery and Trojan, who made the invitations for their shows (O'Byrne 2009).

The last incarnation of this 1980s club culture – and possibly the most excessive– was Kinky Gerlinky, a night started in 1989 by Michael and Gerlinde Costiff in the late 1980s in Legends, Old Burlington Street.

Prior to running the club, the Costiffs had opened World, a shop on Litchfield Street selling a curated selection of artefacts. They regularly flew to New York, Rio or other parts of the world and would collect items they found interesting. The store became a medley of objects or clothing items produced by young creatives – Keith Haring prints, Bodyglove latex clothing, Anarchic Adjustments t-shirts – mixed with unusual one-off pieces found on their travels. As Michael explained, stylists like Kim Bowen, Judy Blame and Ray Petri would regularly come into the store to borrow items for photographic shoots, to be featured in magazines. He claimed they would often take inspiration from the displays that he constructed in the windows or within the store, drawing a comparison between the practices of window dressing, or the 'visual merchandising' of instore displays, with the process of styling:

> It used to annoy me. I am a bit of a stylist myself, so I did all the displays. Something like that [points at a photo of a World shop display], a stylist would just come in and just take that. Lift the whole thing. It irked me a bit but it's almost like a compliment as well.[10]

World was also a meeting place for fashionable Londoners, attracting a similar crowd to the club scene and, like Bazaar, Biba, SEX, Acme Attractions and PX before it, provided a daytime hang-out for young people at a time 'before coffee shops, and mobile phones' (Costiff 2022). The interactions taking place socially were integral to cultural production at the time but the status that involvement in these social scenes accorded is also significant. For example, former stylist Zee Shore defined herself as an outsider to the social scene in London at the time; she felt that her lack of interest in clubbing was detrimental to her career, calling it her 'Achilles heel' (Shore 2017). However, although clubs and clothes shops would seem the most obvious places for style-centred social activity, the creative culture of London at the time took place in other spaces: in educational establishments and domestic environments.

Art School

London's educational establishments provided another key context for easy access to likeminded people with shared values and creative interests. Perhaps the most important hub was St Martin's School of Art, which by 1978 had 650 students and ran courses in art, fashion and graphic design (Llewellyn 2015). This is also where Iain R. Webb, Stephen Jones and Simon Foxton studied fashion; and Robin Derrick and Caryn Franklin, graphic design. During the 1970s and 1980s, the school was situated on Charing Cross Road and at various locations in Soho. This had been London's arty, bohemian area since the 1930s, and in the 1950s had become known for its underground music scene. Thanks to its location, St Martin's naturally interacted with the local art scene. By the 1960s, Soho's vibrant youth culture had attracted the media, publishing, film and television industries, developing an 'offbeat, creative [and] novel' character (Porter 1994: 443).

St Martin's had a strong reputation for art education, and entry was competitive. From 1976, tuition fees (though relatively minimal) were abolished and prospective students would apply to join a course based on the quality of their portfolio alone. To many, being given a place at the college felt like privilege. Webb, for example, remembers strongly aspiring to become a student specifically at St Martin's despite being brought up in a small village in the west of England:

> My favourite designer at the time was Bill Gibb and he'd studied at St Martin's School of Art; he also came from a really big family in rural Scotland so there were quite big similarities between us. So, as soon as I heard about St Martin's School of Art, I thought that's what I wanted to do. I had to go to art school, specifically St Martin's School of Art, to study fashion. So, I applied to do a Foundation course at Salisbury College of Art because at that time we got grants and it had to be a college within the county, so I went there, which was fantastic. It was truly life-changing to be around other people who were also focused on a career in fashion and art. People who thought differently and looked at the world differently. This was 1976, when punk was happening, so it was a very exciting time.[11]

Art school culture has been associated with the origins of punk and it also played a part in the post-punk music and styles, such as New Romantic, that evolved from it. The more spectacular versions of punk style were, according to Nathaniel Weiner, 'products of the British art school system' (2018: 5). The Sex Pistols' bassist Glen Matlock was a student at St Martin's, and the band played their debut performance in its common room. The association of the college with punk was an additional motivating factor for many applying towards the end of the 1970s and the beginning of the 1980s.

St Martin's fostered a sense of interdisciplinarity, which became useful when students graduated and were forced, often due to lack of regular paid work, to do more than one thing to make money. There was also collaboration between students at different institutions, such as Middlesex Polytechnic in north London, which was facilitated by their living arrangements, nightlife and socializing in shops and on the streets:

> When some of my classmates weren't selected for the St Martin's graduation fashion show, the class of 1980, we decided to put on an alternative show, which we staged in an art gallery in Chelsea, the Chenil Gallery. I think it was in August of that year. And it was called 'No Sacrifice'. Melissa Caplan, one of my friends from the Blitz club, had dropped out of the fashion course at Middlesex, she hadn't had a graduation show, so she asked if she could be in the show and was eventually the finale. She got all these people, Blitz club people, from the Warren Street squat to model for her; John Maybury modelled in her show, and David Holah modelled in it because he was at Middlesex and graduated the next year along with Stevie Stewart. They went on to form BodyMap together. So, the scene was incredibly supportive, and I think that even Stephen [Jones] did hats for Melissa at that show as well. Whilst I was at St Martin's, myself and Stephen Jones, who was in the year above, and Fiona Dealy, who was in the year below, were all living as flat mates together. Again, it was that sort of cross-pollination of all these different ages and different courses and different colleges then. I think it was just much more collaborative, the lines between the colleges, the different mediums, the different courses, were blurred a lot more, so you had people from graphics involved with fashion people and fashion people involved with art people and all working together on different things.[12]

Webb notes that St Martin's educational principles, along with an early internship with the fashion and textile designer Zandra Rhodes, had a long-lasting effect on his work ethic (2017). Crucially, those without direct access to art education also benefitted from living and socializing with art students. As Jeffrey Hinton observed:

> I wasn't educated but you get educated indirectly because you're living with people who are. So, they're showing me things too but just in the way that I want them, in the way that I like, rather than a sit-up school sort of scenario. I was never very good in structures. I don't really like authority. I don't function well with being told. I have to understand why it is how it is, rather than just do it because I'm told to do it. I'm stubborn like that. So, I did learn things from John [Maybury] and from Cerith about film. They were working with film, but I really liked working with video. It was very immediate. And fashion. I was with fashion people, and we were dressing up all the time. Or making stuff.[13]

Blame has also said that his friendships with art students, like the graphic designers Malcolm Garret and Peter Saville, expanded his knowledge ('about Bauhaus and Warhol'). He later worked collaboratively with collage artist Linder Sterling (Blame 2016).

Squatting and Collectivism

The geographical proximity of squats, art schools and nightclubs facilitated ease of interaction and a collective identity. This played out through vibrant subcultural activity in both public and private settings. The availability of vacant housing in central London during the late 1970s and early 1980s enabled those involved in the local social scene to find free accommodation within shared, abandoned houses. During the 1970s, the capital had also experienced a drop in population, with more than three quarters of a million people moving out of the Greater London area. The increase in squatting in London reflected a similar trend in other European countries, where the occupation of illegal properties had become more commonplace. Aside from practical and economic reasons, this was also a consequence of the hippies' promotion of communal living (Vasudevan 2017). The area behind Warren Street tube station comprised many empty buildings that, as illegal squats, housed students, artists and prominent figures on the social scene. In London, groups of squatters mobilized themselves to take over empty properties, often in areas that had long waiting lists for social housing. Both domestic and commercial properties were occupied. Rees and German cite an example of a disused bank building in Tolmers Square, on Euston Road opposite Warren Street, that became a highly organized and long-lived squat (Rees and German 2012). This cluster of squats, incorporating communities of creatives, represents just one example of collective resistance to property speculation in London at that time. A protest about the redevelopment by Westminster City Council of the 'Carburton Street Triangle', an area bounded by Great Titchfield Street, Greenwell Street and Carburton Street, was well publicized. The proposal to demolish Georgian townhouses within the triangle was contested for several years – by Save Britain's Heritage, by tenants and by the organizers of the Easter 80 housing collective – before finally being razed in 1983.

Communities of artists and clubbers were constantly migrating and reforming. As a case study, Miles describes the activities in and around one squat on Carburton Street. His description illustrates the diverse, densely populated but transient nature of this community. Home to members of the art collective the Neo-Naturists – Christine and Jennifer Binnie, Wilma Johnson and Grayson Perry – the squat he describes was also occupied by clubbers Marilyn and Boy George, and by the 'music hall double act' Robert Hall and Robert Durrant (Miles 2010: 383). The nature of squatting is that communities are built and rebuilt as people move on, recluster and reconnect. Inhabitants of the Carburton Street squat moved to 65 Warren Street, in the same area, which housed Jeffrey Hinton, the filmmaker John Maybury, and David Holah of the fashion label BodyMap. The house backed on to another building on Euston Road, creating a further direct link to another community of squatters. Binnie and Perry moved again to live in the basement of a building that Marilyn had previously shared with the artist-filmmaker Cerith Wyn-Evans (Miles 2010).

Of those interviewed for this book, Jeffrey Hinton, Iain R. Webb, Mitzi Lorenz and Stephen Jones lived in squats. Stephen Jones was still squatting in the area when he started his millinery business. Juggling work and social life, he said he spent years 'running a hat company but coming home at five with twenty-five people' (Jones 2017). Hinton remembered the living arrangements in Warren Street being quite loose. He often slept in other people's rooms. He noted that Warren Street was divided into two sides, not only architecturally but also socially. One side comprised Georgian buildings, which he claimed was home to artists, while the other side he described as 'kind of druggy' (Hinton 2017). A reality of squatting is the threat of being moved on by the police. After several years, Hinton was evicted. However, he continued to live in 'hard to let' housing, because at the time he was receiving unemployment benefit payments (Hinton 2017). During the first few years of Thatcher's tenure as prime minister, unemployment figures had risen markedly. By the end of 1983 there were three million unemployed people in Britain, more than double the number in 1979. The fact that the stylists and other contributors to the style press were able to fund themselves, through either welfare payments or student maintenance grants, contributed to the facility of freelance working. As did their rent-free accommodation. By the end of the 1980s, though, Margaret Thatcher had introduced an act (the Social Security Act) that made it more difficult for people to receive welfare payments if they were not seen to be actively seeking work.

There were shared values within this community, a collective sense of 'otherness'. Hinton and Webb both referred to them as 'outsiders' (2017; Blackman and Davies 2019: 81). Collaboration happened organically in squats because people spent so much time together and this gave rise to a very particular creative milieu:

> It's also very quick because when you're living with a whole group, you're in each other's lives, so you don't need to make meetings because you're in one big meeting. You're with each other, so things naturally change and adapt and it's really interesting. I think I'm lucky, I've had lots of those experiences because I didn't have to put myself in a place, try and sell myself, try and prove anything, try and do all that competitive stuff. We were put in this unique position of knowing all these things about each other.[14]

This connectivity and sense of creative community also played out in a fashion environment, a sense of informality, camaraderie and anti-professionalism. As Caryn Franklin noted:

> 'Real' has become a different word but going back to being immersed in the BodyMap era and cutting my teeth in a fashion moment, when BodyMap would be on the catwalk and their mums, their aunties and clubland friends would model, there was real life. As a young woman, I saw these amazing-looking women with grey hair doing their thing. And with the clubland contingent, there would be a range of shapes, sizes, body types, also diverse race and queer culture representation. Everyone looking cool, amazing, inspirational. Of course, there'd be some models. Michael Clark [who also squatted in Warren Street] would normally pop up having choreographed a bit of catwalk action. People would

> even get up off their seats in the audience and dance, just like 'It's London! We're having some fun!' and that's what I thought fashion was in the early-mid '80s and that's always been my vision of fashion. Everyone included – looking cool and amazing. So, when it began to change, jettisoning the characters in favour of the homogenized model body, I felt we were seeing a corporatization of appearance, although I can say all this with hindsight. It was as if creatives I'd started out with, were being sucked into a kind of bigger, competitive space in which they were expected to have to behave in a certain way.[15]

It would be convenient to localize creative activity to certain subcultural groups or geographical boundaries as there was clearly migration and cross-pollination between different scenes. For example, the Buffalo collective, which developed slightly later, was formed further afield, although its collaborators were also actively involved in the West End social life of central London. Buffalo member Mitzi Lorenz lived in a squat in Euston, in the same area as the Warren Street communities. She spent part of her time there and the remainder in a house in Primrose Hill she shared with Ray Petri and the photographer Jamie Morgan (Lorenz 2017). Communities travelled to find pockets of activity that suited their musical interests or subcultural affiliations. For example, the members of Buffalo would socialize in both West London and Soho but would also travel to Peckham or Dalston to visit reggae clubs (Lorenz 2020). According to Hinton, the 'energies' of these communities of squatters and clubbers were largely channelled into the production of magazines (Hinton 2017).

Britain, Politics and Publishing

Although this chapter has focused mainly on local cultures and social situations, the political environment in Britain throughout the 1980s deserves a mention. It became a theme in the image-making of many young stylists but was also a factor in the development of opportunities for the emerging freelance stylist. Margaret Thatcher became Conservative party leader in 1975, and prime minister in 1979. She proposed radical changes, a neoliberal response to counter the economic stagnation witnessed earlier in the decade. Her move towards a new mode of, fiercely capitalist, conservatism ended a thirty-year period of social democratic consensus between European states, which had been necessary for societal and economic reconstruction in the aftermath of the Second World War (Hayes 1994). Thatcher's government of the early 1980s instigated a move away from an industrial economy which relied on union-controlled manufacturing industries to a model where services, media and enterprise became new priorities (McRobbie 1998).

Thatcher's policies had an impact on the publishing industries in Britain. Between 1980 and 1988, the government introduced a series of acts that were devised to weaken the influence of the unions and control industrial disputes. The precarious economic situation, along with competition from other media, especially television, had caused a sharp drop in the sales of mass-market magazines. Initially seeking to cut costs in the pre-press and print sectors of the industry, publishers introduced new technology to counter rising print costs and reduce the number of staff. These plans were opposed by the trade unions but, unsurprisingly, supported by Margaret Thatcher's government. The subsequent success of the employers, after a well-publicized strike, weakened the influence of the print unions. The National Union of Journalists also lost credibility throughout the 1980s, and publishers' existing policies on pay, casual labour, redundancy and overtime were progressively withdrawn, leading to 'more flexible, responsive and innovative' forms of production and business organization to maintain or improve profitability (Gough-Yates 2002: 53; also Hayes 1994). Many of those becoming freelance stylists for independent publications were initially not being paid (Lynge-Jorlen 2016; Lifter 2018). However, as the freelance stylist became a known quantity, paid opportunities arose within the editorial teams of established publications.

The move from an economy centred on industrial production to one that is more reliant on service industries was not unique to Britain. As manufacturing declined in the United States and other European countries, there was an increased demand for the creation – or crystallization – of occupational roles in sectors that provided 'symbolic goods and services' (Bourdieu 2010: 359). The freelance fashion stylist represents one of these roles.

Although political influence on the publishing industries actually created openings for freelance stylists, the creatives who initially contributed to early style magazines saw themselves as sitting outside of established forms of publishing. They certainly wouldn't have aligned themselves with the Conservative government's version of enterprise culture or felt themselves representative of global trends in media employment. Many of them were politically minded. This is apparent in the way that London stylists, magazine editors, journalists and photographers chose to work and live. It also informed their attitudes to art, design and fashion. As Blame said, 'We were reacting against our environment, but we wanted to do it creatively' (2016). Political intentions came through in their image-making, or in the collective ethos of the publications for whom they worked at the time. They often responded to perceived inequalities in society or represented protest against the dominant political stance.

The Thatcher government provided further opportunity for protest. Its policies addressed immediate economic issues, but its approach was less concerned with any resulting social inequalities. A 'new racism' was emerging, and this was actively promoted by Thatcher's New Right (Mercer 1994: 8). Government policies were seen as directly contributing to frustration in Black and Asian communities, through her apparent support of anti-immigrant politics, through the elevated level of unemployment that occurred during her premiership, and through initiatives that gave the police more authority to stop and search, all of which caused tensions in urban areas. By contrast, the policies of the left-wing Greater London Council – representing an electorate who had ensured a Labour majority since the early 1970s – had championed an anti-racist agenda (Porter 1994). Yet the early 1980s was seen as a renaissance, as communities created pockets of resistance to ultra-conservative attitudes but also expressed their frustration with the inadequacy of left-wing policies (Mercer 1994). Rock Against Racism and the Anti-Nazi League were youth initiatives that formed in the 1970s in response to racist factions. 2-Tone, a music label formed in the late 1970s, was a 'confederation' of bands from a mixture of ethnic and urban backgrounds across the country, which set out to make a statement about multiculturalism by fusing reggae and punk, both musically and visually. 2-Tone was well represented by *The Face* when it first launched.

The Conservative Party's introduction of discriminatory policies targeting other minority groups also led to community action. Thatcher, as the first female British prime minister, was not well placed to promote patriarchy, but in fact she actively peddled Victorian family values (Porter 1994). Party values were conventionally family-orientated, traditional and based on Christian heterosexual values. She was associated with the introduction of controversial bills such as Clause 28, which prevented schools or local authorities from promoting homosexuality. The bill (also referred to as Section 28) was seen as a reaction to the support given by the Greater London Council to local gay community groups and educational initiatives with an anti-discriminatory focus. Clause 28, understandably, prompted an increase in the mobilization of gay rights activity in Britain at the time. However, many staunch traditionalists felt the Thatcher administration had not done enough to address the continuing liberal attitudes that had dominated British society since the second half of the 1960s (Hayes 1994). Race and identity politics were constant themes in both the journalism and editorial direction of the style press and, as discussed in Chapters 4 and 5, they were explicitly quoted in the styled fashion images appearing in these magazines.

The social environment of London in the early 1980s bred a distinct creative culture that led to the emergence of new practices in the fields of fashion publishing and advertising. Communities of niche interests formed, and these fed the profusion of new styles appearing on the streets and in the clubs. As discussed in the next chapter, these communities provided the talent for the new independent magazines but also the content, as they documented the music they were making, their art projects and creative businesses, and the clothes they were wearing. The specific nature of the fashion system in London both influenced and was fed by the approaches and attitudes to the new wave of fashion stylists. Their activities fed into a culture of street style that existed alongside and in defiance of the established fashion industry, building on a network of boutiques and small-scale fashion businesses that already existed, and developing an alternative fashion culture that gained the attention of international designers and media.

Notes

1 Later, Paul Smith's flagship store in Covent Garden, Pam Hogg's shop in Soho, Modern Classics in Shoreditch and Hyper Hyper in Kensington would be equally instrumental in attracting fashionable retailers and shoppers to other parts of London (Stanfill 2013).

2 Blame (2016), interview by Gregoir Muir, 1 June.
3 S. Jones (2017), interview by Philip Clarke, 12 April.
4 S. Jones (2017), interview by Philip Clarke, 12 April.
5 B. Sharpe (2017), interview by Philip Clarke, 10 February.
6 An area that has since been radically redeveloped to serve the new Elizabeth line rail link.
7 M. Lorenz, (2017), interview by Philip Clarke, 17 January.
8 M. Lorenz (2017), interview by Philip Clarke, 17 January.
9 Z. Golding (2017), interview by Philip Clarke, 6 February.
10 M. Costiff (2022), interview by Philip Clarke, 1 March.
11 I. R. Webb (2017), interview by Philip Clarke, 10 May.
12 I. R. Webb (2017), interview by Philip Clarke, 10 May.
13 J. Hinton (2017), interview by Philip Clarke, 23 June.
14 J. Hinton (2017), interview by Philip Clarke, 23 June.
15 C. Franklin (2016), interview by Philip Clarke, 14 December.

Chapter 3

STYLE PRESS AND THE FASHION IMAGE: 1980–1985

During the 1980s the field of British magazine publishing saw the introduction and influence of a new genre of magazine. The 'style press', as they became known, targeted both sexes and existed as a countercultural alternative to mainstream fashion titles. The production methods and format of these publications evolved from fanzines (or 'zines), which were home-made, limited-run magazines distributed among young people with interests in similar music, dress and leisure activities. This chapter looks at both mainstream and style publishing in the first half of the 1980s. It discusses how they documented style culture in London and how the freelance stylist operated in both fields. In addition to interviewing stylists, fashion editors and their peers, I examined a large sample of monthly publications printed in Britain between January 1980 and December 1989. These included the three style publications, which all launched in 1980 (*The Face* in May, *i-D* in August, *Blitz* in September). To provide comparison, I looked at British *Vogue*, *Tatler* and *Harpers & Queen*, society magazines with a long history and strong focus on fashion. Finally, I chose *Cosmopolitan*, as an example of a women's magazine, and the *Sunday Times* and the *Observer*, which had supplements with fashion content. I was looking for evidence of the stylist's input, to answer specific questions: how were creative roles, particularly the closely related roles of fashion editor and stylist, named in the production of fashion features? How did the acknowledgement of stylists and fashion editors compare to that of collaborators, such as the photographer? Did acknowledgement differ between the style magazines and established mainstream publications, and what opportunity did the materialization of this new form of youth publishing represent for the stylist?

From the early 1960s onwards, British popular culture experienced a gradual decentring of the sources of cultural arbitration. This had been seen in fashion where, as discussed in Chapter 2, trends in youth culture were being generated within local social scenes. These were often located in a specific part of London and gave rise to business opportunities for young, unestablished designers and creatives. In broader terms, this decentring reflected wider cultural shifts in Western art, design and fashion. In art, for example, the 1960s had also seen a re-evaluation of the boundaries and points of overlap between the traditional fine arts and applied or commercial forms of art and design. The influence of youth publishing produced in Britain during the 1980s is a further example of fashion 'bubbling up'. This was evidenced in their choice of content, the format of the magazines and the staffing arrangements, which didn't follow standard editorial conventions. Fresh approaches challenged the traditional tastemakers in fashion media, such as magazines like *Vogue* or *Tatler*, or women's interest publications like *Cosmopolitan*. The 'new and radical' forms of fashion publishing introduced throughout the 1980s laid the groundwork for a further 'explosion' of magazines devoted to, or featuring, fashion in the following decade (Cotton 2000).

This diversification of fashion media enabled the dissemination and validation of a wider range of potential subject positions or identities, in terms of gender, sexuality and ethnicity. It demonstrated the willingness of advertisers or editors to respond to these new audiences, even if at times the motivations of certain publications were commercial rather than entirely ethical. Lynge-Jorlen sees *i-D* and *The Face* as the earliest examples of what she defines as 'niche' magazines, publications that represent an alternative fashion media that 'does not have the immediate attention of the masses' (2017: 25). The transformation of British publishing during the 1980s contributed to recognition of the occupation of the stylist, to an increase in career opportunities, and to more aspiring stylists adopting the job title. The stylist became noticed as a key contributor in the production of the fashion image, in line with a wider reappraisal of the formats and sources of fashion information.

Although the editorial analysis in this book is not exhaustive, it provides a clearer insight into the conventions of crediting creative occupations in British fashion publishing. It has allowed comparison between different types of publication and the structure of their production teams. I collated both masthead (the listing of personnel, usually at the front of the publication) and in-feature credits. In respect of the former, this includes in-house staff and freelance, or contributing, editorial personnel. For each magazine, I looked at all content named as 'fashion' or 'style'. These included written features based on fashion topics, trend features documenting what people wore on the streets or what models were wearing on the catwalk, and fashion 'stories' where models have been dressed and photographed in either studio or location settings, to depict a certain theme or trend. Changes in crediting were not always significant, but they often indicated a change in the structuring of the editorial team, a development in the publication's approach to hiring personnel or a wider shift in the perception of a role.

Nova *and Caroline Baker*

In some ways Caroline Baker is an anomaly in a discussion of the stylist, because she largely worked as an in-house fashion editor. She has only been labelled as a stylist retrospectively (Beard 2013; Webb 2021). Her work for *Nova* in the late 1960s and early 1970s is worth mentioning here because it explored new methods in the construction of the fashion image and because of the influence it had on the style magazines that came later. Lynge-Jorlen sees *Nova* as the first example of a 'style bible' (2017: 24). Throughout her career, Baker has worked across both mainstream and niche, independent forms of media. The way she dressed both herself and the models on fashion pages was presented as a demonstration of feminist intent and as an art statement, predating those made by style publications two decades later.

During the 1960s and 1970s, a need was identified for a British magazine that spoke to the concerns of the 'new woman'. *Nova* launched in 1965 and for a relatively short period of time attempted to plug this gap in the market. Although the magazine was clearly aimed at women, it defined itself as 'gender-ambiguous' (Braithwaite 1995: 79). Its target audience was loosely outlined by its editor as 'twenty-eight or thirty-eight, single with a job or married with children'. She was 'a girl with a university degree, or a girl who never took school seriously' (Braithwaite 1995: 79). The magazine aimed to appeal to educated readers. It had a pioneering approach to design, layout and photography and a critical journalistic perspective (Winship 1987: 48). The fashion images on its pages, produced by Baker and her predecessor Molly Parkin, were deliberately provocative and featured types of women and situations that had not previously been seen in a women's magazine ('fat women, old women, and faux-realist sex scenes', Evans 2004). They were also intended to encourage women to start their own creative projects with clothing, and this element of 'how to' carried through to the features Baker produced for *i-D* in the 1980s. For example, for 'Body Wrap Rap' in issue 4 (1980: 9–11) she showed readers various ways of creating wrapped garments with found fabric.

The launch of the British version of *Cosmopolitan* in 1972 is viewed as the main contributing factor to the closure of *Nova* a few years later in 1975. 'Cosmo' was instantly more successful because its market was more clearly defined and because it spoke to a broader audience. The price and the types of advertising in *Nova* made it a direct competitor of *Vogue*, *Queen* and *Harper's Bazaar*, but the inclusion of more risqué material would not have appealed to the reader of these magazines, which attracted conservative women (Braithwaite 1995). The models that Baker styled for the pages of *Nova* were presented as individuals, as real women. Their unique, eclectic looks suggested they were independent thinkers and creative dressers, as opposed to the models seen in *Vogue* dressed head-to-toe in a designer outfit (2013). Interviewed for this book, Baker feels that *Nova* was considered influential, despite not achieving widespread popularity or high readership figures at the time, because it resonated with what many British women felt about society:

> This was the beginning of the women's liberation movement and women were being recognized to be intelligent, to be consumers, to be able to have jobs with the boys; that they might perhaps want to read a magazine that wasn't just about cooking and fashion.[1]

By the 1970s, it had become more acceptable to question the validity of 'top-down' fashion and for magazines to suggest that women didn't need to be told what to wear. Still, most fashion and women's titles were still heavily influenced by designers and brands and were required by their advertisers to show full looks from the latest collections (Steele 2013: 24). After *Nova*, Baker held editorial positions at

Vogue, *Cosmopolitan* and the *Sunday Times*, worked freelance for *i-D*, and collaborated with the fashion designers Vivienne Westwood and Katharine Hamnett. Her methods and influence, principally the ways she presented dress as a political or art statement, are discussed in Chapter 4.

The Birth of the Style Bible

The style bibles, *i-D*, *The Face* and *Blitz*, challenged accepted modes of fashion communication and image-making. The freelance fashion stylist was considered, perhaps for the first time, to have contributed to this. Certain relationships between photographers, stylists and editors were key in stretching the boundaries of fashion photography (Williams 1999: 104). Established fashion and women's publications had well-founded formulae in the ways that they constructed and presented editorial content, and in the ways that they staffed their businesses. The founder of *i-D*, Terry Jones, claims the style magazines 'formed a new micro-sector in the magazine publishing industry' (Gorman 2017: 19). They spoke to a new type of reader. Despite initially being based on the format of home-produced, punk 'zines, these titles were more 'upmarket' than previous youth market magazines. They were more ambitious in terms of projected audience and in their vision of consumer goods (York 1980: 146; also Mort 1996: 23). *The Face* in particular is often regarded cynically, as an example of 'authentic' youth culture being recuperated by the mainstream. Frank Mort suggests that editor Nick Logan's principles, reflected in the editorial stance of *The Face* and its take on both consumer culture and local subculture, originated from his own background as a mod. Mod culture mistrusted the mainstream but viewed itself as a form of elite. This is also a common theme among members of other British postwar subcultures. Mods saw themselves both as tastemakers and consumers, but not consumers of mainstream culture. This perspective very much informed that of the young, freelance stylists working in the 1980s (Mort 1996).

The style magazines were published independently and on a relatively small scale. They relied on the contribution of predominantly unpaid teams of freelancers or those whose involvement was offered on a part-time basis. Contributors often had another paid job or depended on benefits or a student grant to fund their lifestyle. As a side note, Judy Blame claims that the reason many of them adopted pseudonyms was because they were signing on and didn't want to be caught working. It would be convenient to claim that these new modes of staffing and production were affected by the wider changes in the publishing industry discussed in Chapter 2. Yet although the ascendance of the freelance stylist represents an example of the fluctuating landscape of employment in Britain, these magazines were first launched in 1980, before the industry experienced any notable changes. The link between punk culture and enterprise has been noted elsewhere in this book, and their initial ways of working have more in common with subcultural business models. Small-scale youth industries were integral to the punk music scene, in producing artwork and promotional materials, but also short-run, low-budget publications (McRobbie 1994: 153). As the British labour market gradually became a more competitive field, short-term or one-off projects became more commonplace in many areas of the media industry. With less availability of in-house, permanent roles, young freelance creatives relied on alternative ways of finding jobs (Hayes 1994).

The Face has been the most debated magazine and is often credited for the emergence of the stylist (Hebdige 1988; Mort 1996; Lorenz 2000; Gorman 2017). It was first published in May 1980 by Wagadon, a company conceived by Nick Logan specifically to launch the magazine. He had found the funds needed to pay for the magazine's launch from personal savings and the remortgaging of his flat. Logan had previously been editor of both *Smash Hits* and *New Musical Express*, and *The Face* was also primarily a music magazine for the first couple of years. In the beginning, most of the editorial content focused on reviewing the latest music releases and live performances, and interviewing musicians. Over the first few years, the format and content evolved to incorporate a range of political, cultural and style features. Like *Nova*, *The Face* has been critically acclaimed for its innovative design and for presenting imagery and text in a way that challenged norms. Despite being framed as both a product of and reaction to Thatcherism, *The Face*'s philosophy was less directly political. Its methodology has been likened to that of avant-garde artists. It is also described as postmodern, for its ironic view on popular culture and irreverent mixing of styles (Hebdige 1988). The art director Neville Brody was fascinated by the Bauhaus and the typefaces of Herbert Bayer, but these were just ingredients in a complex bricolage of diverse reference points. Despite the apparent counterculture of the content it presented, *The Face* was acutely aware of contemporary marketing and promotional tactics: the magazine was as lauded for its advertising strategies as well as for its editorial content. The two were intrinsically linked, as the cultural capital that association with *The Face* represented made it highly desirable for advertisers.

When it launched, the core editorial team of *The Face* was minimal, with the editor Nick Logan and the in-house design team being joined by a long list of contributors. Most of the photographers listed in the early issues had worked with Logan for the youth music titles *New Musical Express* (*NME*) and *Smash Hits* (Gorman 2017). Although *The Face* started as a specialist music publication, Logan claims that he had always been as keen to focus on the clothes that the groups were wearing as on the music they were playing. The term 'style' was used as a label for clothing-related features. Although it included fashion content, and gradually expanded its remit to feature catwalk coverage and the work of young designers, the emphasis on style signalled its aim to attract a mixed audience, in terms of gender and class, in a way that youth publications had not previously explored. Some 60 per cent of *The Face*'s readership was male and the gender ratio of the production teams on the magazine reflected this (Mort 1996: 44). The original style features in *The Face* were usually modelled by musicians, such as Suggs from Madness, The Polecats, Brian Setzer of The Stray Cats, and John Cooper Clarke. A feature called 'Techno Pop', photographed by Sheila Rock for the July 1981 issue (see Fig. 3), is a good example of this, featuring various members of Japanese pop bands in a constructed setting. The outfits were obviously contrived, as the sources of the clothing were credited. So too were the suppliers of the chrome-coated furniture and accessories that surround the musicians. The first acknowledgment that these photographic portraits of musicians were fabricated, and that someone was responsible for dressing the models or creating the scenario, is a feature entitled 'The Beat Goes on' in September 1981. According to the caption, it was 'staged and photographed' by Rock. Further acknowledgement of the behind-the-scenes production of the features appeared in issue 23, when Jacqui Lefton received a mention for make-up. This led in subsequent issues to hair and models receiving a credit, as further confirmation that these scenarios were manufactured rather than natural.

A credit for 'styling' was first included in issue 27 of *The Face* in 1982. Sheila Rock was named for 'photography and styling' in a feature modelled by Glenn Gregory of the electronic pop group Heaven 17 and Green Gartside of Scritti Politti. Exceptionally, in December of the same year, the art director Jean-Paul Goude was listed for 'photostyling'. If one considers the form of his other creative projects at that time, which were mainly cut-up and airbrushed photographic imagery, it is likely that his input related more to image manipulation than dressing the model. But the use of the term does suggest that the notion of 'styling' as an activity related to image production was gaining currency. These early credits for styling in *The Face* should not automatically lead to the assumption that those doing the styling were stylists. In Rock's case, for example, she was known as a photographer and had built a reputation photographing musicians. What the styling credits did, however, in all style magazines, was reinforce that someone apart from the photographer had been specifically involved in creating the overall look, even if most people still did not understand what their input had been.

From issue 38, styling was consistently credited for almost every style feature. Helen Roberts is said to have instigated the magazine's transition from music to style, and Ray Petri's arrival a couple of years later formalized it (Nick Knight, in Gorman 2017). The recognition of the stylist, through crediting in the style press, provided an opportunity for them to demonstrate their occupational status, leading to greater awareness of their role, both within the fashion and publishing industries and further afield. For many of the stylists interviewed for this book, it was their first opportunity in styling work. Conversely, the photographers who started working for *The Face* at this time had often acquired a more 'formal training', by assisting photographers (like Harry Peccinotti). They gradually replaced the jobbing music photographers who had previously contributed the image content (Gorman 2017: 104). Nonetheless, despite their experience, they were equally grateful for the opportunity. *The Face* provided a platform and a considerable amount of cultural capital. Roger Charity, who was already established as a freelance photographer, is an example of this:

> We thought 'Wow, this is really exciting, let's just keep going.' And as soon as *The Face* picked up on it, we were away, basically. They started to publish our stuff. We weren't commissioned, we just went out, did what we did, and presented it to

> them. And if they took it, they took it and if they didn't, they didn't. They didn't publish every story we brought to them, but we did a lot of shoots at that time. Everybody did it for nothing. Obviously, I had to pay for film and processing, but we just sort of winged it really and there was Nick Logan with *The Face*, guiding us along. That was the beginning really. There was no commissioned work, which was great. There was a sense of freedom and excitement.[2]

Like *The Face*, its competitor *i-D* was equally aware of the value of 'style' as an alternative to fashion and as a way of attracting a wider audience, of both young women and men. Although it initially labelled itself a fashion magazine, it changed the tagline to 'Manual of Style' on the cover of issues 7 to 13, then later to the 'Worldwide Manual of Style'. *i-D* magazine was first published by editor Terry Jones in August 1980 in a staple-bound, landscape format. There is a clear link between the 'cut-and-paste' aesthetic and format of these first issues with Jones's 1978 publication *Not Another Punk Book* (Smedley 2000; Lynge-Jorlen 2016). Like *The Face*, *i-D* was first produced by a small team of core staff, supplemented with a fluctuating rota of freelance or voluntary creatives. Many of the original *i-D* team were relatively inexperienced, like Caryn Franklin, who had already found work experience for a magazine while still a student:

> When I went to St Martin's I began working for *New Sounds, New Style*, which was, I think it was Caspar De Graaf, who ran that. I got the job through a fellow student called Laura Hardy. She used to go out with Howard Devoto of the happening group Magazine and so she, in my mind, was very cool. She was the journalist, and I would go with her to photograph things for her page in the magazine. I would also photograph stuff happening at college. It was a kind of 'funky London' report. Then my next job immediately after graduating was *i-D*. I took my magazine work and knocked on the door.[3]

As Simon Foxton explains, he earned very little money for his contribution when he first started working for *i-D*, but appreciated the value of the work in other ways:

> People often think, naively, 'That's good, you got photos in magazines, you must be making a bomb' and they don't realize that we literally didn't get a cent from the magazines. Further on they were a bit more generous and, you know, we got fifty pounds a page or something, but back then there was absolutely nothing. So, shoots cost us money, but it was enjoyable, and it was kind of nice to do. It was a good vehicle.[4]

Caroline Baker was also among the few experienced contributors to early issues of *i-D*. Already known as a fashion editor, her inclusion could be seen as giving credence to what was at the time an unknown, self-published magazine. The first acknowledgement of styling in *i-D* was for Frankie, in the masthead of issue 14 in March/April 1984.[5] This was two years later than the term first appeared in *The*

Face. In the following issue, Ola and Nicki Trulocke were credited in 'Buy and Wear' trend features, which is the first time that styling is mentioned within a feature. The apparent lack of styling credits throughout the earliest issues of *i-D* is perhaps not surprising. Large portions of the publication were devoted to the features that documented youth culture, recording a tribe, a pub or a club night. *i-D* was keen to present itself as a snapshot of the youth-cultural scene at the time. When it launched, most of the editorial content followed the format of the 'straight-up' documentary style that Jones had used in his book. A 'straight-up' showed the whole outfit of clubbers or young people scouted on the streets. Street styles were recorded in an almost anthropological way, stood against a wall, facing the camera. As the magazine started to include more 'styled' fashion, it was necessary to find sources for clothing and to cast and dress models. Caryn Franklin explains how she started working for *i-D* and how her methods of styling for photographic shoots evolved:

> Steve Johnston who made the [*Not Another*] *Punk Book*, he'd had that published in about '77, I think, was working at *i-D*. He and I would go out to the clubs, and I would pick out people I wanted to photograph because of the way they looked, and their attitude, which made them intriguing. The fun of writing up what they were wearing, where they got it from, and why they had chosen it. I think that that's where I was able to make a connection with the power of identity through self-styling. And I would also style looks for the magazine based on street casting; getting people together to wear stuff from the young designers we wanted to feature. I wasn't very organized at all, I didn't understand the skill of styling, which is a very exact vision. For me it was just about being in the studio and having fun creating a narrative with clothes. Youth culture and young designers were having a moment, and I was simply part of the documentation process.[6]

From 1985, an expanded team was credited in the masthead of *i-D* for styling, including Baker, Foxton and Petri, but also Toby Anderson, Georgina Godley, Hellen and Reb. This indicated that the magazine, or the contributors themselves, wanted the role to become more recognized. Also comparable with *The Face*, it became progressively more common for the magazine to credit the agencies that represent the stylist, or make-up and hair team. The Buffalo collective received a credit as an agent, as did Ziggi Golding's Z agency, which also featured heavily in the second half of 1985 for supplying make-up artists and models. The services of the freelance fashion stylist were now becoming a commodity.

A third style title, *Blitz*, is often overlooked because its commercial success, readership and time span were eclipsed by those of *i-D* and *The Face*. The magazine was first published in September 1980 by two twenty-year-old university students, Carey Labovitch and Simon Tesler. The lack of job opportunities for young people in Britain at that time motivated them to provide a platform for those who wanted to turn their 'hobbies or interests – such as photography or writing or styling or performance art – into professions' (Webb 2013: 10). They were driven by similar principles, and operated in a comparable way, to the other two style magazines.

Iain R. Webb, for whom this was his first career opportunity, describes how the inclusion of fashion, then style, content evolved at *Blitz*:

> One of the people I lived with on a sink estate in Hackney was a guy called Greg Davis, who had his own fashion label, had started his own label. He was part of that 'London Goes to Tokyo' and 'New London: New York' collective that was pulled together by Susanne Bartsch, and so I would use some of his stuff to shoot in fashion stories, or it might be people like BodyMap, who I knew from the clubs. So, I did this one story together with photographer Mike Owen and they actually used one of the images for the cover. That was the first kind of 'fashion' I suppose that I did within *Blitz* magazine. Previously, I used to do a monthly column called 'People', which was basically me profiling people, my friends, I knew from around town, and that went on for quite a while; then that morphed into a double-page spread, called 'Style' pages. Each month I would construct maybe three or four different little stories on this double page, and that might be a story about a new designer and there'd be one picture and a bit of blurb about them, then there might be a piece on new make-up – I once got Leigh Bowery to do his glam make-up on boys from the clubs but then also I'd sort of style a little fashion story. It might only have been two pictures, and again they might be used really tiny, but it was just that whole idea of putting together a story. It was like I wanted to create my own mini fashion magazine each month.[7]

However, compared to the other style publications, the format of *Blitz* magazine, if not the content, aligned more with that included in traditional fashion publications. Furthermore, it was keen to be a commercial success and had a similarly rigorous approach to allowing certain types of advertising as *The Face*. The magazine developed a core editorial team, which was largely responsible for the production of all fashion content. *Blitz* differed from the other two titles in that it was more embedded in fashion, and less focused on documenting street or youth culture. From February 1985, Webb was listed as 'fashion editor' in the masthead, as he explains:

> At first, they didn't pay for anything; different freelance stylists and photographers would come to the magazine with fashion stories, maybe only two or three pictures that they'd created, and the editors would take the stories and that was how the fashion content was pulled together in the magazine. There was no overall vision. So, I went to see the editor one day and I said, 'I think you need to have a fashion editor, to give the magazine credibility but also to give it a unified look because at the moment some of those stories are weaker than others, some of them are stronger, some of them are not as good as they should be, or just not going together within the magazine.' So, they turned around and said, 'Well, if you want to be the fashion editor then you can be the fashion editor. There isn't any budget.' I think it was that I had twenty-eight pages a month to fill so then that literally was the start of me being at the magazine full-time. I styled all the fashion stories unless I occasionally commissioned something.[8]

Many who became freelance stylists at the time, particularly those working on an ad hoc basis for smaller independent publications like *The Face*, *i-D* and *Blitz*, did not fully understand what the role involved. They were often not even aware that it existed as an occupation. The parameters of the stylist, and the process of styling, continued to be defined as the role became recognized and further legitimized throughout the 1980. For Simon Foxton, becoming a stylist was not a conscious decision. When he realized it could be a career, he was attracted by the immediacy of the styling process. Working within a culture where roles were not fixed or a salaried, it was necessary for the contributors to these publications to develop relationships and network to gain career opportunities. Foxton attributed his initial success to a chance meeting with *i-D* editor Terry Jones, through a friend who was already contributing to the magazine. His first opportunity in styling was with the photographer Mark Lebon, who at this stage was also relatively inexperienced (Foxton 2017). Paul Frecker, who became a stylist in 1984, learnt what styling entailed through his role at the PR company Marysia Woroniecka. Frecker says:

> Amanda Grieve, now Lady Harlech, used to come in, and the first time I met her I absolutely fell in love with her. She complimented me on a Vivienne Westwood Pirate collection waistcoat that I was wearing, that was sort of horizontal stripes, shantung silk. And I just took it off and gave it to her. She said to me one day, 'All these middle-aged journalists who are coming in here, you're putting the outfits together for them, before you send them out. You're doing their job for them. You should be doing it yourself.'[9]

By the mid-1980s, the style press had also started to write about stylists. A feature in the July 1985 issue of *i-D* includes interviews with Frecker and Frankie. They were asked to respond creatively to a prescribed theme, providing a styled image and commenting on their creative process. This type of feature gave an insight into the styling process but also improved the perception of the role among the readership. The fashion stylist was becoming legitimized as an occupation and their opinion as experts in a specialist field was being valued.

Buffalo

The influence of Ray Petri in raising the profile of the stylist, or establishing styling as a valid occupation, has been widely documented. Even before his collaborator Mitzi Lorenz had produced a lavish book of Buffalo's photographic work (2000), Frank Mort had published a thirty-page reflection on Petri's relevance with a detailed visual analysis of 'The Harder They Come', a cover story that Petri produced for *The Face* with Jamie Morgan (1996; also Nixon 1996; Jobling 1999). More recently, Shaun Cole's essay on Petri in Lynge-Jorlen's *Fashion Stylists*, and Carol Tulloch's chapter on Buffalo in Glenn Adamson and Jane Pavitt's *Postmodernism: Style and Subversion 1970–1990* have refreshed and recontextualized Petri's legacy (Lynge-Jorlen 2020; Adamson and Pavitt 2011).

Simon Foxton claims that seeing a Petri shoot for *The Face* impressed him and inspired him to become a stylist, as does David Bradshaw. Stephen Jones, speaking as a designer who worked with both stylists and fashion editors, says that both Petri and Foxton hold equal responsibility for 'putting the role together', that they defined the practice of styling and the way that the role was understood. Although there had always existed a similar role in that of the fashion editor, Petri's notoriety was an important contributing factor to the increase in recognition of the freelance stylist (Jones 2017).

Buffalo was an agency and collective, not a subculture, although it is occasionally referred to as such. The influence of its image-making was obvious in contemporary fashion design in the late 1980s and early 1990s, particularly in menswear trends. Buffalo was initially a relatively localized phenomenon; it was formed by Petri with an extended group of twenty-one photographers, models, musicians and stylists. The style magazines provided an opportunity for Petri, Lorenz and the other members of Buffalo to project their collective vision for contemporary image-making and style. *The Face*'s change of focus from music to style from the beginning of 1984 coincided with an increase in prominence of the Buffalo team. There was mutual benefit: Nick Logan recognized the importance of Petri's input and worked closely with him and Neville Brody when he decided to launch the men's publication *Arena* in 1987. The culture of the collective was based on that of the Jamaican sound system, where groups of DJs, engineers and MCs (microphone controllers) work together in the production of a live event (Cole 2017: 104). The interchangeability of roles and responsibilities could be seen as a reflection of this. Tulloch says that the core of Buffalo was not its professional techniques but its attitude, its 'emphasis on the personal' (2011: 184). The members' anti-fashion stance underpinned this: Buffalo took the values and principles of subculture, claiming to oppose the structures and systems of mainstream fashion. However, it also knowingly constructed a tribe that embodied the values of the postmodern culture it saw around it. In this way, it aligned perfectly with *The Face* and its dual perspective on subculture and fashion, on style and consumerism. Petri became regularly credited for styling features in *i-D*. I interviewed Buffalo members Roger Charity, Mitzi Lorenz and Jamie Morgan for this book. Charity explained how he and Ray started working together:

> Ray came along and he actually started out as my agent. We met through mutual friends, and he got interested in my work and said 'Do you fancy having an [agent]?' I had one the year before and that finished because nothing really happened. He said 'Just give me a go. I'll take your work around. I'll help edit your portfolio to what I think I can sell.' And we started to do quite a lot of advertising and through that we progressed, with Mark Lebon, Jamie Morgan and the likes of those photographers. We started working through Ray, pretty much for *The Face*, and then after that *Arena*.[10]

The front cover of issue 45 of *The Face*, in January 1984, appeared to symbolize a change of direction for the magazine. It was the first that did not include a portrait, styled or otherwise, of a famous musician. The image was one of a series styled by Petri (listed as 'aka Stingray') and was photographed by Jamie Morgan (see Fig. 4). Morgan had originally been asked by Nick Logan to shoot portraits for the magazine but said that he and Petri were increasingly asked to shoot style stories. Petri was subsequently credited in magazine features in a variety of different ways: as a stylist, but also as the agent of an expanded group of Buffalo members being employed by the magazine (for example, for the illustrator Tony Viramontes, in issue 65). In the work he produced for *The Face* and *i-D*, Petri developed themes. He selected, juxtaposed and accessorized clothing that drew on existing masculine tropes (lifeguard, cowboy, boxer), but found ways to subvert these forms of dress to explore new masculinities (Cole 2020). I have established that style is more associated with men's clothing. The fact that Petri worked almost exclusively as a menswear stylist contributed to his success, at a time when magazines were starting to target male readers and recognize them as consumers.

The Stylist in British Mainstream Fashion Publishing

Despite establishing itself as a key role in style publishing, there is very little evidence of the freelance fashion stylist working for mainstream British magazines during the 1980s. I use the definition 'mainstream' for established titles that represent the dominant culture in fashion publishing and to which the independent, style press proposed an alternative. Overall, these titles followed traditional editorial formats, relying on teams of salaried staff with specialist editorial or directorial roles, and supported by further teams of assistants and secretaries. Of those interviewed for this book, several had worked as a fashion editor for a magazine. Some had worked for mainstream publications prior to 1980, such as Baker or Sarah Miller. I looked at examples of both fashion and women's magazines. Features on the latest clothing trends were a staple of women's magazines and specialist fashion magazines. Historically, a women's magazine would be expected to include fashion, as appearance and dress were fundamental to definitions of femininity, and conversely a fashion magazine would predictably target women. Agnes Rocamora acknowledges that the distinction between women's and fashion magazines has never been clearly defined and settles for a definition that classes fashion titles as a 'sub-genre' of the former. However, she concedes that fashion titles could equally now be classed as a sub-category of men's magazines, and it is this expanding field that it is discussed in Chapter 5 (Rocamora 2009: 60).

A fashion editor, working on a salaried basis for a magazine, was responsible for the production of the fashion features. It is a role that required awareness of current trends, developed through access to designers' collections or retailers' product ranges, and by attending their promotional events (catwalk shows and presentations, press events, etc.). In the magazine, these trends were communicated to the reader through fashion 'stories' (series of photographic images presented with captions) or written features, or both. As Caroline Baker explained, a fashion editor held a privileged position, one where they could 'tell everybody what was right or wrong'

(Baker 2017). Having said that, allegiance to one magazine had its constraints. The fashion editor could be seen to have less freedom than a freelance fashion stylist, as they often had an obligation to adhere to their publication's editorial direction. David Bradshaw, who has worked as a fashion editor for several men's titles during his career, says:

> There isn't a straightforward definition of what a stylist is. It will overlap with ideas of being a fashion editor. As an editor, you are much more involved in the business, and the magazine itself will be a business. You have to act as part of that business. You are a cog in that machine. As a stylist, it's incumbent upon you to be a little bit freewheeling, more creative, to push the agenda a little bit. To push ideas of fashion forward. If I'm working for one magazine that has a strict advertisers' list, you can only be so creative within that list, but it's part of the job of being a fashion editor.[11]

Although very few fashion editors write, there are exceptions. Debbi Mason suggests that these disparities in the occupational remit of a fashion editor stem from differences in American and British publishing. When she started working at *Mademoiselle*, in New York, she saw that fashion editors adopted an organizational role and oversaw the rest of the fashion department, that they 'weren't producing their own styling' (Mason 2017). Mason's comment suggests that the term 'styling' is used to describe what a fashion editor does, when they source the clothes and dress the model, although it is unclear whether this term had always been commonly used, or whether it gained traction when the stylist became a more recognized role. For instance, the uses of the terms 'styling' in *Cosmopolitan* occur much earlier than in *The Face* and *i-D*, but were those doing the styling in-house fashion editors?

In contrast with the constantly changing team of freelance or unpaid contributors operating for *The Face* or *i-D*, most mainstream titles continued to rely on salaried editorial roles throughout the 1980s. No stylists were named in British *Vogue* during this period. British *Vogue* was first published in 1916, during the First World War. It is an example of a structured production network at an established fashion magazine; by the early 1980s, the team responsible for its fashion content had a well-defined hierarchy, with specific roles and responsibilities. In the January 1980 issue, Grace Coddington was listed as the Senior Fashion Editor and a full Fashion department was named in the masthead credits. There were six members of the Fashion team, with quite specific specialist roles. Amanda Clapperton was credited for 'Fashion Promotion' and Linda Pearson as 'Fabrics Editor'. The developed structure and range of fashion roles listed in *Vogue* is perhaps not surprising, as fashion was its key focus. Curiously, no fashion editorial credit appears within the features themselves. This is because, in contrast to the commissioned photographers and make-up and hair, the responsibility for sourcing the clothing and styling each feature lay with the salaried staff, who had already received a credit in the masthead of the magazine. There would be the assumption that everything was produced in-house.

Harpers & Queen magazine had a similarly standardized format to *Vogue* in this period. It was a magazine with an equally long history – prior to merging in 1970, *The Queen* first appeared in 1861, while *Harper's Bazaar* had launched in 1929. As with *Vogue*, fashion editors were not credited in features. Exceptions to this were features with a degree of written content, where someone was being acknowledged for their journalistic contribution (an example in April 1984 is tagged as 'edited by Hamish Bowles'). Where *Harper's* differed from *Vogue* was in its use of the term 'style'. In February 1982, the magazine named the socialite and writer Peter York as its 'Style Editor'. York's musings on the growing importance of the concept of style had been published in *Style Wars*, and in adopting the title, he reinforced his status as an authority on the subject and a contributor to London style culture (York 1980). I reference *Style Wars* several times in this book, and although York's treatment of contemporary culture is more journalistic than academic, his opinions on popular culture are a useful counterpoint to those of Dylan Jones, Robert Elms and other style press writers.

Tatler was another example of an established mainstream title that maintained a conventional fashion editorial format throughout the 1980s. Yet it also demonstrated awareness of the currency of style culture. The original *Tatler* launched in 1709, as a literary journal, but only lasted two years. The current version, which shares its name but little else, emerged in 1901. It became *Tatler & Bystander* from 1977 to 1982 and experienced a further change of direction when it was bought by *Vogue* publisher Condé Nast, rebranding again as *Tatler*. It has been claimed that Michael Roberts, who joined the magazine in 1979, was the first to use the term 'stylist'. Although I found no evidence of this credited in print, Maggie Alderson namechecked him in a 1986 feature for *Honey* magazine (see Fig. 1). At the time, she called him 'the reigning king of the stylists'. Roberts was a writer at the *Sunday Times* in the 1970s and, although he may at one point have defined himself as a stylist, he worked in various media. As well as being a journalist and illustrator, he was given a long list of titles during his career. His editorial experience enabled him to transition from the level of fashion editor to higher status positions (Design Director of British *Vogue*, Paris Editor of *Vanity Fair*, Fashion Director, Art Director and Style Director of *Tatler*). But neither he nor Baker, who also produced features for *Tatler*, was credited as a stylist for the magazine during the 1980s. Paralleling the adoption by *Harper's* of a style specialist, it was Joe McKenna who became 'Style Correspondent' for *Tatler* in May 1985. The front cover of the June 1985 issue, photographed by Andrew MacPherson, was listed as 'styled by' McKenna, and this trend continued. McKenna had started out as a contributor to *The Face* and is an example of a freelance, style press stylist working freely across mainstream titles. This practice became more common in the late 1980s and into the following decade. Janice Winship (1987) notes that 'style' was also acknowledged beyond fashion or lifestyle titles, giving the feminist title *Everywoman* as an example, which included a 'Style' section from its launch in 1985.

Cosmopolitan is perhaps the most significant of the mainstream titles in that it credited the stylist in features before the others, even the style titles. Typically classed as a women's magazine, it targeted a broader, more middle-class readership than *Vogue*, *Harper's* and *Tatler*. When it first appeared in 1972, its aims were like those of *Nova*, wanting to appeal to 'real women'. Originally an American publication, it was heavily promoted and its first print order of 300,000 sold out on the day of its launch. The second issue, which saw sales step up to 450,000 copies, took only two days to sell out (Braithwaite and Barrell 1988). Sales quickly eclipsed those of competitors, attracting their advertisers and appealing to a wider audience. By comparison, the combined circulation figures of *Vogue*, *Queen* and *Harper's Bazaar* were only 150,000 in 1970. The front cover of the August 1980 issue of *Cosmopolitan* credits the 'styling' of an image earlier than any other British magazine. The listing 'cover styled by Kezia Keeble and Paul Cavaco' was included amongst the credits on the contents page at the beginning of the publication. Following this, the October and December issues of the same year also included 'styled by' credits for the cover, both for Freddie Leiba, and again in March 1981. Miller, when interviewed for this book, suggests that Keeble, Cavaco and Leiba worked for American *Cosmopolitan* in New York. The images were bought from the US version of the magazine, which may indicate that the term was used in US fashion publishing before it was widely used here (although I found very little evidence of this apart from *Interview*). The crediting of styling for cover images continued throughout the first half of the 1980s, naming Sean M. Byrnes, Donna Jordan and Rachel Crespin. Crespin is also the first to be named as 'stylist' in *Cosmopolitan*, again for a cover image.

Caroline Baker started working for *Cosmopolitan* in the early 1980s. She was both 'Style and Beauty Editor' and 'Style Editor'. Her job titles indicate that, despite essentially doing the job of a fashion editor, she could maintain her anti-fashion stance. She associated herself with style culture. She was, for the same reasons that *i-D* had enlisted her help, recruited because of her status and prior experience with successful publications. Miller says:

> At that point she really was perceived as very hot, even though it was *Cosmo*. *Cosmo* UK then was hot, it's hard to believe now, because it's a mass-market publication. Caroline was trying to make it edgier. She'd worked on *Nova*, that was her big pull. That's the thing with journalism, you work on a prestigious title such as *Nova*, which can be edgy but doesn't get any might nor huge revenue, and of course you get poached by the bigger ones.[12]

Miller herself was also credited for styling (from December 1983), coinciding with her inception as 'Style Reporter'. She explains that the label 'style' was introduced by her to reflect her interest in covering other aspects of lifestyle than merely fashion:

> So, we came up with this idea of doing a Style column every month. And from the Style column it meant that I got to express myself through the interests that I'd always had in fashion, design, art and architecture. Having started this Style File, I was sent to Milan in, I think, 1983, to interview [architects and designers] Ettore Sottsass and Alessandro Mendini, and also [fashion designers, or *stilisti*] Giorgio Armani and Gianfranco Ferre, for an 'Italian special' style section.[13]

Throughout the 1980s, *Cosmopolitan* included several features that gave an insight into the working life of the stylist. A feature on Zee Shore, a freelance 'photographic stylist', was included in the November 1982 issue of the magazine. Shore was featured in a career profile article but did not work for the magazine. Her first experiences as stylist were in catwalk production, and she initially worked for London Fashion Week. Interviewed for this book, she said that she was not aware of the term before 1980 but noted that her agent started promoting her as such at that time (Shore 2017). Later, another feature called 'Your Cosmo Stylists' appeared in the May 1984 issue, this time covering two 'stylists', Vivienne Lynn and Julia Fletcher, both of whom were employed by *Cosmopolitan* as fashion editors. Lynn and Fletcher were asked to define their own tastes, the latest trends and their sartorial habits. The feature indicated some of the responsibilities of the job, including choosing the clothes, 'often making some of the outfits', pressing clothes for the camera, and mentions that they attend the prêt-à-porter shows in Paris. It also implies that they have well-paid roles, describing the stylists/fashion editors as 'struck-lucky women who spend their lives swanning up and down South Molten Street, homing in on clothes only they can afford' (Kelsey 1984: 55–61). The feature suggested that the terms stylist or fashion editor could be used interchangeably and demonstrates the magazine's awareness of the currency of stylist as a job title.

In addition to fashion and women's publications, the weekend magazine supplements of popular British newspapers included fashion features. Iain R. Webb comments on the relevance of these magazines to an audience who would otherwise not have had access to fashion because they were too young to buy magazines:

> There's a lot of emphasis put on the style magazines; what you have to remember was that those colour supplements that came with the Sunday broadsheet newspapers [the *Sunday Times* and the *Observer*], right from the 1960s when they started, really had some amazing fashion imagery in there and were one of my biggest sources for fashion inspiration. Looking back, I have realized that my fashion information, inspiration, didn't come from *Vogue* or other glossy magazines but from the *Daily Mirror* (my parent's newspaper of choice) or the Sunday supplements from the *Sunday Times* newspaper, that my sister had. Even though it might only be a double-page fashion story, or perhaps three pages, it could be some of the most amazing imagery.[14]

Supplements also included stylist credits from the beginning of the 1980s, before the freelance stylist became popularly known. Where style titles were later keen to promote that they were employing stylists, the supplements credited the role discreetly at this time, ensuring that their editorial team were given prominence. I looked at both the *Observer* magazine and the *Sunday Times*. The latter was the most useful for tracking the involvement of the stylist in the production of editorial content. As both magazines failed to include a masthead, it was not possible to gain insight into the status of contributors. Although styling was infrequently credited, a feature in a January 1981 issue of the *Sunday Times* supplement called 'All Things Bright and Beady' named the stylist Anne Drummond. Meriel McCooey was named after the main text as the fashion editor responsible for writing the feature, and Drummond's credit was printed in the gutter of the feature, along with the photographer's name. Drummond appeared again in a similar way, in further features in April and May 1984, listed as 'stylist' and 'styled by'. Miller started working for the *Sunday Times* newspaper in the mid-1980s. She gave an insight into the commissioning process and explained the way that freelancers worked with the core editorial team:

> Just over a year after I'd joined *Elle*, I got poached to go to the *Sunday Times* Look pages, which were the women's feature pages in the newspaper at that point. It was at the end of 1985, 1986, and Liz Jobey was running them. I became her deputy and I used to do help her with all the fashion for the *Sunday Times* Look pages. Then Liz left, and I took over as the Look page editor, and I would commission all the fashion. I brought on Jane Procter, who was freelance then, Marian Hulme, Colin McDowell, and there were others as well. Peta Hunt, Iain R. Webb, there was a whole roster of fashion writers-cum-stylists and we used to work together; by that time, I would go on the odd shoot, but I was really editing.[15]

To conclude, the conventions followed by established mainstream women's and fashion publications in the 1980s show little deviation from the tried and tested formats they had followed for decades. There is little or no evidence of the input of freelance stylists. However, as the trio of new, independent youth publications (*The Face*, *Blitz* and *i-D*) gained credence for advocating 'style' over 'fashion', the former term was seen more frequently in the mainstream press. Style was used as both a label for types of content ('Style' sections) and editorial roles ('Style Editor' in *Cosmopolitan* and *Harper's*, 'Style Reporter' in *Cosmopolitan*, 'Style Correspondent' in *Tatler*). Despite a common assumption that the style publications invented the stylist, even those involved in the production and promotion of these new, independent youth titles were aware of its existence as a role beforehand (Jones 1987). Nevertheless, their interest in promoting the role gave individual British stylists a status they had not previously encountered. Although Petri's career was cut short before he could gain wider commercial success, he was arguably one of the first stylists to gain professional acclaim for his contribution to image-making, as evidenced in the crediting of his work in editorial features, in the tributes to him when he died and in the subsequent coverage in academic texts (Mort 1996; Nixon 1996; Jobling 1999; Tulloch 2011; Cole 2020). The styled stories being generated by Petri and his peers for *i-D, The Face* and *Blitz* created looks with combinations of clothing (and often other materials) that reflected the influence of punk and post-punk subcultural dress and were performatively, deliberately 'styled'. Lynge-Jorlen calls this 'experimental styling'. The role of the stylist in the production of the images is made explicit because the clothing has been visibly manipulated (Lynge-Jorlen 2017: 63). These new modes of image production are covered in the next chapter, which looks at the way experimental styling drew attention to the freelance stylist as an artist and political commentator.

Notes

1 Baker, C. (2017), interview by Philip Clarke, 13 January.
2 Charity, R. (2018), interview by Philip Clarke, 13 February.
3 Franklin, C. (2016), interview by Philip Clarke, 14 December.
4 Foxton, S. (2017), interview by Philip Clarke, 3 February.
5 *i-D* was published bi-monthly at the time.
6 Franklin, C. (2016), interview by Philip Clarke, 14 December.
7 Webb, I. R. (2017), interview by Philip Clarke, 10 May.
8 Webb, I. R. (2017), interview by Philip Clarke, 10 May.
9 Frecker, P. (2018), interview by Philip Clarke, 4 January.
10 Charity, R. (2018), interview by Philip Clarke, 3 February.
11 Bradshaw, D. (2023), interview by Philip Clarke, 11 July.
12 Miller, S. (2018), interview by Philip Clarke, 23 March.
13 Miller, S. (2018), interview by Philip Clarke, 23 March.
14 Webb, I. R. (2017), interview by Philip Clarke, 10 May.
15 Miller, S. (2018), interview by Philip Clarke, 23 March.

Chapter 4

STYLING AS STATEMENT: BRICOLAGE, ART AND POLITICS

This chapter explores how the 1980s stylists, and their peers, understood their work, and discusses their attempts to create meaning through dress. These attempts related to their immediate social scene in London, as well as their wider awareness of politics, art, fashion and popular culture. The images in the pages of style magazines were a mix of self-styled outfits photographed on the streets of London, and those constructed by freelance stylists in a contrived setting. However, both exemplified a new experimental approach to fashion editorial. This approach drew attention to the style press, to the images themselves and to the stylists that made them.

The early issues of the style magazines promoted styling as art. A feature in *i-D* in October 1984 suggested that 'all stylists are artists, and all artists have style' (1984: 34–43). To reinforce the comparison, the article ('Different Strokes') included collaborations between stylists and artists. Joe McKenna created images with the artist David Band, and Keith Haring with Mario Testino. More recently, Penny Martin has compared Simon Foxton's practice of constructing looks with random ephemera to that of assemblage or collage artists, who themselves 'challenged accepted definitions of art through designating found objects' (Martin 2009). Many of the stylists I interviewed referred to their own creative practice as art, although at the time, this was often questioned. 'While most now recognise the validity of photography as an art form', asked Dylan Jones, 'who would make such a claim for something as ephemeral as styling?' (1989: 10)

The idea that a fashion image could convey a profound meaning did not, of course, originate with the style magazines. There was feminist political messaging in the pages of *Nova*, and throughout the 1970s mainstream fashion magazine included stories with serious narratives, incorporating what Jobling calls 'discursive or rhetorical themes' (1999: 23). In the late 1960s, feminist critique largely considered fashion patronizing and banal (Steele 1997). Therefore, the more meaningful examples of 1970s fashion image – even if they were still essentially selling clothes – were conceived in response to the critique of the previous decade. They demonstrated that fashion could be intelligent, thought-provoking and artful. The incorporation of complex narratives was considered pioneering when seen in Baker's fashion features of the late 1960s and early 1970s (Beard 2013). Yet at the time, the fashion editor's contribution to the image – however major – was not valued as highly as that of the photographer. If anything, the idea that fashion could be artistic or political was gently mocked in popular media:

> [Caroline Baker] started saying fashion was irrelevant, left her job and described herself as anti-fashion. She got involved, so she said, in politics in 1977, style as a statement; into this eclectic trip where she'd be expressing her creativity by juxtaposing those legwarmers, different colours, with the shoes (like the Black kids wore in Harlem), with Vivienne Westwood's bondage suits, and the whole big thing became not just making herself an art object but one that meant something. In the 1970s, fashion became very intellectual, ironic, political and artistic and fragmented.[1]

Only a few years later, the freelance stylists gaining a name for themselves in the style press were determined to ensure that their work was taken more seriously (even if many people still didn't understand what they did). So, how did these stylists come to be a recognized as image-makers and vital players in the 1980s fashion industry? It was not only the novel ways of constructing a look, of pulling together clothes and objects to make an artistic or political statement, it was also a new identity the freelance stylists carved for themselves. These stylists considered themselves avant-garde artists. They presented looks that blatantly evidenced cultural and historical references. They challenged gender boundaries. The forms of assemblage they created were purposefully eclectic and intended to be read as bricolage, as a mix of visual or 'vestimentary' messages presented as a new style. Their 'experimental styling' was often intellectually motivated,[2] making an art statement with clothing (Volonté 2020; Lynge-Jorlen 2020: 65).

By contrast, their work is also frequently presented as an example of the superficiality of the postmodern image, as are the publications in which it appeared. The style magazines of the 1980s, particularly *The Face*, have been criticized for adopting political and cultural themes as mere stylistic ingredients. They mixed serious news items with fragments of visual and textual information about architecture, sex, fashion, music and philosophy (Hebdige 1988). Although their methods of creating new identities with dress were often equally eclectic, the stylists of *The Face* and *i-D* were, however, often genuinely motivated by political beliefs. Despite being accused of prioritizing style over substance, they were keen to communicate certain messages. Regardless of how it was perceived, the stylists themselves saw their work as having 'transformative and subversive significance' and it was this that drew attention to them (Tulloch 2011; Lynge-Jorlen 2017).

Juxtaposition, Assemblage and Disruptive Dressing

I have chosen two spreads from publications produced in 1978 and 1984 (see Figs 5 and 6) to illustrate the ways young stylists used clothing to make statements, and how their methods were influenced by the subcultural styles seen on London's streets. The first is *Not Another Punk Book*, produced by Terry Jones and Isabelle Anscombe. Despite being panned as an inauthentic document of punk, it piloted a template for the presentation of street style photography that was adopted in the first issues of *i-D* (1978). Most of the book was filled with full-page photographs of young people, wearing their everyday clothes, standing upright against a neutral background in a public place. The format of recording a full fashion look would become known as a 'straight-up'. This way of showing real people wearing their own outfits in public spaces had not been seen in British magazines – the idea had been pioneered by the American magazine *Rags* earlier that decade.

One of the *Punk Book* photographs featured shows two men, each wearing a self-styled outfit complete with sunglasses (rarely a necessity in 1970s London) and jackets adorned with chains, safety pins, badges and scribbled slogans. The man on the right-hand page has deliberately buttoned his jacket incorrectly, to create an uncomfortable asymmetry. He wears a black PVC glove on one hand; the other is covered with a half-sleeve of a similar material. Both outfits have been demonstrably 'styled', with the wearers clearly keen to show they have purposefully manipulated their clothing. It has been adapted and customized to disrupt clothing conventions.

The second spread was taken from a ten-page feature ('The Challenge') in *i-D*'s tenth issue from July/August 1984 (Jones 1984). Dylan Jones's introductory text described the premise of the feature. In a sense, this was a styling competition. Six teams of designers and stylists were given the task of creating a fashion image with groups of models in a studio location, which was then captured in a single image by the Buffalo photographer Mark Lebon. Their brief was simply to use found clothing. Each team was given a maximum of £1,000 to source objects, clothes and props. The provenance of each item was credited, and in doing so the contrived, 'styled' nature of the images was made explicit. Jones referred to their methods as 'juxtaposition'. The aim was to see how the teams, each known for a different aesthetic, would 'juxtapose' the items they sourced to create a scene that epitomized their view of London style (Jones 1984: 28).

One of the double pages shows facing photographs (page 36) styled by Ray Petri and Caroline Baker respectively. Both situations are shot in a photographic studio, but there are parallels between the fashion content of these images and the straight-ups of Jones and Anscombe's *Punk Book*. They feature atypical combinations of conventional clothing items that have also been customized and adapted. Positioned to complement each other, Petri's image is headed 'Boy versus Girl', whilst Baker's is titled 'Girl versus Boy'. The styling of the images in this spread, and the accompanying clothing credits, make unambiguous statements about gender and multiculturalism. In Petri's image, on the left-hand page, the model Nick Kamen appears in an outfit that combines a designer garment with woven fabric and found objects. An expensive black coat by the Japanese designer Yohji Yamamoto is worn over a Nigerian 'kanga', a striped fabric which has been wrapped like a skirt around the model's waist. Horse bandages, 'from a shop in Mayfair', are crisscrossed over the model's chest. The look is finished with 'rings from New York', a 'French legionnaire's badge from Covent Garden Market' and flip-flops which, the credits indicate, were found in Eastbourne. The look combines objects in ways that are not expected to be seen together. The editorial credits highlight the fact that they are from different cultures and situations. The contrast of reference points and mixing of messages is made clear: Japanese designer fashion is combined with French military, British seaside, and so on.

Baker's look is presented in a similar format to Petri's. A crumpled fabric backdrop hangs behind the model, Gabby. Like Nick, she stands on a wooden palette. The image is similar because it intermingles ideas that do not conventionally belong together. The willful androgyny of the looks is reinforced by the credits: 'Gabby wears cotton gloves from men's shop in Pembridge Road.' A black swimming costume, tied with a leather belt, is worn over a large pink t-shirt, with striped tights, pink socks and heavy worker's boots. The model's hair is cut into a boyish bob and her t-shirt sleeve is pulled back to reveal a hairy armpit. Again, the credits reveal a mix of mismatched clothes: the bathing suit is from the charity shop Oxfam, the tights from Pineapple Dance Centre, the stockings are by designer Mary Quant, and the monkey boots are from Laurence Corner, a second-hand clothing supplier.

Petri was at this point a relative newcomer (his first credit was in the January 1984 issue of *The Face*). As others have argued, Baker directly influenced the younger generation of stylists, and this double-page spread which presents their work side-by-side makes this point explicit (Beard 2013). The intentions of Petri and Baker as the images' authors is further iterated by statements from them, included on the page. Intended to add further layers of meaning, Petri's statement relates to spirituality, reflected in the pose of the model, who is holding his hands together, as if in prayer, whilst Baker's talks about the problems of over-consumption.

The stylist's method of combining heterogeneous clothing and found objects – much like the subcultural practices of dressing up from which it is derived – is frequently referred to as 'bricolage' (Clarke 1976; Hebdige 1979; Mort 1996; Jobling 1999; Lynge-Jorlen 2017). While all subcultural dress appropriates pre-existing clothing and reworks it to construct new meanings, punk experimented with the possibilities of bricolage more than anything before. For Hebdige, punk was at the centre of his 1979 book, *Subculture: The Meaning of Style*, because at the time its methods represented a new development in subcultural styling. The first punks didn't conform to one style. They lifted every form of postwar, subcultural style – styles of dress which had themselves also cited existing forms of dress (Clarke 1976; Hebdige 1979: 26). The notion of bricolage is central to the experimental styling of the 1980s and it shares many of punk's practices. More broadly, it is commonly associated with postmodern design and with the late-twentieth century tendency to combine, recycle and reconfigure stylistic motifs, as witnessed in much of the art, design and architecture. Bricolage has also been used to define the processes of assemblage artists (dada, situationist, arte povera), who amalgamate everyday objects in different contexts and who, like stylists, often made political statements through their choice of components.

The word bricolage is used in everyday French to refer to what the English would call 'Do-it-Yourself', a bricoleur being an unskilled, amateur decorator or builder who uses any available materials. Prior to being applied to subcultural dress and postmodern design, the term was appropriated by Claude Levi-Strauss in an anthropological context (1994), to refer to the way that indigenous societies create myth, meaning and symbolism using available resources.[3] It can also translate as 'a makeshift job', which would seem apt in a discussion of a practice as transient as fashion styling. Judy Blame and Simon Foxton talked of using found objects to create looks and to both customize and create hybrids of existing clothing, accessories and materials they had scavenged or otherwise acquired (Blame 2016; Foxton 2009). Bricolage could be seen in the images produced by other stylists at that time, such as Amanda Grieve (now Harlech) or Debbi Mason (see Fig. 7), whose ensembles reconfigured otherwise incompatible materials. Evans and Blame both use the term 'magpie' to describe this type of styling – there is a myth that the birds steal trinkets and shiny objects to line their nests (Evans 2003: 25; Blame 2016).

When stylists pull together various sourced materials to create a look for a shoot, they consider how the image will be understood by the reader. The disruption created by bricolage is only perceived as such if the original meanings of the garments or objects being combined are widely recognized: 'their relocation and transformation' must be 'understood as a transformation' (Clarke 1976: 177). Bricolage can, of course, be seen in a less ephemeral format in fashion design, in the choice of garment shapes, details and textile patterns. Each aspect of a garment may have been inspired by (or directly copied from) a pre-existing cultural form or type of dress. I have discussed the role of the *stilista* or *styliste* in the design of ready-to-wear fashion, and in broader terms, the introduction of ready-to-wear and promotion of the sale of 'separates' encouraged mix-and-match outfit construction. In the *i-D* feature, Jones wrote that both Vivienne Westwood and Jean-Paul Gaultier's fashions were 'juxtaposition'. He suggested that Gaultier had been taking inspiration from Westwood, but arguably both were influenced by the stylists with whom they worked and/or interacted socially – Westwood with Baker and Gaultier with Petri (Jones 1984).

Malcolm Barnard, it should be noted, warns against overstating the importance of bricolage in fashionable or subcultural dress. He points out that in everyday life there has always been a level of improvisation or juxtaposition of clothing items. For most people in everyday life, he says, 'clothes are acquired, chosen and worn in a variety of ways'. Many wardrobes are full of clothes that have been gifts or cast-offs from other people (2002: 184).

Styling can be viewed in the context of other forms of 1980s bricolage, including the then-emerging styles of music and new media formats. Hip-hop music is a form of bricolage, as it edits together samples of existing music and sounds to create new music (Thornton 1995; Adamson and Pavitt 2011). Similarly, when the global music channel MTV launched in 1981, it broadcast a relentless stream of music video clips. The pace and quantity of content shown on the channel encouraged competitiveness. Video makers looked to an increasingly diverse range of stylistic references to create promotional clips that differentiated them from other artists. Some included multiple references in the same clip. Peter Gabriel's stop-motion video for his 1986 hit 'Sledgehammer' (directed by Stephen R. Johnson), for example, showed the singer in more than fifty different scenarios, as a constantly evolving bricolage. Jeffrey Hinton saw similarities between fashion styling and his own processes when making films, as he frequently cut together and mixed material from different sources. As Hinton put it:

> I used to work on the music with Jeremy [Healy] and then chop up the video. That term 'scratch video' has started being used. I was kind of an originator of that. We hired two VHS video machines. And I'd just do lots and lots of 'pause' editing. It would take hours and hours. I was obsessed. I loved editing. I loved to juxtapose. It was the same with music, and how you could just mess things around and chop them up. Because TV was much slower then. I guess, talking about the visual side, it was very important to me, I didn't differentiate between the sound, the visuals, the energy, the look, you know. If you want to talk about styling, it's all about bringing all those things together.[4]

Customization of clothing can be a form of bricolage. It takes the process further by embellishing or adapting the form of an item, again changing the meaning. The process of customization is central to the logic of fashion styling. It was common amongst the young British stylists of the early 1980s. Caroline Baker's styling for *Nova* had also relied heavily on customization. Her features were frequently accompanied by texts that explained a new look or trend to the readers, but also encouraged them to customize their own clothing resourcefully, with safety pins or brooches, or accessorize with bangles, veils or hats. They were asked to experiment. The adaptation of clothing by stylists in the 1980s, and before, was also due to the lack of variety of products in high street stores at the time. According to Robin Derrick, it was the scarcity of interesting clothing that prompted stylists to be creative:

> You get the Caroline Baker school of styling, which is to make things, dye things yellow, cut-off jeans, and customize the clothes, and that becomes interesting because it transmutes into Simon Foxton's styling, and other stylists I worked with. I did the tenth anniversary of punk shoot for *The Face* magazine, the punk cover of the white-haired girl with the red dog collar, I did it with Nick Knight, and I gave myself some really fancy credit on there, like 'concept and creative direction'. We street cast the shoot and used a girl that Nick knew from college. He said she had this amazing white hair, but when she turned up, she had black hair that we had to bleach back to white. She must have been bald the next day! Simon turned up with bloodied hands because he'd spent all night banging studs into trainers.[5]

Derrick called this way of working, 'making stories from the product'. In this sense, the stylist was developing concepts for new products, or variants of existing products. They were working in ways that would become more common as stylists became collaborative partners in the design process of fashion designers. Webb says that he would also adapt or customize clothing when working on commercial projects, for advertising or for musicians' promotional appearances:

> Also, there was another band that Tom [Watkins, music promoter] got me to style. They had denim jackets that we kind of washed and roughed-up and studded, then we put these huge, long fringes on the arms and across the backs of the jackets. You know, they were those kinds of tassels that you buy from the furnishing department at John Lewis that go on the bottom of curtains, which we unravelled to make these dramatic fringes. It was all about using things, anything, and changing up things to get the look you wanted to achieve.[6]

Punk dress was unashamedly countercultural and disruptive. Its juxtaposition of items of clothing – each communicating a different message – into new and previously untested combinations was an attempt to dislocate and reconfigure meaning (Hebdige 1988). As well as highlighting their creativity by adopting artistic and countercultural methods, the stylists taking part in The Challenge were making obvious political statements. Demonstrating a critical approach to the construction of fashion image, the themes they incorporated into their message-making reflected local cultural practices, such as subcultural dress, but also an understanding of broader, global, postmodern themes in art and design. Using the diptych of styled fashion images presented by Baker and Petri as a starting point, I now explore three further key themes: historicism, multiculturalism and androgyny – stylistic themes which were conspicuous in much of 1980s art, design and fashion, but which were interpreted by stylists to promote themselves as artists and communicators.

Historicism, or Recycling the Past

The clothing credits in style magazines of the early 1980s named many suppliers of second-hand items. These included both fashionable boutiques and charity shops stocking used clothing. Yet the stylists were not merely using second-hand clothes as ingredients in their image-making but also historical styles – either exaggerating them, faithfully recreating them or mixing them together.

This historicism represented the culmination of a progressive trend for recycling past styles that had gained traction in the late 1960s. In British fashion, there had been a decisive shift away from the modern styles that dominated the early 1960s. For example, the designs of Barbara Hulanicki for Biba heavily referenced the past, in particular Victoriana and the textile motifs of the Arts and Crafts movement (Breward, Ehrman and Evans 2004: 127). However, this trend predates the 1960s. Raphael Samuel points out that much of the nostalgic design attributed to the 1960s and 1970s was already becoming popular in the 1950s. Laura Ashley's Victorian prints were first produced in 1953. William Morris wallpaper and fabric also experienced a revival at the time – albeit as a 'minority taste' (Samuel 1994: 92). Nostalgic themes became especially noticeable in Western fashion during the early 1970s, with designers systematically reworking styles from the 1920s, 1930s and 1940s. Caroline Baker sees Yves Saint Laurent's 1971 collection 'Scandale', which referenced the 1940s, as a moment when the fashion press started paying attention to the nostalgia trend (Webb 2021). The style of the 1930s was being seen in films, such as Arthur Penn's *Bonnie and Clyde* (1967), Luchino Visconti's *The Damned* (1970) and Bob Fosse's *Cabaret* (1972). In France, the term 'retro-chic' was used to describe this growing taste for period styles, 'retro' in the United States and Britain (York 1980; Samuel 1994). Yet the direct allusion to historical periods seen in the 1970s could in some ways be considered a transitional trend. It mutated into a 'random cannibalisation of the past', witnessed in subcultural dress of the lates 1970s and 1980s, and in editorial style. Historical themes, motifs and clothing pieces were thrown indiscriminately into a scramble of visual reference points (Jameson 1984: 65; also Evans and Thornton 1989).

Historicism was at the heart of postmodern debate in the 1970s and 1980s. It was not unique to fashion and was first discussed as a trend in architecture, as architects increasingly incorporated past styles into their building designs. Referencing of the past in fashion, or indeed any form of art and design, took a variety of different forms. Many writers continue to recycle definitions used by Frederic Jameson in his 1984 essay *Postmodernism, or the Cultural Logic of Capitalism*. The acceleration of consumerism witnessed in the later decades of the twentieth century led to a re-evaluation of the legitimate sources of cultural citation, and the volume and pace of artistic and commercial production (Jameson 1998: 135). Jameson defined postmodernism as an application of the principles of fashion to all areas of culture and lifestyle. The cannibalization of historical styles was partly prompted by this increased demand for new sources of design, for new images. This manifested in various ways: as parody, pastiche, nostalgia, or bricolage. According to Jameson, parody imitates the past but in a satirical or mocking way. Pastiche is parody without satire (he calls it 'blank parody'). Nostalgic art or design is pastiche with sentiment: it represents a yearning for the past. Bricolage, as just discussed, may incorporate historical materials or motifs but in an attempt to create new meaning. Bricolage transforms rather than replicates. The term pastiche is often used in comparison with bricolage, and there are commonalities, and points of contention, in the various ways that each is defined (Jameson 1979; Barnard 2002).

Elizabeth Wilson has questioned parts of Jameson's postmodern manifesto. Although she accepts his definitions, she points out that pastiche has been apparent in fashion since the turn of the twentieth century. As an example, she notes that the London department store Liberty was already offering women's dresses in a range of historical styles (Wilson 2009).

Wilson nevertheless concedes that the hippies of the late 1960s contributed to the increase in historicist ways of dressing that became popular in the early-to-mid-1970s. They reappropriated old clothes and styles in new contexts, but in response to the wastefulness of consumerism as a form of protest (Wilson 2009).

This extended beyond historical styles, to include dress from other global cultures. The first examples of second-hand clothing appearing in printed fashion stories were those styled by Baker for *Nova*. In some fashion stories, she integrated historical themes in a congruous way, creating nostalgic 'costume dramas'. In others, she mixed used clothing into bricolage, to create completely new looks. She presented vintage clothing in a way that had not been seen in fashion magazines before, largely because there was an expectation from designers and advertisers that their clothing would be featured. Baker's methods were tolerated – and indeed encouraged – by *Nova*, who had a reputation for presenting unconventional editorial content, but were less well-received when she worked for mainstream titles:

> 'Cheap Chic', that was it, I was cheap chic [laughs]. The stories I did in *Vogue* were really fun, though. I did girls in pyjamas. I think that was the last straw for [*Vogue* editor] Bea Miller. We photographed them in places, rooms with cracks on the walls, she couldn't cope anymore. My career at *Vogue* didn't last very long.[7]

Descriptions of the night life in and around London in the mid-1970s suggest that the past was being cited in the theming of club nights, an example being a Glenn Miller revival night at The Goldmine in Canvey Island, which was attended by clubbers in '1940s glam' (Smith 2011). The interest in the 1920s, 1930s and 1940s seen in the early 1970s segued into a renewed fascination with the 1950s that was visible in aspects of punk dress. The original British punk aesthetic was more pastiche or parody than bricolage. Many of the first punks directly referenced pre-existing youth cultural styles, such as mod, or ted or rocker. In fact, Vivienne Westwood and Malcolm McLaren had been selling new versions of teddy boy clothing since 1971, along with second-hand clothes. Their shop, Let it Rock, lifted 1950s styles and resold them to new audiences. It was an immersive retail environment that incorporated furniture and décor from the same era. The appeal of 1950s looks continued into the 1980s and was notable in the style of many post-punk bands. Many of the styled images of musicians featured in early issues of *The Face* are examples of historical pastiche in image-making. A feature on The Polecats, a rockabilly band, in the April 1981 issue (see Fig. 8) showed the band members in a 1950s-style domestic setting, and outside against the backdrop of an appropriately streamlined convertible car. The bequiffed guitarist Boz Boorer was posed in front of a mirror in a red and blue bowling shirt, holding a Gretsch Chet Atkins guitar. The bassist Phil Bloomberg, in a black leather jacket and open-necked shirt, stood brushing his equally impressive quiff. The clothing, the interior decoration of the home and the make of the car are consistent with the theme.

The first stylists working for style publications supposedly relied on second-hand clothing because of their lack of access to designer clothing. It has been argued (Lifter 2018) that unlike fashion editors, they did not have the essential PR connections. This, however, may be a limited viewpoint, as many of them just didn't want to be associated with designer fashion. In this respect, Jones' introduction to The Challenge was telling. In it he outlined the foremost fashions of the London social scene. The first, of which he was clearly not a fan, he called 'label junkies' – lovers of branded fashion ('you have to put your rubbish in a Gianni/Yohji/Issey bag on top of the dustbin'). The second, which he called 'camp', embodied the style culture seen in nightclubs, on the streets and on the pages of *i-D*. Lovers of camp, he says, would happily mix high-street clothes with designer or second-hand. The fact that the style magazines permitted the use of shop-bought or found clothing was the antithesis of the mainstream fashion monthlies. They were strictly seasonal and would only use samples of future collections provided by their PR contacts.

The acceptable use of second-hand clothing as a fashion statement rather than just affordability was not merely a direct consequence of the anti-consumerist, hippie culture of the late 1960s. Since the war, certain subcultural groups had been wearing second-hand styles as a form of rebellion, to shock the older generation, who associated used clothing with poverty and disease (McRobbie 1998). The trend for recycling history, both on a subcultural level or in popular fashion, benefitted from the availability of second-hand clothing, and this provided opportunities for those with clothing businesses. In the 1960s the trend for recycling clothing led to the opening of specialist shops in London (McRobbie 1994). Baker says that she got a lot of her clothes from the army surplus store Laurence Corner in Camden, and Acme Attractions on the King's Road, where she would buy second-hand American sporting gear. Laurence Corner modelled itself on Westwood and McLaren's Let it Rock but presented a mix of influences: it sold second-hand clothing and furniture, reggae and rock records, and new versions of retro clothing. Flip in Covent Garden was a popular source of vintage clothing for young stylists, but magazines also credited charity shops, such as Oxfam or Help the Aged. In 1978, Roger Burton set up Contemporary Wardrobe as a resource supplying second-hand street fashion to the television and film industries.

Barrie Sharpe and the Duffer of St George team initially built their business from trading reworked second-hand menswear. The reappropriation and reinvention of types of clothing, notably the knitwear brand John Smedley, was key to their success:

> We were basically going to Oxfam shops, picking up old Burberry macs, silk scarfs, brogues, blazers, for pennies. There was four of us, and we had so much gear in the end that we thought, let's sell it, let's start selling it. So, we went down Camden with a suitcase. The High Street was closed on Sunday in 1984, and we wrote out a receipt, for the front of a shop, to show the police that we'd hired it, put the products in the shop and we started selling out of suitcases.[8]

Sharpe says that they profited from the publicity given to them in *The Face* and *i-D*, and that Petri and the Buffalo team regularly visited the Duffer store to borrow clothing for photo shoots. He claims there was mutual admiration between the two teams.

The increased use of second-hand clothing amongst young Londoners, and the revival of historical motifs seen in fashion, can be viewed as a form of postmodern 'omnivorousness'. There emerged an increasingly undiscerning demand for cultural and historical quotation in Western art, design and fashion (Jameson 1984; Evans and Thornton 1989; Bauman 2011). McRobbie, though, warns against simplistically framing 'retro-dressing' as another example of the postmodern fashion for nostalgia or period pastiche, as it also sits within a continuum of British, postwar youth cultural styles (1994). The people I interviewed spoke of their own interest in nostalgic fashions, fed by the availability of army surplus and second-hand clothing. They were aware of popular global trends in music, fashion, filmmaking or other arts, but they were equally motivated by stylistic experimentation among those in their own subcultural spheres.

Multiculturalism

The cannibalization of styles seen in both street fashion and magazines extended beyond the appropriation and regurgitation of historical dress. Although multiculturalism can be seen in broader terms as another example of global, postmodern practice, those I interviewed had a specifically London-centric view on the relevance of racial and ethnic diversity (Bauman 2011). For example, Buffalo styling often placed emphasis on the mixing of clothing associated with non-Western cultures. They looked to clothing adopted by local immigrant communities, but also combinations that reflected aspects of their own heritage, or other global styles of dress. Sometimes the reference was blatant, such as accessorizing a men's suit with a feathered Native American headdress or topping it with a straw hat and a Peruvian knitted chullo. At other times, the point of reference was more subtle, combining a pork pie hat – as worn by British Jamaican rude boys – with a black tailored designer suit customized with medals. In another image, modelled by Mitzi Lorenz, a wide-lapelled red satin suit with a Union Jack patch was paired with a turban. She had a red bindi on her forehead, making a statement that combines various aspects of Indian heritage with the cut-up British nationalism seen in mod dress.

The stylists or designers incorporating non-white models or non-Western clothing into their image-making saw it as a way of representing the cultural mix of the capital. Describing her awareness of racial difference growing up, Mitzi Lorenz jokes that she and her siblings were referred to as the 'United Nations' because each of the daughters was of different ethnic origin. By 1981 a sixth of London's 6.6 million population was born outside the United Kingdom (Porter 1994: 433). The postwar period from the early 1950s to the early 1970s marked an increase in migration from Commonwealth countries to the United Kingdom. This was especially significant in London. The formation of West Indian communities was specifically concentrated in the Notting Hill and Brixton areas (Panayi 2010). In fact, the highest population of West Indian people in 1971 was 21.26% in Kensal Rise, a neighbouring ward to Ladbroke Grove and Notting Hill.

The influence of the West Indian community in these areas of West London was key to the formation of the Buffalo collective, of which Lorenz was a member. They socialized in venues that catered for Caribbean clientele. Buffalo claims to have followed the model of the Jamaican 'sound system' in their decision to operate as a collective. The members of the collective were, says Lorenz, brought together by the fact 'that none of us fitted into any class, race or social background that we could feel was our own' (2000: 13).

The representation of cultural diversity promoted in the style press evidenced the political motivations of the contributors. There had been a great deal of overlap between punk and reggae styles. 2-Tone, which was a fusion of British and West Indian cultural references, was prominently featured in *The Face* when it first launched (see Fig. 9). Jerry Dammers of The Specials, a Coventry-based 2-Tone band, appeared on the front cover of the first issue. Nick Logan is said to have rushed through the launch of the magazine in 1980 because he wanted to support the scene's increasing mainstream success. Other 2-Tone bands were regularly featured, as were stores selling its styles, such as The Modern Outfitter, which had opened in 1978 on the King's Road (Gorman 2017). When *The Face* transitioned from focusing solely on music to including a broader range of lifestyle (or 'style') content, the themes of multiculturalism and 'social commentary' continued to be reflected in the written features and in the styling.

Ziggi Golding grew up in Jamaica and is of German and Jamaican descent. As a former model and casting agent, she had clear opinions on the acceptance of multicultural themes in fashion and the casting of models. She claimed that attitudes started to relax in the 1970s and viewed the 1980s as a period of 'individualism', where difference was celebrated. Golding credited the art director Jean-Paul Goude for showing ethnic difference in American magazines in a way that had not been seen before. His tableaux of ethnic groups ('Hispanics', 'Blacks', 'Whites') could be seen as a precursor to Benetton's advertising series a decade later. The influence of Goude's image-making can also clearly be seen in the styled ensembles of Simon Foxton. For example, 'New England', in the August 1986 issue of *The Face*, featured parodies of London types ('Yuppie', 'B-Boy', 'Roma', 'Eastender', 'Ninja').

Throughout the 1980s, multiculturalism started to be seen in the ways that established global brands chose to advertise their products. Caroline Baker styled the Benetton campaigns with the photographer Oliviero Toscani in the mid-late 1980s, and they regularly featured multicultural themes. The integrity of the 'United Colours' advertisements has since been questioned for naively conveying an ideological version of multi-racial and multi-ethic harmony (Sardar 1998). However, Iain R. Webb defends Baker and Toscani's approach, claiming that their intention was to foreground the wider debate on racial equality. He concedes that the campaign 'would by modern values been deemed stereotyping' yet feels that at the time the images championed equality and diversity in ways that were not reflected in most other advertising (2021: 14). Indeed, Baker herself was motivated by her own strong political values and a desire to show different ethnicities and cultural motifs.

For those who were raised and educated in the city, the diverse cultural nature of London was inherent to their upbringing, their choice of social circle and most importantly their relationship with clothes. Barrie Sharpe noted the crossing of Jamaican style with 'British working-class attitude' (2017). He defined the environment that he grew up in and how it shaped his views on style:

> When I was ten, I went down to Petticoat Lane, to the Electric Light Store – an electric store that sold reggae records – and there were these geezers outside, Black geezers, with sheepskin coats, rolled up Levi's, cropped Levi's, actually, expensive shoes or loafers and red socks and braces, and I wanted to look like them. The fact that they were Black was irrelevant, they were the most stylish people I had ever seen, I wanted to look like that.[9]

The style magazines are also credited with introducing street casting as a common practice in fashion editorial. Initially documenting subculture, club fashion or musicians, the magazines habitually used non-professional models. Although model casting did not always fall within their remit – the responsibility of selecting the models for a photographic project was often the stylist's. As with their approach to sourcing clothing, the decision to street-cast was also motivated by their stylists' limited access to agencies or the funds to pay them. The fact that Petri so frequently cast Black models was, as he himself admitted, predominantly motivated by his own sexual attraction to Black men. The way that Black men have been fetishized by white image-makers, such as Robert Mapplethorpe, has also been viewed in a more critical light in recent years (Mercer 1994). Nevertheless, at the time he was praised by his peers for showing Black male sexuality in a way that had rarely been seen in fashion imagery before (Lorenz 2000; also Tulloch 2011). The move away from conventional (traditionally white) model casting was not unique to Buffalo. As an example, the double-page spread 'Soul Train', which was shot by Nick Knight and styled by Simon Foxton for the December/January 1986 issue of *i-D*, featured eight street-cast Black men. Foxton has throughout his career regularly cast non-white models (see Fig. 10).

Ziggi Golding's agency Z was, along with Buffalo, seen as being key to a shift in attitude to the types of models that were being used. There was a certain homogeneity in modelling before this point. Golding stated that she often took models with no prior experience and worked with them to build a professional portfolio. However, Caryn Franklin, who had previously worked for *i-D* magazine, found that the diverse representation in independent youth publishing was not reflected in other media. When working for *The Clothes Show*, which was broadcast by the BBC and reached a much wider audience, she remembered times where her suggestions to diversify were rejected:

> I interviewed a stylish Muslim guy who had specific things he wanted to say, and I remember fighting in the edit to keep some of it in. He was talking about the significance of the African leather medallion necklace he was wearing, but it was deemed not mainstream enough. I sometimes felt like an outsider trying to

> bring exciting people in. In this instance I would be told 'Well, not everybody lives in Brixton', which I did at the time.[10]

The perspective on race, ethnicity and diversity amongst the interviewees reflected, in some cases, wider debates seen in global visual media. The term postmodern was itself used by many of them. As young people living in a cosmopolitan city, they would also have experienced the bricolage of cultural styles that is evident in immigrant communities, the creolization of music and visual languages. These influences were also reflected in their subcultural heritage. Certain features of punk had been absorbed from West Indian rude boy and rasta style (Hebdige 1979), while 2-Tone also represented a fusion of cultural influences.

Androgyny

A third common theme in early style press image-making is its challenging of binary gender norms. Many of the stylists I interviewed spoke of playing with gender, using clothing to present unisex identities or new versions of masculinity and femininity. I cover the latter in the next chapter, discussing how stylists were involved in the formulation of the 'new man' and 'new woman' being presented in the media and advertising. The nuanced, feminized versions of menswear being produced by Petri for *The Face* or *Arena* or the shoulder-padded new women seen in the pages of *Elle* were more gently radical. The extravagant experiments with gendered styling seen in clubs – which filtered through into editorial features – were way more extreme. They were, as Dylan Jones acknowledged, a form of 'camp' (Jones 1984; also Breward, Ehrman and Evans 2004), but they were also asking much more pertinent questions about the relevance of gender norms.

According to Cole, androgyny – the manifestation of a neutral or mixed gender identity – 'was the buzzword in the 1980s' (2000: 165; Davis 1992). The 'ambivalent androgyny' of the New Romantics was seen by some as a trigger, destabilizing the idea of distinct masculine and feminine sexualities for the remainder of the decade (Jobling 1999). The style magazine readership was not gender-specific, which provided an opportunity for exploration of non-gendered identity construction in a way that would be discouraged in a magazine targeting a male or female audience. Having said that, the level of experimentation with gender stereotypes seen in styled editorials was disputably less boundary-pushing than that seen in the more radical club nights. The more scintillating looks were seen in *i-D*, *Blitz* and *The Face* in reports that documented parties and club nights. In the fashion pages, whose function was essentially to endorse new trends for its readers, the styling was generally more subtle. The magazines perhaps realized the unfeasibility of the more flamboyant looks for the majority of their young readers. However, self-styled androgynous looks were being embraced by popular musicians, gaining them publicity in style and fashion magazines, but also in the British tabloid press. For example, Annie Lennox (close-cropped orange hair, tailored suit, pink lipstick, painted eyebrows) and Boy George (loose brightly-coloured overalls, feminine make-up, braids twisted with ribbon) both attracted media attention for their 'gender bending' styles. The latter is an example of the cross-pollination between designers, stylists and clubbers. George heavily quoted the editorial and commercial styling of Caroline Baker – the rasta-inspired looks she made with Westwood and for Malcolm McLaren's pop group Bow Wow Wow, and the outfits worn by Haysi Fantayzee.

Susan Sontag's important essay *Notes on Camp* (2018) was no doubt a reference point for Jones when writing the *i-D* feature. Written in the 1960s, her definitions of camp in contemporary culture fed into the postmodern debate. Camp is a celebration of artifice. It prioritizes style over substance. It takes styles or art forms previously considered bad taste and celebrates them, in a knowing, ironic way. Much of the pastiche in postmodern art and design could be considered camp. 'Camp,' says Sontag 'sees everything in quotation marks' (2018: 9). It is also, she claims, an androgynous phenomenon.

Sontag stresses that the display of campness is not inherently homosexual. This perspective is certainly relevant in defining the stance of these clubbers, stylists and performers on dress and identity construction. Although many of the young clubbers were gay and treated these spaces as somewhere they could behave freely (see Chapter 2), they were often treated as outsiders by the gay scene. Yet they enjoyed their outsider status, which was another facet of the elitism that permeated their club culture. For example, the club night Cha Cha's was run in a venue near Embankment, in a small space that was attached to the back of the gay club Heaven. It enforced a similar door policy to Louise's, Billy's and the Blitz and, despite there being an interconnecting door, would not allow the mainstream gay crowd to enter unless they wore an appropriately clever look (Blame 2016). According to Jeffrey Hinton, both the camp and 'asexual' aspects of early 1980s styling can be traced back to punk, which he felt was also a gender neutral, sexless subcultural space.

Leigh Bowery, who never worked as a professional stylist, was probably the most obvious example of styling as art statement during the 1980s. Bowery's personas were almost entirely androgynous. He sometimes simultaneously exaggerated both masculine and feminine characteristics, or created costumes that did not acknowledge either biological sex or gender constructs. Some looks did not even acknowledge his human form. His oblique approach to outfit construction was firmly situated in, and always in dialogue with, the late-1980s club culture. Yet the 'hyperbolic' artificiality of his costumes and the ways they both denaturalized and over-emphasized gender placed them firmly in the realm of camp, surpassing many of his contemporaries in club or drag culture (Granata 2021: 26). Although styled fashion became less performative in the style magazines as the decade progressed, club dressing in venues such as Taboo and Kinky Gerlinky became more so. Bowery was the ultimate tastemaker for this scene and eventually was accepted into the art world. In 1988, he staged a five-day performance in Anthony d'Offay's gallery window in Dering Street. The shop front was glazed with one-way mirrors, so Bowery could only see himself. Changing his position every few seconds throughout the shows, he enacted a succession of fashion poses.[11] The show reinforced his status as both a contemporary artist and dandy, placing the styled body centre-stage. Bowery's looks have since been an essential source of inspiration for experimental stylists and designers, from Alexander McQueen's 2009 'Horn of Plenty' show, styled by Katy England, to Matty Bovan's Spring/ Summer 2019 show, staged in collaboration with stylist Katie Grand.

Various factors informed these examples of gender play. For the younger stylists, David Bowie is a cardinal stylistic reference, as an example of both androgyny and camp. His style and outlook throughout the early 1970s are cited as 'ingredients' of British punk. The expectation that every look would be different, individual and unique, as well as an irreverence for gender norms, fed both post-punk club etiquette and editorial approaches to fashion styling. There had been an element of camp and transvestism in early punk. It became permissible among young punks to dress up, to dye their hair and wear too much make-up. In some ways, the Bowie-esque club nights in London in the late 1970s and 1980s were a form of 'gay punk' that didn't fit anywhere else. Bowie was openly bisexual. This statement, combined with his adoption of androgynous stage personas, was considered controversial by the British media but, unsurprisingly, appealed to young gay people who had previously very few role models in contemporary pop culture. Bowie's early looks, such as the brocade, calf-length dress by designer Mr. Fish, worn with knee-length leather boots and loosely flowing curls, on the cover of his 1971 album *The Man Who Sold the World*, had been mildly non-conformist. This was superseded by less understated, more provocative styles. Bowie developed a reputation for changing his look regularly, taking the principles of fashion and accelerating them. For many of the young stylists of the 1980s, he had been an idol and style reference from an early age. Iain R. Webb says even his mother was acutely aware of his tastes:

> She used to go shopping every Saturday morning and one weekend she came home with a brown paper bag, and I thought maybe it's a fake Ben Sherman shirt from the market, but it turned out to be a fox fur. I then sat watching *Match of the Day* on TV with my dad, wearing this fox fur and mum said 'Well, I thought you'd like it because I know you like that Roxy Music and all that kind of thing.' So, in that period, especially with Bowie, Roxy and glam stuff like that, it was all about that kind of nostalgic fashion that was around at the time, heavily referencing the Hollywood version of the 1930s and 1940s.[12]

Other local forms of drag stimulated the culture and attitude to dress of the young gay men of the London club scene. Drag had played a part in more public forms of protest by Gay Liberation Front members in the early 1970s. Shaun Cole cites an example of GLF members arriving, in October 1972, at a court hearing in drag ('an ankle-length black satin dress with a pill box hat and net veil' and 'a pink polka dot dress and glitter around the eyes') to protest against a Notting Hill pub's refusal to serve gay clients (2017). Jeffrey Hinton, whose older brother was also gay, was taken to performances by Bloo Lips when he was a teenager. Bloo Lips was formed in the mid-1970s by Gay Liberation Front members, and Hinton recalls this spirit of activism being a motivator in their incendiary performances. He refers to their forms of drag as 'gender-fuck' or 'gender-fluid'. Using the same term, Cole suggests that the genderfuck of the more radical drag queens fed into the styling of glam rock pop stars like Bowie and Marc Bolan (Hinton 2017).

More of an art happening than a blatant political protest, the Alternative Miss World, which was first hosted by the artist Andrew Logan in his studio in 1972, is another precursor of the camp experimentation of later clubbers and stylists. The events were also performatively queer, at a time when homosexuality had only just been made legal in Britain. They attracted a mixed crowd and celebrated the 'diversity and difference' of all forms of non-heterosexual gender and sexual identity (Gezcy and Karaminas 2013). The event continued to run,[13] and later in the 1980s was attended by regular clients of club nights like Taboo and Kinky Gerlinky. Leigh Bowery appeared in the 1986 show with collaborator Fat Gill. Gill appeared completely naked with a shaved head. Bowery wore a home-made frou-frou mini dress of layered red tulle, with a clown-like black grin painted ear-to-ear, eyes glued onto National Health issue spectacles and an upturned red bucket as headgear. Initially the Alternative Miss World centered on the social scene I have referred to elsewhere as Them, the group of artists and fashion designers comprising Zandra Rhodes, Duggie Fields, Kevin Whitney and Derek Jarman. There was continuity and overlap between style cultures within London. When interviewed in 2016, Blame spoke of his friendship with Derek Jarman, whom he visited many times at his flat in Soho. Webb interned with Zandra Rhodes as a young graduate. Principles and practices were passed on through working relationships and across social circles.

The type of stylist described in this chapter would seem completely at odds with historical versions of the role; the stylists of the American automobile industry or Italian ready-to-wear were commercially focused. They considered what styles would appeal to a mass audience. They responded to and influenced trends but were essentially concerned with selling product. The new freelance stylists were anti-fashion and claimed to be anti-consumerist. They were motivated by a desire to make a political or artistic statement, informed by the subcultural and art communities from which they emerged. There methods were, in many ways, distinctly postmodern. They pillaged the past, or other cultures, to find new styles to incorporate into their image-making. They created pastiche or bricolage. Their experimental methods gained them attention and acclaim. As the next chapter will discuss, the launch of the style magazines was followed in the late 1980s by the introduction of publications that targeted new male and female audiences and new types of consumers. These magazines allowed opportunities for styling new sexual identities, and alternative versions of masculinity and femininity, in fashion photography.

Notes

1 P. York (1980), *Style Wars*, Chichester: Sidgwick and Jackson Ltd.

2 It can be compared with the deconstructed, 'experimental fashion' of Rei Kawakubo for Comme des Garçons in the 1980s or Martin Margiela's recycled collections in the late

1980s and early 1990s – both of which presented fashion as an art statement (Lynge-Jorlen 2020; Granata 2021).

3 This definition of bricolage has been criticized for failing to recognize that all forms of cultural production make use of available language, materials and tools, regardless of their cultural setting (Derrida 2014).

4 J. Hinton (2017), interview by Philip Clarke, 23 June.

5 R. Derrick (2017), interview by Philip Clarke, 17 February.

6 I. R. Webb (2017), interview by Philip Clarke. 10 May.

7 C. Baker (2017), interview by Philip Clarke, 13 January.

8 B. Sharpe (2017), interview by Philip Clarke, 10 February.

9 B. Sharpe (2017), interview by Philip Clarke, 10 February.

10 C. Franklin (2016), interview by Philip Clarke, 14 December.

11 Alexander McQueen referenced this idea in his Spring/Summer 2001 show, 'Voss'. In it, the models were contained in a large glass-fronted space with a one-way mirror so they could only see themselves.

12 I. R. Webb (2017), interview by Philip Clarke, 10 May.

13 The Alternative Miss World event was last hosted in London in 2022 and has taken place every few years since the first show in the early 1970s

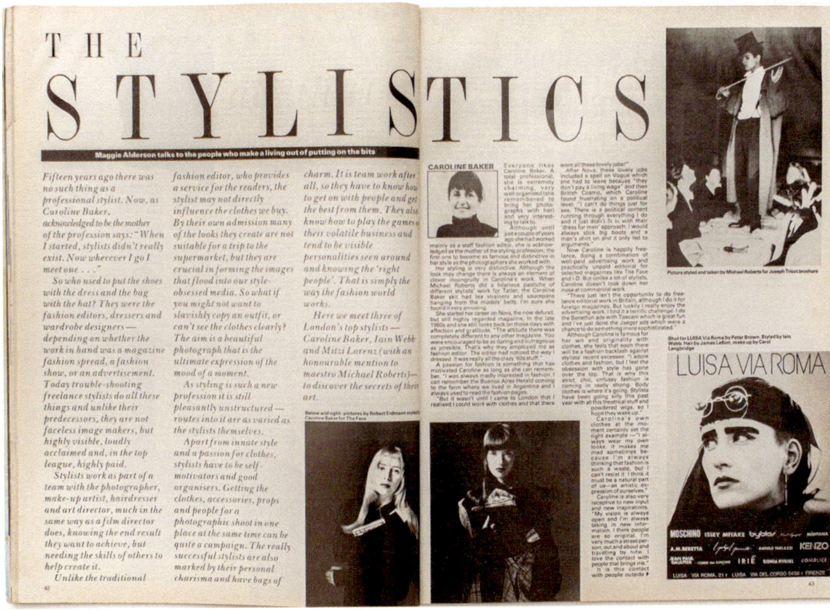

THE STYLISTICS

Maggie Alderson talks to the people who make a living out of putting on the bits

Fifteen years ago there was no such thing as a professional stylist. Now, as Caroline Baker, acknowledged to be the mother of the profession says: "When I started, stylists didn't really exist. Now wherever I go I meet one . . ."

So who used to put the shoes with the dress and the bag with the hat? They were the fashion editors, dressers and wardrobe designers — depending on whether the work in hand was a magazine fashion spread, a fashion show, or an advertisement. Today trouble-shooting freelance stylists do all these things and unlike their predecessors, they are not faceless image makers, but highly visible, loudly acclaimed and, in the top league, highly paid.

Stylists work as part of a team with the photographer, make-up artist, hairdresser and art director, much in the same way as a film director does, knowing the end result they want to achieve, but needing the skills of others to help create it.

Unlike the traditional fashion editor, who provides a service for the readers, the stylist may not directly influence the clothes we buy. By their own admission many of the looks they create are not suitable for a trip to the supermarket, but they are crucial in forming the images that flood into our style-obsessed media. So what if you might not want to slavishly copy an outfit, or can't see the clothes clearly? The aim is a beautiful photograph that is the ultimate expression of the mood of a moment.

As styling is such a new profession it is still pleasantly unstructured — routes into it are as varied as the stylists themselves.

Apart from innate style and a passion for clothes, stylists have to be self-motivators and good organisers. Getting the clothes, accessories, props and people for a photographic shoot in one place at the same time can be quite a campaign. The really successful stylists are also marked by their personal charisma and have bags of charm. It is team work after all, so they have to know how to get on with people and get the best from them. They also know how to play the games of their volatile business and tend to be visible personalities seen around and knowing the 'right people'. That is simply the way the fashion world works.

Here we meet three of London's top stylists — Caroline Baker, Iain Webb and Mitzi Lorenz (with an honourable mention to maestro Michael Roberts) — to discover the secrets of their art.

CAROLINE BAKER

LUISA VIA ROMA

Plate 1 'The Stylistics', *Honey*, February 1986; written by Maggie Alderson.

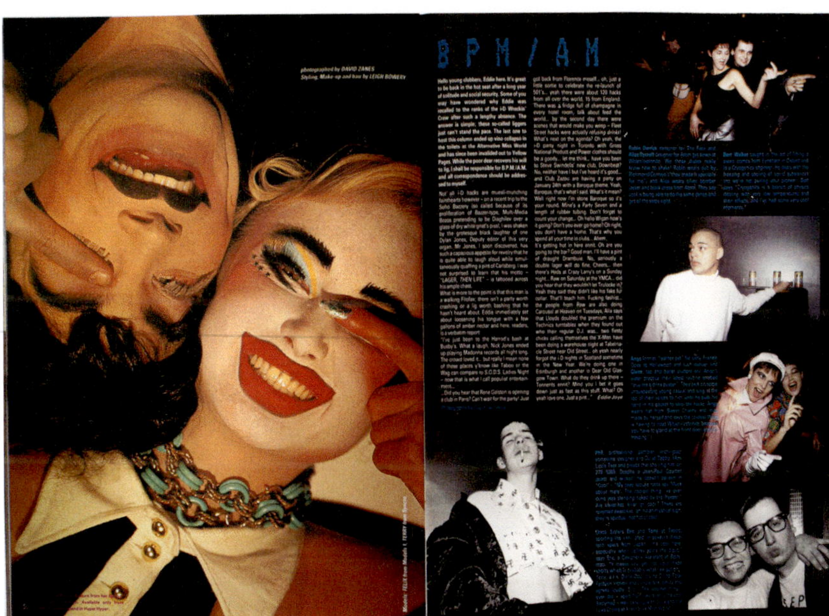

B P M / A M

Plate 2 'BPM/AM', *i-D*, February 1986.

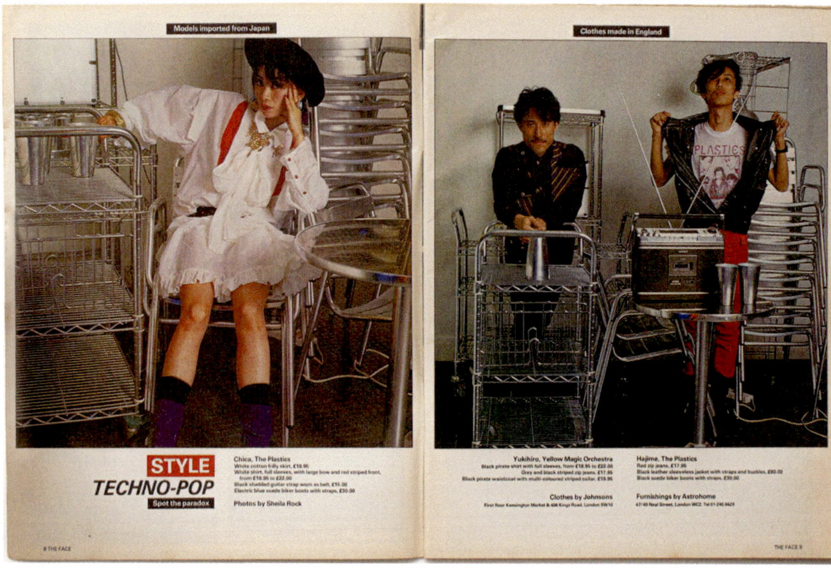

Plate 3 'Style: Techno Pop', *The Face*, July 1981; photographed by Sheila Rock.

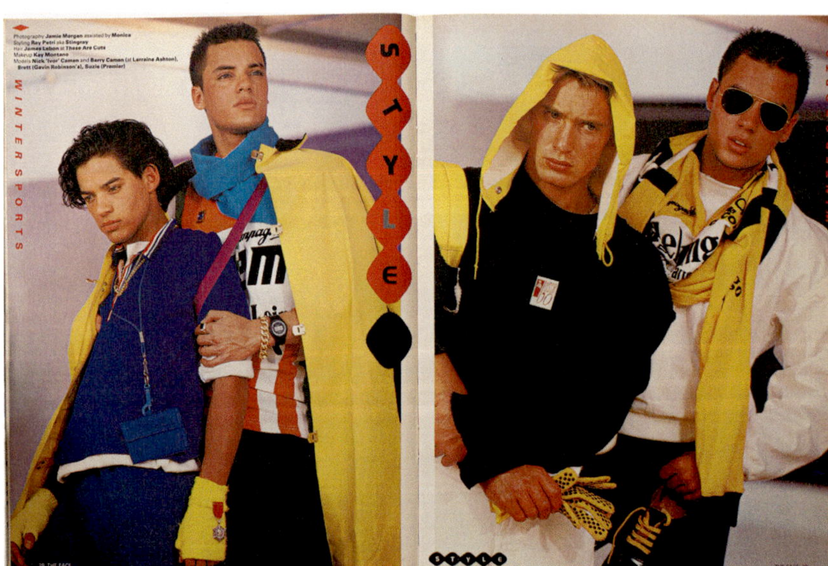

Plate 4 'Winter Sports', *The Face*, January 1984; photographed by Jamie Morgan, styled by Ray Petri aka Stingray.

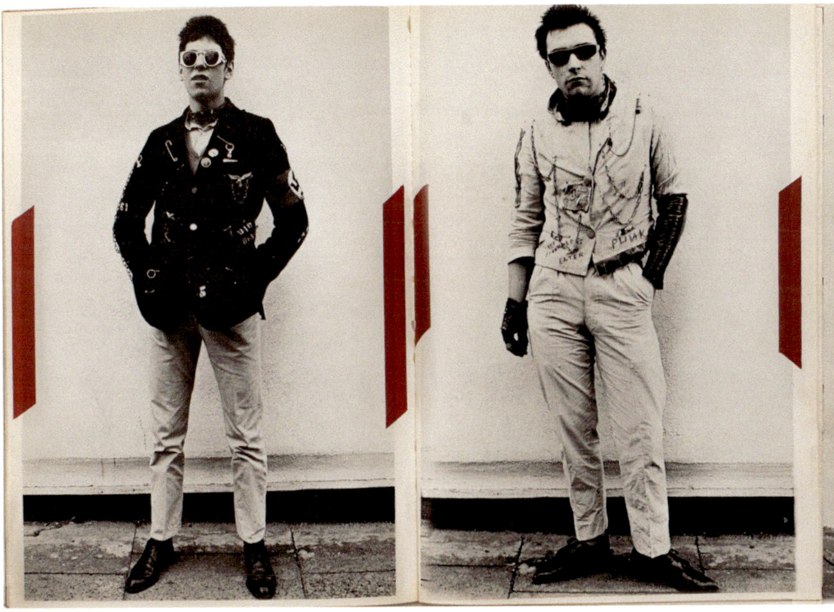

Plate 5 *Not Another Punk Book*; photographed by Steve Johnston.

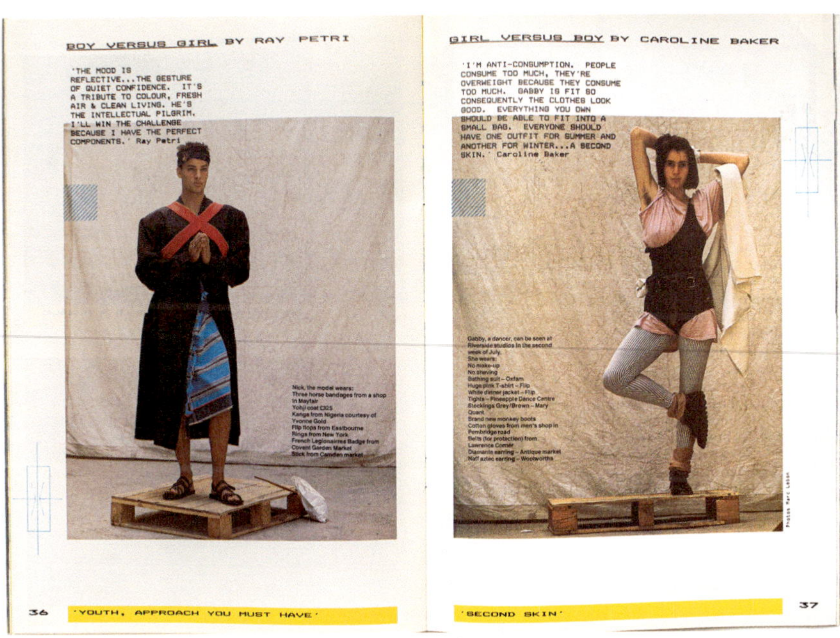

Plate 6 'Boy versus Girl', *i-D*, July/August 1984; photographed by Mark Lebon, styled by Ray Petri and Caroline Baker.

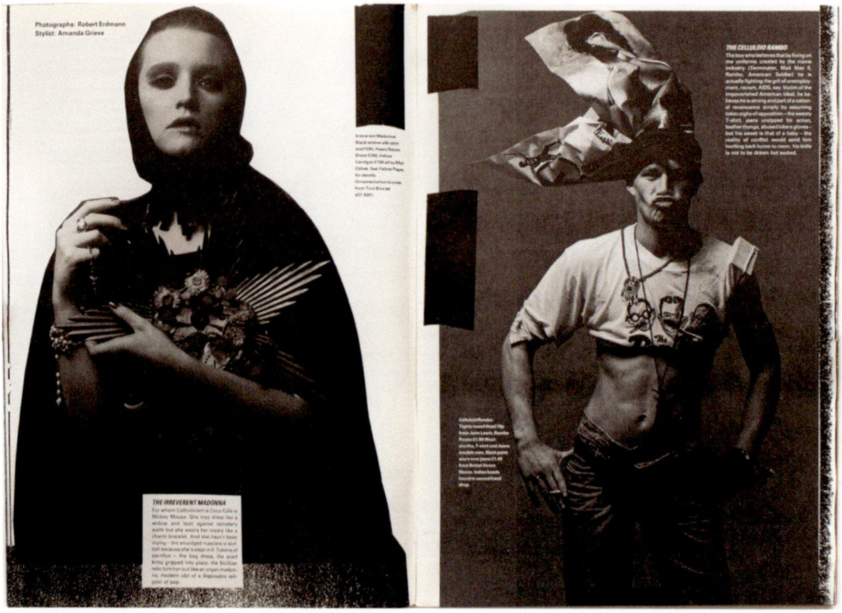

Plate 7 'The Irreverent Madonna', 'The Celluloid Rambo', *i-D*, March 1986; photographed by Robert Erdmann, styled by Amanda Grieve.

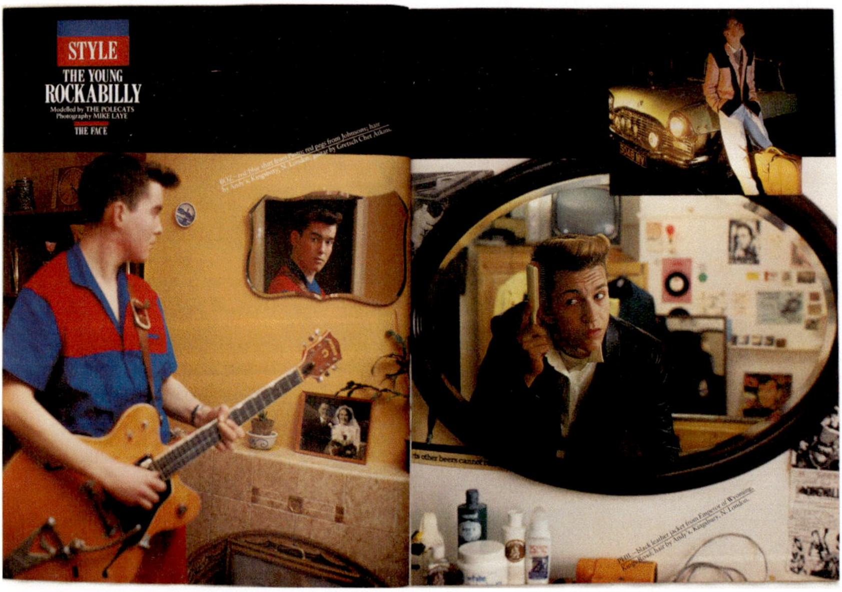

Plate 8 'The Young Rockabilly', *The Face*, April 1981; photographed by Mike Laye.

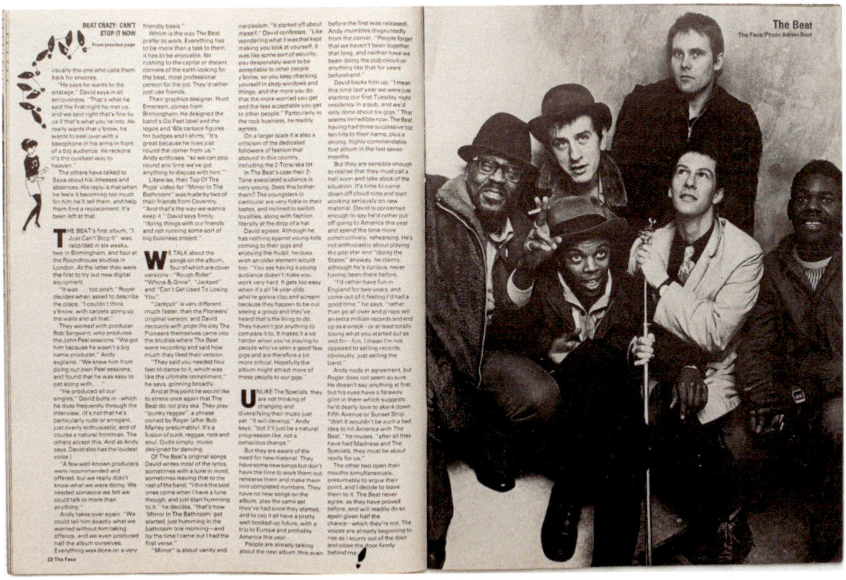

BEAT CRAZY: CAN'T STOP IT NOW

From previous page

usually the one who calls them back for encores.

"He says he wants to die onstage," David says in all seriousness. "That's what he said the first night he met us, and we said right that's fine by us if that's what you're into. He really wants that y'know, he wants to keel over with a saxophone in his arms in front of a big audience. He reckons it's the quickest way to heaven."

The others have talked to Saxa about his illnesses and absences. His reply is that when he feels it becoming too much for him he'll tell them, and help them find a replacement. It's been left at that.

THE BEAT's first album, "I Just Can't Stop It", was recorded in six weeks, two in Birmingham, and four at the Roundhouse studios in London. At the latter they were the first to try out new digital equipment.

"It was . . . too posh," Roger decides when asked to describe the place. "I couldn't think y'know, with carpets going up the walls and all that."

They worked with producer Bob Sergeant, who produces the John Peel sessions. "We got him because he wasn't a big name producer," Andy explains. "We knew him from doing out own Peel sessions, and found that he was easy to get along with . . ."

"He produced all our singles," David butts in—which he does frequently through the interview. (It's not that he's particularly rude or arrogant, just overly enthusiastic, and of course a natural frontman. The others accept this. And as Andy says, David also has the loudest voice.)

"A few well-known producers were recommended and offered, but we really didn't know what we were doing. We needed someone we felt we could talk to more than anything."

Andy takes over again: "We could tell him exactly what we wanted without him taking offence, and we even produced half the album ourselves. Everything was done on a very friendly basis."

Which is the way The Beat prefer to work. Everything has to be more than a task to them, it has to be enjoyable. No rushing to the capital or distant corners of the earth looking for the best, most professional person for the job. They'd rather just use friends.

Their graphics designer, Hunt Emerson, comes from Birmingham. He designed the band's Go Feet label and the logos and '60s cartoon figures for badges and t-shirts. "It's great because he lives just round the corner from us," Andy enthuses, "so we can pop round any time we've got anything to discuss with him."

Likewise, their Top Of The Pops' video for "Mirror In The Bathroom" was made by two of their friends from Coventry. "And that's the way we wanna keep it," David says firmly, "doing things with our friends and not running some sort of big business project."

WE TALK about the songs on the album, four of which are cover versions—"Rough Rider", "Whine & Grine", "Jackpot" and "Can't Get Used To Losing You".

"Jackpot" is very different, much faster, than the Pioneers' original version, and David recounts with pride the day The Pioneers themselves came into the studios where The Beat were recording and said how much they liked their version.

"They said you needed four feet to dance to it, which was like the ultimate compliment," he says, grinning broadly.

And at this point he would like to stress once again that The Beat do *not* play ska. They play "punky reggae", a phrase coined by Roger (after Bob Marley presumably). It's a fusion of punk, reggae, rock and soul. Quite simply, music *designed* for dancing.

Of The Beat's original songs David writes most of the lyrics, sometimes with a tune in mind, sometimes leaving that to the rest of the band. "I think the best ones come when I have a tune though, and just start humming to it," he decides, "that's how 'Mirror In The Bathroom' got started, just humming in the bathroom one morning—and by the time I came out I had the first verse."

"Mirror" is about vanity and narcissism. "It started off about meself," David confesses. "Like wondering what it was that kept making you look at yourself, it was like some sort of security, you desperately want to be acceptable to other people y'know, so you keep checking yourself in shop windows and things, and the more you do that the more worried you get and the less acceptable you get to other people." Particularly in the rock business, he readily agrees.

On a larger scale it is also a criticism of the dedicated followers of fashion that abound in this country, including the 2-Tone/ska lot.

In The Beat's case their 2-Tone associated audience is very young. Does this bother them? The youngsters in particular are very fickle in their tastes, and inclined to switch loyalties, along with fashion, literally at the drop of a hat.

David agrees. Although he has nothing against young kids coming to their gigs and enjoying the music, he does wish an older element would too. "You see having a young audience doesn't make you work very hard. It gets too easy when it's all 14-year-olds who're gonna clap and scream because they happen to be out seeing a group and they've heard that's the thing to do. They haven't got anything to compare it to. It makes it a lot harder when you're playing to people who've seen a good few gigs and are therefore a bit more critical. Hopefully the album might attract more of these people to our gigs."

UNLIKE The Specials, they are not thinking of changing and diversifying their music just yet. "It will develop," Andy says, "but it'll just be a natural progression like, not a conscious change."

But they are aware of the need for new material. They have some new songs but don't have the time to work them out, rehearse them and make them into completed numbers. They have no new songs on the album, play the same set they've had since they started, and to cap it all have a pretty well booked-up future, with a trip to Europe and probably America this year.

People are already talking about the next album (this even before the first was released). Andy mumbles disgruntedly from the corner. "People forget that we haven't been together that long, and neither have we been doing the pub circuit or anything like that for years beforehand."

David backs him up. "I mean this time last year we were just starting our first Tuesday night residency in a pub, and we'd only done about six gigs." That seems incredible now, The Beat having had three successive top ten hits to their name, plus a strong, highly commendable first album in the last seven months.

But they are sensible enough to realise that they must call a halt soon and take stock of the situation. It's time to come down off cloud nine and start working seriously on new material. David is concerned enough to say he'd rather put off going to America this year and spend the time more constructively, rehearsing. He's not enthusiastic about playing the pop star and "doing the States" anyway, he claims, although he's curious, never having been there before.

"I'd rather have fun in England for two years, and come out of it feeling I'd had a good time," he says, "rather than go all over and p'raps sell an extra million records and end up as a wreck—or at least totally losing what you started out as and for—fun. I mean I'm not opposed to selling records, obviously, just selling the band."

Andy nods in agreement, but Roger does not seem so sure. He doesn't say anything at first, but his eyes have a faraway glint in them which suggests he'd dearly love to skank down Fifth Avenue or Sunset Strip. "Well it wouldn't be *such* a bad idea to hit America with The Beat," he muses, "after all they have had Madness and The Specials, they must be about ready for us."

The other two open their mouths simultaneously, presumably to argue their point, and I decide to leave them to it. The Beat never agree, as they have proved before, and will readily do so again given half the chance—which they're not. The voices are already beginning to rise as I scurry out of the door and close the door firmly behind me.

22 The Face

The Beat
The Face/Photo Adrian Boot

Plate 9 'The Beat', *The Face*, July 1980; photographed by Adrian Boot.

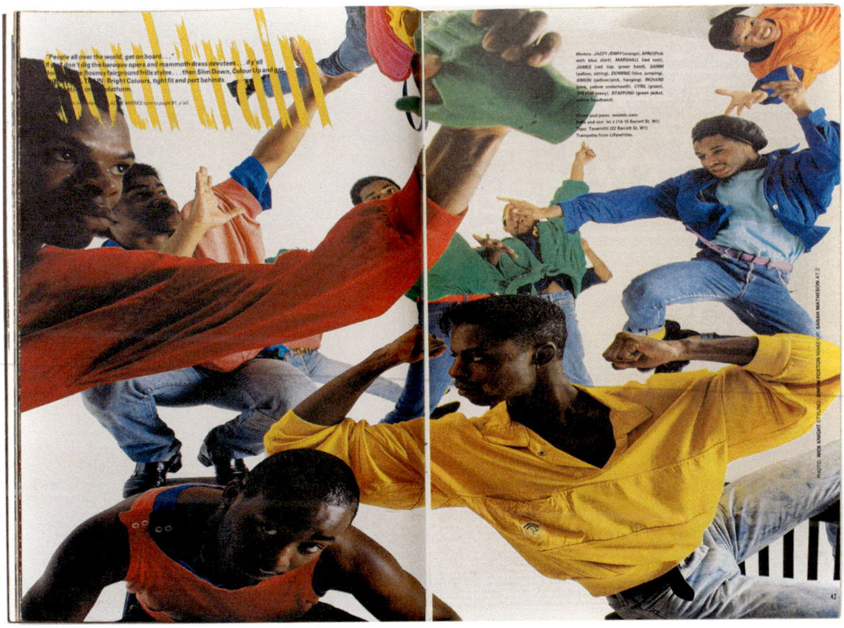

Plate 10 'Soul Train', *i-D*, December/January 1986; photographed by Nick Knight, styled by Simon Foxton.

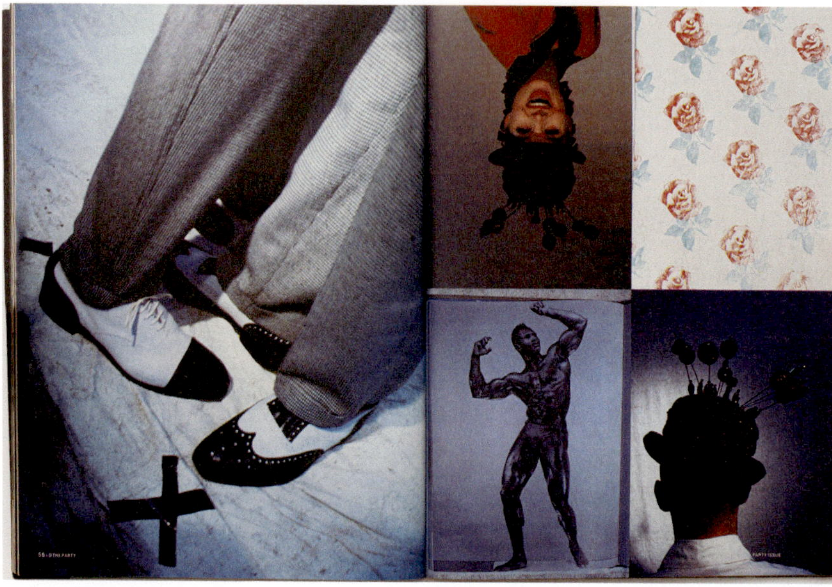

Plate 11 'Party Up', *i-D*, September 1988; photographed by Mark Lebon; creative direction by Judy Blame.

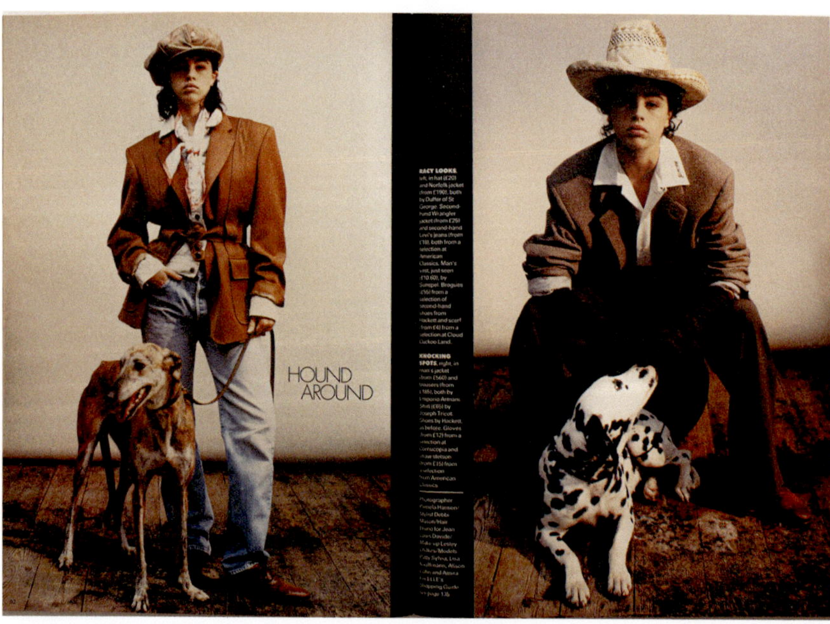

Plate 12 'Hound Around', *Elle*, February 1988; photographed by Pamela Hanson, styled by Debbi Mason.

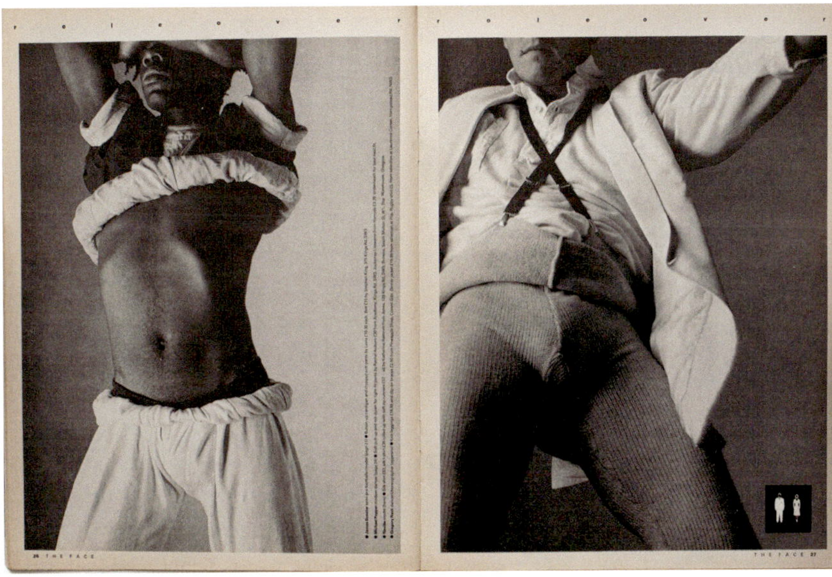

Plate 13 'Role Over', *The Face*, September 1984; photographed by Robert Erdmann, styled by Caroline Baker.

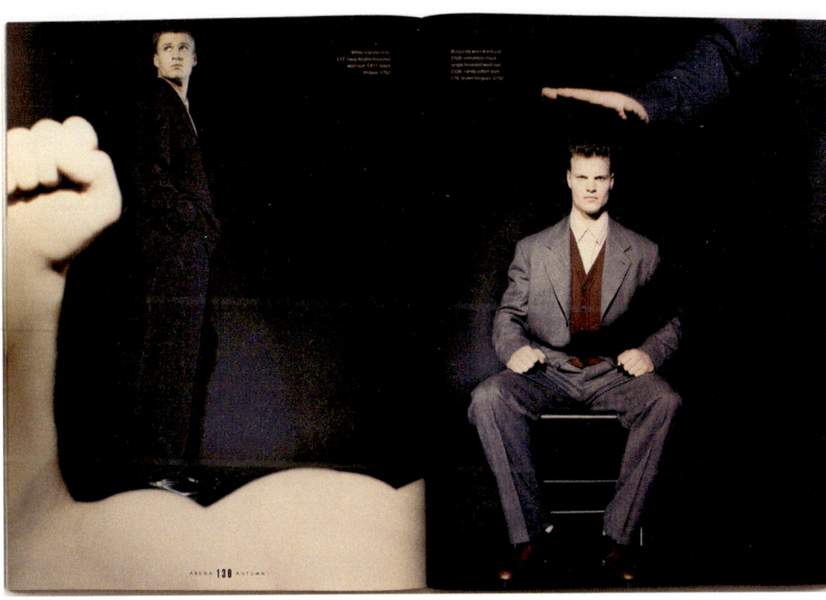

Plate 14 'Big', *Arena*, Summer/Autumn 1989; photographed by Christian Thompson, styled by Christian Logan.

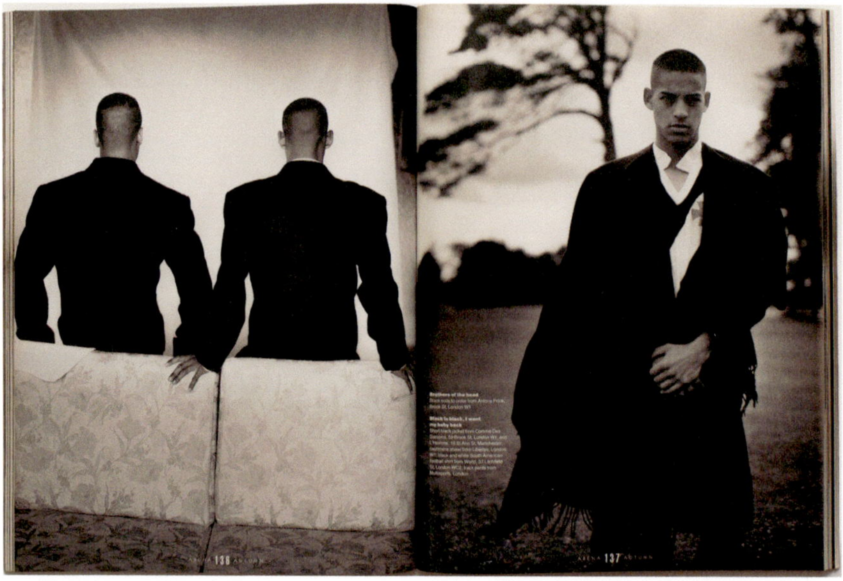

Plate 15 'The Long Goodbye', *Arena*, Autumn/Winter 1989; photographed by Roger Charity, styled by Ray Petri.

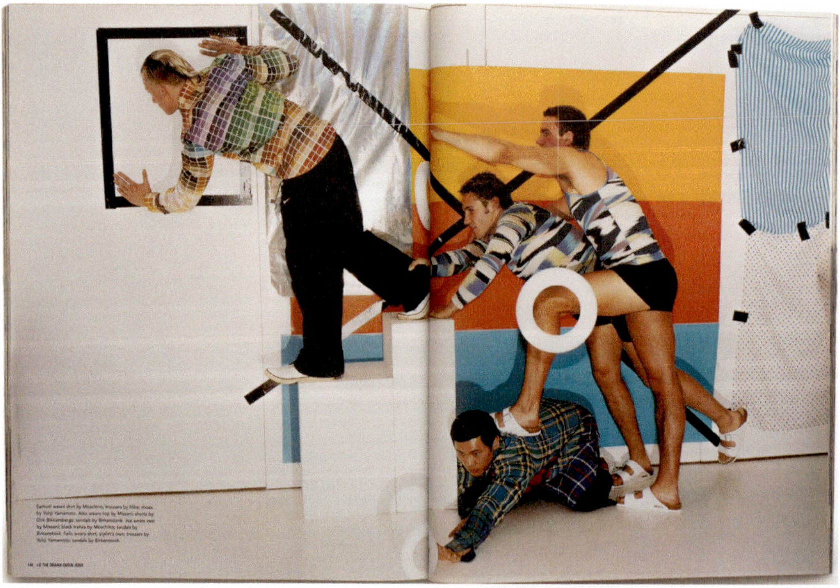

Plate 16 'Hey There, Fancy Pants', *i-D*, May 2004; photographed by Jason Evans, styled by Simon Foxton.

Chapter 5

NEW MAN, NEW WOMAN, NEW STYLE: 1985–1990

> At the end of the last decade, not many people understood what a stylist actually did. It was one of those jobs hovering in the grey area between journalism, fashion design and photography – 'I mean, what does a stylist do?' Well, these days it seems that stylists do just about everything. Stylists used to just pick the clothes for models or celebrities to wear for photographs or personal appearances, but this is the age of media overload – the age of endless photo shoots for album sleeves, singles bags, promotional posters, fashion spreads, videos etc. This ubiquitous designer existence – styling has become one of the most important professions in the entertainment and consumer markets. A stylist can literally make or break a person or product.[1]

The second half of the 1980s heralded a further increase in the acknowledgement of styling in British fashion editorial. The style magazines had given the role significance. They had enabled established fashion editors to build on their reputation and for unknown stylists to consider a new type of career. Moving into the second half of the decade, new titles, such as *Elle*, *Marie Claire* and *Arena*, credited styling from the outset. The idea that an image had been 'styled' became more widely recognized. There was a greater awareness – at least within the fashion industry itself – of what a stylist contributed to the construction of a fashion image. *The Face*, *i-D* and *Blitz* continued to define 'style' both visually and through journalistic commentary. Style also became the currency of new titles targeting men. Fashion was a woman's domain. It was frivolous, transitory and linked to excess consumption. Style was associated with more fixed personal tastes and lifestyle choices, so was considered a more appropriate way of addressing male consumers.

Writing for *i-D* in 1984 (see Chapter 4), Dylan Jones had suggested that the stylist's culture existed as an alternative to that of designer-obsessed 'label junkies'. Nonetheless, writing for the same magazine in 1987 he placed the stylist at the heart of the designer lifestyle. He asserted that their input was essential to the successful promotion of a new product, or celebrity (1987: 85). This chapter discusses how the style press adapted towards the end of the 1980s and how they prompted the introduction of both new men's and women's titles, aimed at intelligent readers who also had a keener awareness of their spending power and tastes. *Arena* and *Elle* employed stylists from the moment they launched. Collaborating with the art director, they were crucial to the coherence of the magazine's overall visual identity. They also ensured that the curation of fashion products on its pages would respond to the tastes of an increasingly style-conscious and consumption-driven readership.

As in Chapter 3, the themes covered in this chapter are structured around a review of editorial content, and the ways that stylists were credited for their contribution in the masthead and within the printed features they produced. I reflect on the ways that the British style magazines evolved, their influence on new magazines for new types of men and women, and the place of the stylist in each of these fields.

Establishing the Style Bible

The freelance stylist had gained a place as a valued collaborator in the conception and production of the fashion image. The style magazines had ensured that their contribution was respected. The introduction of many new magazines in the second half of the 1980s led to movement of personnel between titles. This opened opportunities for new stylists. Many were as inexperienced as their predecessors had been but, all the same, they offered fresh perspectives on the form of fashion.

The success of the style press and Nick Logan's previous venture *Smash Hits* had created a more diverse and dynamic environment for magazines targeting the youth market. The content and focus of the new teen magazines came from the street. They referenced real people and documented youth culture in a way that had been pioneered by the style titles. Keen to ride on the waves of these new genres, *New Sounds, New Styles* launched in 1981. Although it had a comparable format to *The Face*, the remit of *New Sounds, New Styles* was limited. It focused mainly on the New Romantic club scene and on the music acts and fashions that had developed from it. The pilot issue featured Blitz club host Steve Strange, the German electronic band Kraftwerk and, inevitably, David Bowie and Roxy Music. *Just Seventeen*, *Etcetera* and *Mizz* arrived in 1985. These were publications that attempted to target teenage girls, viewing themselves as competitors for existing titles like *Jackie*. *Etcetera* closed after a year due to poor circulation figures (Winship 1985; Braithwaite and Barrell 1988). *Looks* magazine was also launched by Emap, intending to build on the success of *Just Seventeen* and targeting fifteen to twenty-two-year-olds. None of these new titles used stylists. An exception was *The Hit*, which was introduced by IPC Media in 1985. It contained a small element of fashion and, following the example of the style press, enlisted the services of a freelance stylist to produce it. Essentially a music magazine, its format could be compared, like *New Sounds, New Styles*, to the earlier issues of *The Face*. It targeted young men, hoping to kindle the kind of interest in male readers that magazines like *Just Seventeen* garnered in teenage women. *The Hit* included a regular double-page feature ('Hit the Street') that showed some of the latest trends. The magazine valued the style content enough to have a 'style editor', and named those responsible for the styling, including freelancer Paul Frecker.

The style magazines, of course, maintained the practice of crediting stylists and gave them even more prominence. Furthermore, the magazines had moved beyond cult status to being noticed by the mainstream. *The Face*, for example, was the subject of a 1985 exhibition at The Photographer's Gallery in London. Much of the literature assessing its cultural relevance appeared in the mid-1990s (Mort 1996; Nixon 1996; Jobling 1999). However, in 1988 Dick Hebdige included an essay on *The Face* in *Hiding in the Light*, a book which looked at case studies of examples of postmodern culture. *i-D* had less attention in terms of academic critique than *The Face*. Although the design of *i-D* became progressively slicker through the late 1980s, and its format transitioned from stapled to perfect bound, it stayed true to its street style origins.

i-D continued to credit 'styling' throughout the magazine for any fashion editorial images. The masthead named a core team responsible for the fashion content (Caryn Franklin, Robert Leach, Fred Poodle, Georgia Gunn and Simon Foxton), while additional stylists were named in features, especially Caroline Baker. The listing of agencies representing creative personnel also became even more apparent in the later part of the decade. This indicated that freelance stylists were valued as a marketable service. Almost all the stylists named in *i-D* from 1986 onwards were represented by an agency (Cloutier, Pin-up, Unique, Max Presents, Satellite, Synchro, Select), a practice that had started to be evident in earlier issues but became the norm. Demonstrating their affiliation with the magazine, Simon Foxton and Judy Blame were elevated to 'Contributing Fashion Editors', alongside the magazine's permanent Fashion Editor, Beth Summers. Foxton, collaborating more and more with the photographer Nick Knight, continued to create fashion that combined street looks – mod, hip-hop or skinhead – with sportswear. Their visual language was recognizable from issue to issue.

Despite being considered one of *i-D*'s key fashion editors, Judy Blame was rarely named in the credits of 1980s fashion and style publications. This was unexpected as he is often closely associated with the creative culture of this period. Blame has since been cited as influential by many stylists and photographers and was the subject of a one-man, retrospective show at the ICA in 2016. In fact, throughout the late 1980s much of Blame's styling work was credited under the alternative pseudonym of 'Fred Poodle' (Judy Blame was already an alter-ego). One of the most extensive features produced by Blame during this period was the five-page 'Recycled Pioneers'. Shot by Mark Lebon for *i-D*, each page featured outfits created using upcycled materials, refashioned into jewellery. Blame was a big advocate of recycling. The principles of the House of Beauty and Culture, with whom he crafted jewellery and accessories, were very much centred on scavenging and gathering used or decayed objects and repurposing them as art pieces or functional furniture or clothing. Blame (2016) recalled that Terry Jones, the editor of *i-D* magazine, was the only person to support his use of salvage in fashion stories. He was strongly motivated by a desire to make the readers think about the damaging effects of pollution, in a way that was not commonly promoted by the mainstream fashion industry at the time.

That Blame would choose to be credited by his professional name for the jewellery, but by a lesser-known pseudonym for styling, suggested that at the time, the styling was a secondary activity that he valued less than his role as designer. An exception was a stylist credit in the April 1988 issue of *i-D* and – an indication of his rapid ascension to higher profile roles – a credit for the 'creative direction' of a feature in September of the same year, where the stylists Adam Howe and David Thomas were also named for their contribution (see Fig. 11). The feature involved a full team in its direction and production. Style magazines were gradually progressing to have more structured hierarchies, similar to the old-school fashion and women's magazines.

During the late 1980s, Blame and Lebon collaborated with the East London design collective House of Beauty and Culture; with the shoemaker John Moore; fashion designers Richard Torry and Christopher Nemeth; photographer Cindy Palmano; Fric and Frack, who designed and made furniture; and the illustrator Dave Baby. The collective was among the first to make a statement about global environmental issues and commonly reused waste products in their design and craft. The group dissipated after Moore's death in 1989 and the relocation of Nemeth to Japan. Blame claims that his ongoing collaboration with Lebon 'filled that gap', and it was at this point that he shifted focus from making jewellery 'towards the style side of it'. Interviewed by Gregor Muir for the ICA retrospective of his work, Blame says that Lebon and Ray Petri encouraged him to style more, and he worked with Petri on some of his shoots, accessorizing the outfits with his jewellery. The films and photographic imagery he made with Lebon led to Blame becoming better known as a stylist and creative director. Following this, music became a focus (he claimed that 'everybody was a bloody pop star' at the time) and, having already worked with Boy George, he became the stylist of the singer and rapper Neneh Cherry when she started to achieve success (Blame 2016). Young stylists were using their association with style publications to find better paid commercial work and their influence in creating trends could be seen in both.

If *i-D* spent the late-1980s strengthening its identity as a street style magazine and bolstering the reputation of existing stylists like Foxton and Blame, *The Face* moved in a different direction, both in terms of focus and staffing. This was in part a result of various contributors and core team members leaving to join new titles, such as *Elle* and *Arena* (Gorman 2017). The subsequent influx of fresh journalistic and editorial talent clearly affected the types of content being featured, but the changes in British youth culture during this period were also a factor. *The Face* was one of the first publications to comment on the arrival of MDMA or Ecstasy, as the drug of choice in the new club scene. The magazine began to report on new forms of nightclubbing and subcultural activity, in particular the burgeoning House music scene. Like *i-D*, *The Face* progressively adjusted its editorial structure to incorporate more traditional roles. By the end of the decade, it had also employed a permanent fashion editor, Kathryn Flett. She has since suggested that the decision was prompted by the desire to attract more advertisers, in the belief that that the allocation of more traditional roles gave the publication more gravitas. Despite seeming to adopt conventional staffing arrangements, both *i-D* and *The Face* continued to rely on a large pool of freelancers, even for official roles. According to Flett, the role of fashion editor had always unofficially belonged to Ray Petri. When he died of AIDS in 1989, the level of coverage in both *The Face* and *i-D* demonstrated the impact that his brief career had in authenticating the fashion stylist as a fundamental figure in the increasingly respected field of British fashion photography. *The Face* labelled him a 'visionary and a trendsetter', as someone who had made a substantial contribution to the style of menswear in the 1980s (Gorman 2017). Both magazines devoted several pages to showing the images he had produced as a stylist. Petri's death prompted reflection on the standing of the stylist and by the end of the decade, others were accorded similar praise and recognition. For the final issue of the 1990s, *i-D* credited Simon Foxton as being 'the man (alongside Nick Knight) responsible for some of this decade's most memorable images' (1989: 73). That a stylist would be considered an equal, in terms of collaborative contribution, to the photographer in the conception and production of an image suggests how the relevance of the role had gained traction.

Blitz continued to be published until 1991, but towards the end of the 1980s it had already started to lose momentum. The recession of 1990–1 made it difficult to attract advertisers and, unlike *The Face* and *i-D*, *Blitz* did not seek financial backing from larger publishing companies. Iain R. Webb left in 1987 and the stylist Kim Bowen took over as its fashion editor. The magazine's editors also attributed the launch of new 'fashion oriented' women's and men's magazines, like *Elle* and *GQ*, as a factor in *Blitz*'s demise. To compete with these more mainstream, commercially focused titles, they decided to concentrate on showing designer fashion, forfeiting the more 'radical or unconventional' approach to image-making seen in earlier issues. If anything, *Blitz* had retained the playfulness and DIY aesthetic of the earlier style press for much longer than *The Face* and *i-D*. However, tastes among the younger readers had changed and those who originally read them had moved on (Webb 2013: 13). Despite its highly creative image-making, the magazine consistently receives fewer mentions in coverage of 1980s style culture. This is no doubt because it folded so soon but could also be attributed to its overall adherence to a more predictable editorial model. Stylists like Petri, Foxton and Blame were known quantities as stylists and their work has been continually debated as an example of styling practice; Webb's career has been more varied, and he is now seen as a journalist, illustrator and curator, as much as a stylist.

Elle and the Shifting Feminist Perspective

As the style press and the freelance stylists working for them gained commercial success and cultural capital throughout the late 1980s, their editorial influence could be seen in other magazines. The targeting of a mixed demographic had been key in establishing the style publications, and this informed the approach of new magazines for female and, increasingly, male readers. The British version of *Elle* magazine launched in November 1985 and credited the stylists Lucinda Chambers, Debbi Mason, Harriet Jagger and Amanda Cochrane from the very first issue. The publishers of *Marie Claire* also decided to launch in the UK in 1988, and although there was less emphasis on the stylist's input, Catherine Bailey appears in the masthead as 'Freelance Fashion Stylist' from issue one onwards.

Elle, published by News International and Hachette, intended to transform glossy women's publishing in Britain, declaring war on the circulation figures and advertising revenues of many established women's titles, especially those published by National Magazines, who were responsible for *Cosmopolitan* and its sister title *Company* (Gough-Yates 2003). During the 1980s, *Cosmopolitan*, despite remaining the market leader, had far fewer readers than during its peak a decade earlier. *Elle* was the first to realistically challenge its status as the number one women's title, and other competitor publications launched during the 1980s had so far failed to attract readers. For example, *Options* was introduced in April 1982 by IPC and was accorded a similar expensive media campaign to both *Cosmopolitan* and *Company*. Although it claimed to be targeting an 'entirely new breed of consumer', it was clearly aimed at the same, if slightly updated, female market to its predecessors (Braithwaite and Barrell 1988: 37). Hardly revolutionary, the magazine was, according to Janice Winship, aimed at 'the grown-up *Cosmo* girl with domestic responsibilities' (1987: 155). Another prospective competitor, *Working Woman*, had launched in October 1984, and was a version of an American title. Slightly more ambitious than *Options*, it set out with the intention of appealing to executive women but did not perform well. It closed in 1987, having failed to reflect the real lives of its readership in its editorial direction (Braithwaite and Barrell 1988).

Gorman claims that *Elle* was '*The Face* for women' (2017: 133), and when it launched, the publication had strategically employed members of *The Face* editorial team, taking on Lesley White as deputy editor and employing writers Robert Elms and Tony Parsons. In *Elle* features, creative roles were given equal weighting on the page, and the stylist was listed alongside the photographer, hair, make-up, models and model agency. Of those interviewed for this book, both Sarah Miller and Debbi Mason were at British *Elle* during its formative years. Miller joined *Elle* whilst continuing to work at *Cosmopolitan*, moving soon after to launch *Blueprint*, a design and architecture magazine. Her working pattern is indicative of the increasingly flexible nature of employment across all the publishing industries in the UK (Gough-Yates 2003). *Elle* had a more dynamic approach to the allocation of editorial roles. Miller fulfilled both features and styling roles because she was a writer but had experience of dressing and working on a shoot. Mason explains how the various responsibilities were allocated when she was first recruited and how she managed the role alongside other freelance commitments:

> To begin with, Lucinda Chambers and I were given equal status. I can't remember what the job titles were, but we were both equally in charge. And Sally didn't find that was a very effective way of working, she wanted one person to take responsibility, so she promoted me, and I became fashion editor there. Harriet

> Jagger was one of the fashion editors at that time. We worked closely with the art department, and that was Clive Crook, with the art team under him. That might have been about it at the start. And then we used to produce periodic menswear supplements and get different people in freelance to produce that. And beauty also came under fashion too. I [worked solely for *Elle*] in the beginning and then they allowed me to become freelance and remain fashion editor. And then I was contributing to all sorts of things; I worked for *The Face* quite a bit, *Arena*, Italian *Vogue*, Italian *Marie Claire*. Yeah, lots of different people.[2]

Elle followed the lead of *Nova* and *Cosmopolitan* in previous decades, attempting to directly address the 'new woman' (Winship 1987). According to editor Sally Brampton, its reader was the antithesis of the 'Sloane Ranger', a popular stereotype of the upper-middle class, West London woman, who read established society titles like *Tatler* and *Harpers & Queen*. *Elle* was considered noteworthy from the outset because of its relevance to the contemporary British, middle-class woman. It had previously been successful in other countries and readers were familiar with its format and its quality (Winship 1987). The magazine's launch team had conducted thorough market research and had identified a considerable percentage of women who had benefitted from higher education and expected more intelligent editorial content. Focus groups conducted a year after its launch indicated that the prior existence of *Elle* elsewhere was advantageous and it was felt the brand identity already embodied 'European-ness, stylishness and adventurousness', qualities that would help to market it to a British readership (Gough-Yates 2003: 102). The magazine was introduced to the public through 'tasters' that were placed in the May and September issues of the *Sunday Times* colour magazine, and the launch was given a budget of £1 million to be advertised on national television and through a public poster campaign (Barrell and Braithwaite 1988). It averaged circulation figures of 230,000 over its first six issues which, although *Cosmopolitan* was still reaching circulation figures of 375,000, indicated that it was a popular title.

Elle presented fashion and lifestyle content that suggested a new-found freedom for women, even if, as Miller concedes, they still recognized inequalities. *Elle* employed advertising in a way that women's titles like *Cosmopolitan* had not done before:

> *Elle* came along with a completely new, fresh attitude. Largely inspired by Sally, for whom I have a huge regard, who'd just been fashion editor of the *Observer*, and it was like the next wave. It wasn't women fighting for equality anymore, it was just the assumption that they had it, and that you could be that. So, it wasn't pummelling feminism, in the same way that *Cosmo* was still doing, and it had taken a whole generation leap. I felt much more akin to this new attitude, than *Cosmo*; it still felt slightly old for me, to be honest. *Elle* went 'all out' in a way that wasn't about long features and staged photographs, it was like 'Here are the gadgets, the gizmos, the items, that you must buy and have' and it was a completely consumerist acceptance that women had spending power. *Young* women. So, the

> difference about *Elle* was that it was a fashion magazine for young women who wanted to express themselves visually, knew the value of their spending power, were affluent, were very hip. Achingly hip. Whereas *Cosmo* was, I think, for a slightly less hip reader and more for people interested in relationships. There was a lot about, you know, 'Does your man satisfy your longings?' [laughs].[3]

British *Elle* was eager to offer a new format of women's editorial that reflected the paradigm shift brought about by the style press. The visual language of *Elle*, as a franchised title, had an obligation to align with the graphic identity of the publication's other international partners. It could not be as avant-garde as the style magazines, but the way it presented fashion nonetheless acknowledged the hand of the stylist. As an example, Fig. 12 shows 'Hound Around', a feature styled by Mason for the February 1988 issue. In it a young model poses with a succession of different dogs. The clothing items have been manipulated to create certain shapes, to suggest certain silhouettes. On the left-hand page, a men's, rust-coloured, Norfolk jacket (from Duffer of St George) has been knotted at the waist then drawn open to show the layers of denim beneath. On the opposite page was a wide-shouldered men's jacket (Armani), worn over an embroidered shirt (Joseph). The sleeves have been pushed up and folded to reveal the satin lining, held up by a pair of ruched, black opera gloves from Cornucopia, a second-hand clothing store in Pimlico, South London. The looks, created largely with menswear items, encourage the reader to think about new styles for women, that are perhaps not yet available in womenswear stores (see Fig. 12). Like Baker's work for *Nova*, the styling is not intended to patronize or dictate to its readers. The freedom to choose *how* to wear clothes is implicit in the way the looks are presented.

Stylists were starting to be seen as individuals. They were building reputations for themselves and the personal style of their work was being recognized. The designer Stephen Jones said that 'types' of stylist were emerging. The idea that a stylist's way of selecting and combined clothing could communicate their creative identity became accepted. This acceptance was a step towards being acknowledged in a similar way to their peers, to designers or photographers. Jones suggested there were two camps of stylist. He classed Debbi Mason and Lucinda Chambers as one type, as mainstream, and Mitzi Lorenz and Ray Petri as the alternative. But it was not that clear cut. Mason's approach to dressing a model was often as inventive as stylists working for independent magazines. As a freelancer she worked for both mainstream and style magazines. She said that Sally Brampton gave her permission to 'break the rules'. Despite advertising being important to the publishers, *Elle* allowed stylists to be irreverent. Rather than showing a designer or brand's full outfits from head to toe, Mason would put Armani with Comme des Garçons, or 'whatever she felt like doing'.

Mason asserted that *Elle*, despite its acknowledgement of consumer culture, was prepared to style fashion in a way that reflected new feminist perspectives, as Baker had done for *Nova* two decades earlier. Yet one could argue that *Elle* was postfeminist, rather than feminist. The *Elle* reader was primarily a consumer, keeping abreast of the range of available lifestyle choices, rather than having a particular political stance or belief system. The fashion featured in the magazine was addressing women who – as Miller claimed – had established their equality, whereas the *Nova* or *Cosmopolitan* readers were aspiring to it (Miller 2018). In both cases, however, the stylists played a part, through the way they dressed women to make a statement, in reaffirming the ethos of the publication and communicating this to its readership.

New Men

The development of consumer culture among British men in the 1980s and 1990s has been directly attributed to the evolution of magazines targeting men. Supposedly, the 'foremost function' of these magazines was to encourage men to shop, and stylists played a part in this development (Edwards 2016: 74). I have noted that Sarah Miller made the same point in relation to British *Elle* when it was introduced. By the mid-1980s, Britain had experienced six years of Margaret Thatcher's aggressive reforms and, at least superficially, the economy was healthier than it had been a decade earlier. A neo-liberal economy benefits from the promotion of a more diverse marketplace, which can lead to the creation of niche markets and new opportunities for manufacturers and service providers. The 1980s saw a broader range of masculinities presented in the media and these included the 'new man' (Mort 1996; Nixon 1996). The new man was an anti-stereotypical version of manhood; he was 'gentle, emotional and communicative'. Also, he shopped. Shopping had always been associated with women, so the idea that men might shop for pleasure, and build a personal identity through their own retail choices, was a fresh idea (Gill 2007).

Partly prompted by evolving feminism, the arrival of the 'new man' of the 1980s was said to have been motivated by a need for sexual equality in the workplace and domestic sphere. The changing role of women should, it was argued, be reflected by a similar change in the role of men in society. Yet the British journalists responsible for reporting on the lifestyle choices and consumer interests of these new forms of masculinity were less willing than their US counterparts to recognize that changes in gender representation had any link with the feminist movement. There had been a similar refusal by socialist, radical British feminism to engage with consumer culture in the way that American feminism had been doing since the 1970s (Mort 1996). There was also suspicion and criticism of 'new mannism' amongst feminist writers. Some claimed that heterosexual men had adapted to retain their status as a dominant force in society, and that rather than challenging the gender hierarchy, they had extended patriarchy into areas that had previously been the domain of women (McCauley Bowstead 2018).

New gay identities and gay consumer markets were aware of, but also helped shape, the new versions of manhood being discussed and presented in magazines (Cole 2000). Caroline Baker said that the 1980s was a 'huge evolution' for gay men, particularly in relation to fashion and the way that they expressed themselves (2017). Despite the British government's anti-homosexual policies, there was arguably more public acceptance of gay rights. Among advertisers there was a readiness to consider that gay, frequently single, men with no families to support, had high levels of disposable income to spend on leisure activities and on cultural and material goods. Within the gay community itself, identities had shifted during the 1980s. The appropriation of 'new masculine images' among younger homosexual men was as prevalent as for their heterosexual equivalent. New looks replaced the 'clone' styling of the gay men of the previous decade, that is, bomber jacket, worker boots, short hair, beard or moustache. In London, the overtly camp dress styles of the New Romantic, post-punk clubs remained relevant in the late 1980s, and new nights were opening that also catered for a mixed gay and straight audience (Cole 2000). As discussed in the previous chapter, the extreme forms of dressing up and provocative new gender identities seen in these clubs were localized phenomena. Although they were translated into more commercially viable trends by designers – or worn by musicians for performances or promotional videos – these looks were not likely to be adopted by the wider gay community, even in London. Rockabilly and skinhead, both previously decisively heterosexual subcultural forms, became the reference points in the development of new homosexual identities in the 1980s. They epitomized aggressive versions of masculinity and, notably with the latter, had become associated with sadomasochistic sexual practices. Doctor Martens work boots, Levi's 501 jeans, cropped hair and the bomber jacket became synonymous with the fashion conscious, urban gay man (Cole 2000). Menswear stylists like Petri and Simon Foxton were formulating new looks and ensuring they featured prominently in fashion media. For Petri, the bomber jacket was a recurring theme. Roger Charity, with whom he collaborated regularly, says that his looks were feeding back into both straight and gay culture:

> One of the iconic looks that Ray put together was the classic nylon army jacket, the MA1, I think, paired with 501s, and a t-shirt. It had an orange lining, so he used to turn it inside-out. That was one of the looks that he nurtured and then put all sorts of things with it. That came to be called the Buffalo jacket. Magazines used it, manufacturers used it, but we used it first, it was our jacket.[4]

In describing the transition of popular gay identity from the 'clone' look of the 1970s (bomber jacket, worker boots, short hair) to the new looks of the 1980s (also bomber jacket, worker boots, cropped hair), I am aware that they do not sound drastically different. However, the clothes were styled differently, and it was *how* they were worn that affected the way they were perceived. The slicker, more groomed, more effeminate looks produced by Petri and mimicked by both heterosexual and homosexual men were sexy and self-confident. There was 'two-way influence' between Ray Petri's styling and the young men seen cruising the streets of London's Soho, but other international styles had fed into the look. Paninaro, an Italian youth culture that originated in the coffee shops of Milan, was referenced in pop music by the Pet Shop Boys in 1986 and there were parallels between its urban casual style and the type of masculinity that inspired both

Petri and Simon Foxton. I have noted that *The Face* documented the influx of American hip-hop and House music during the late 1980s, and the clothing styles they brought with them were also apparent in both Buffalo style and the dress of gay men.

Nonetheless, Petri's mixing of conventional menswear with unexpected items of clothing ensured that he retained his reputation as an innovator (Cole 2000). He often dressed men in skirts, an aspect of his styling that reflected his desire to present non-Western masculinities, rather than representing a new queer identity. It was more a demonstration of multiculturalism. Interviewed for this book, Jamie Morgan claimed that Buffalo wanted to present men as peacocks, citing more colourful, expressive African, Indian and Native American dress as examples of the diversity of global masculine dress. Petri's work consistently quoted both Western and non-Western masculine stereotypes, such as the West African 'sapeur', the boxer, the Jamaican 'rude boy', the gangster, or the entrepreneur (Tulloch 2011: 183). Buffalo looks influenced London's gay clubbers but were also gaining international attention, with fashion designers showing interest in the style. Morgan recalls that Jean-Paul Gaultier had invited them to his Paris catwalk show because he admired their work. It is not difficult to see the link between the dress codes of Gaultier at that time and the editorial styling of Buffalo, particularly the men in skirts, but also the eclectic mixing of sportswear with tailoring.

The portrayal of male models as sex objects was also a relatively new development in men's publishing. It clearly marked the intentions of magazines, advertisers and stylists to speak directly to the gay consumer. The outfits constructed by Petri and Foxton eroticized the male body, and it was often the positioning of the clothing, rather than the choice of items, that reinforced the sexual message. For 'Heavy Metal' by Petri and Jamie Morgan, in the April 1986 issue of *The Face*, the model Zane appeared half-dressed, in black shoes and socks, with a knitted long-sleeved jersey and little else. He sported a customized black jockstrap, tugging up his sweater provocatively to reveal a further glimpse of tanned stomach. The crotch was the focus, and various metal accessories (a knuckle-duster, gold buckles on the strap) were added to draw the reader's attention to it. In other images, he turned to reveal his bare buttocks, looking over his shoulder at the camera.

Baker was also prepared to sexualize men in a way that was usually associated with women, and for her it was motivated by a need for sexual equality. 'Role Over', in the September 1984 issue of *The Face*, showed male models with the shirts rolled up or pulled back to reveal the nipples or bellies. She deliberately pulled up their trousers to accentuate their 'boys' bumps'. The statement of intent was made clear by the captions: 'Men's fashion reflects a changing attitude to body revelations. The new look is soft, the attitude openly sensitive' (see Fig. 13). She is clearly describing the 'new man'. *Nova* had also often tried to provoke debate by presenting men as objects of desire. For example, the cover of the October 1973 issue, which required no styling, featured a naked man with the slogan 'Lucky you, you can ogle me.' The year before, the American version of *Cosmopolitan* had featured a centrefold of a naked, hairy Burt Reynolds. *Nova* and *Cosmopolitan* magazines were aimed at women, though, and in the 1980s the focus had shifted to address the tastes of gay men. Even if the representations of masculinity in 1980s style magazines did not necessarily reflect a wholesale shift in male representation elsewhere in society, both 'aspirational and narcissistic' versions of masculinity surfaced in all media that had never been seen before.

For Him, *Arena* and *GQ*

It is important not to exaggerate the reach of 'new mannism'. As Bob Pease points out, it was a typically Western discourse and at the most only applied to 'five per cent of the world's population of men, in one region of the world, at one moment in history' (2000: 29). However, British publishers were sufficiently motivated to launch new titles to cater for this new phenomenon. Considering the extraordinary range we now see in contemporary print and digital media, it is difficult to imagine that the representation of men's fashion in British publishing was a relative novelty at the time. Historically, it was a genre of publishing that had not fared well in this country. *Esquire* had failed in the 1950s, and *Men in Vogue* ran for a short while in the late 1960s before folding after five years. *Man About Town* launched in 1952, as an offshoot of the trade magazine *The Tailor and Cutter*. It was restyled in the 1960s, changing its name to *About Town*, then *Town*, but only lasted until 1968. Until the 1980s, British men, if they were interested, mainly found men's fashion in imported titles and trade publications.

Among the first magazines to address new men was *For Him*, in 1985. The fact that it was originally considered a style magazine at its inception is perhaps surprising, as it later became one of the first, blatantly misogynist, British 'lads mags'.[5] Its title a direct English translation of the Italian men's magazine *Per Lui*, it was initially a complimentary magazine distributed in menswear stores. The magazine became quarterly in 1987 and, for a while during the later part of the 1980s, could be a considered a competitor with *GQ* and *Arena*. I examined issues of *For Him* printed from 1985 to 1990 to look for the stylist's input. Although the format mainly followed that of conventional fashion editorial, with an in-house editorial team, there is evidence of the influence of the style press in the labelling of roles and responsibilities. 'Style' was often used to label features that would be classed as 'beauty' in a comparable women's publication (haircare, perfume, cosmetics) and from the outset, Steve Whatley was credited as grooming and style editor. That a men's magazine would openly credit 'grooming', and admit that the beards, skin or hair of the men featured in its fashion pages had been styled, was meaningful. It corroborated the unashamed narcissism of the new man.

In the same year, *Unique* magazine launched, published independently and edited by Jonathan Obadia. It provided a springboard for the stylist David Bradshaw, who later became fashion editor of *Arena*, but the launch of the latter arguably contributed to *Unique*'s closure in 1987. *Unique* was very much a fashion publication, and without the breadth of lifestyle features presented by its competitors it could only appeal to a limited readership.

Of the new menswear magazines of the 1980s, *Arena* was by far the most significant to the development of the stylist and the evolution of the menswear styling. Editor Nick Logan had originally intended to produce a sports magazine when he first considered expanding on the success of *The Face*. Like *Elle*, *Arena* used many personnel that had previously contributed to *The Face*. Logan retained the art director Neville Brody and Ray Petri, the two members of the creative team who had helped to give it a distinctive, unique aesthetic and format. As well as Petri and Brody, Simon Foxton and Mark Lebon, the photographers Davies and Starr and Robert Erdmann, Joe McKenna, and the writer Robert Elms had also been regular contributors to style publications. Caroline Baker, who by this stage had accumulated almost twenty years of fashion editorial experience, was yet again included in the team. *Arena* acknowledged styling for all fashion features from the outset. Foxton and Petri were joined by Marcus von Ackerman, Debra Berkin, Paul Frecker, Nick Logan's son Christian, Venetia Scott and Bradshaw. A further indication of the increased status of the role was the crediting of the stylists' assistants in features. Assisting was becoming a route into a styling career, and it enabled aspiring stylists to understand what the role entailed.

The fashion in *Arena* was disputably more restrained than that seen in *The Face*. However, the synergy between the design and image content, overseen by Brody and art director Robin Derrick and complemented by the participation of a team of increasingly experienced contributing stylists, gave it a bold graphic identity that was pioneering in men's publishing. Like *Elle*, it was directed at consumers, and editorial features were crammed with product and lifestyle suggestions. Even if the clothing featured was sometimes traditional, there was innovation in the composition and style of photography, or in the layout of text and pictures. As an example, 'Big', which appeared in the Summer/Autumn 1989 issue was essentially an advertorial for the French designer Nicole Fahri (see Fig. 14). Styled by Christian Logan and photographed by Christian Thompson, it showed over ten pages a succession of semi-formal menswear looks, with suits, and coats in autumnal shades layered over light wool sweaters, cardigans and t-shirts. In this situation, where the clothing was all supplied by one designer, there would seem to be little scope for creativity. Yet in the posing and placement of the models and clothing, some directly in the foreground and others far in the distance, the photographer created illusions of scale, and these were exaggerated by the strategic placement of giant text on the page. Conversely, 'Twenty White Shirts' in the Autumn/Winter 1988 issue was an exercise in styling. Photographed by Kevin Davies with the stylist William Gilchrist, it featured twenty mildly different white shirts. Variety was achieved through the accessorizing of each white shirt and the way that each one was worn. In 'Medallion Man' the shirt had been tied around the waist, opened to reveal a lightly hairy chest and World necklace (from Michael Costiff's store); for 'Student' the shirt was open over a white t-shirt and chain, with striped braces adorned with a variety of badges with slogans ('love', 'God', 'high'); 'Cowboy' featured a Western-style, collar-tipped shirt and ribbon tie; in 'Mod' the shirt was buttoned with a pencil tie with a target motif from American Classics in Carnaby Street; and in 'Chef' the model held a fish.

Although the status of fashion stylists remained prominent in the late 1980s, with their input in the construction of the fashion image being a given, a new trend for realism in photography required a different slant on styling. Despite the obvious – and credited – input of a team of creative contributors, photographs were increasingly made to look unstyled, like a film still or documentary image rather than something self-consciously staged (Smedley 2000). Although stylists were employed to create these faux-natural looks, each image was contrived in a way that made it look like a snapshot of 'real life'. 'The Back Loft', a fashion story styled by emerging stylist Venetia Scott for the September/October 1989 issue of *Arena*, was shot by Michael Haddi and modelled by a handful of Hollywood hopefuls in various backstreet locations in Los Angeles. The models are caught in motion, largely ignoring the camera. There is nothing unconventional about the way the clothes are worn. Nothing is cinched, strapped, reversed or repurposed. Although attention has clearly been paid to the choice of outfits that comprise each look (an 'Americana' theme, with cow print, a red fifties-style Yohji Yamamoto shirt, a silver suit that echoes those worn by Elvis), the models have been dressed in a careful, convincing way. Shirts have been tucked in and collars unbuttoned. Contrary to this, much of the styling in the early 1980s – particularly that featured in the style press – had been blatant. The clothing and context were obviously contrived, and it had been easy to detect – in the way that the clothing items had been combined – that the situation had been styled.

More interested in creating fantasy, this move towards documenting or replicating reality led Simon Foxton to focus on menswear consultancy during the 1990s. He felt that editorial work had become less fulfilling. To look at most of Foxton's features in *Arena* in the late 1980s, there was an eccentricity in the styling that is not seen in the other spreads. 'Tweedy Pie', styled by Foxton and photographed by Richard Croft, presented a quirky parody of British hunting culture. Although centred on a real-life situation, everything was mismatched and deliberately awkward. Foxton juxtaposed pastel wool jackets and cable-knit sweaters with a traditional Scottish kilt and sporran. Waders and walking accessories were paired with an oversized designer jacket, layered over a chequered waistcoat and a rollneck. The models' hair was gelled into unusual shapes. It has a slap-stick quality. Elsewhere in the same issue, even the cinematic 'South of the Border', by Ray Petri and photographer Norman Watson, restyled existing masculine conventions or cinematic tropes. However, what became increasingly recognized was the craft of creating something authentic. Petri's versatility arguably lay in his ability to be both authentic and experimental (see Fig. 15). Bradshaw said when he joined *Arena* he wanted to present real men in his fashion stories, versions of the men he grew up with, which feels very much at odds with the deliberately disconnected surrealism styled by Foxton.

The introduction of *For Him* and *Arena* magazines was followed by the launch of *GQ*. Condé Nast had been planning to launch a British version of *Gentleman's Quarterly* for several years. Initial market research had not been encouraging, but the success of *Arena* had prompted them to commit to the idea, releasing the first issue in 1988. The men in *GQ* were, according to Nixon, 'more mainstream, successful men' than the 'style leaders' featured in *Arena* (1996: 160). Although the magazine did not typically credit stylists in the 1980s, in the two years that fall within the remit of this book, there was a clear focus on style in the magazine – for example, in their decision to include a 'style and substance' section. At least a third of the editorial space was devoted to fashion coverage (Nixon 1996). Nevertheless, it lacked the flair of *Arena*. Jay McCauley Bowstead says that *GQ*, along with the American publication *Esquire* and Italian *Uomo Vogue*, in fact promoted 'more monochrome, normatively masculine, and much less formatively innovative menswear' than had even been seen in the previous decade (2018: 55).

By the end of the 1980s, the stylists who had cut their teeth in style publications were able to broaden their remit and make more money. A second wave of British style press emerged during the 1990s, including *Sleaze Nation*, *Raygun* and *Dazed and Confused*, and these afforded further opportunities for stylists, both as freelancers or in editorial positions (Lynge-Jorlen 2017). The drug culture and hedonism that had been reported in *The Face* towards the end of the 1980s became intrinsic to the editorial style and content of these new magazines, reflected in both their journalism and fashion images. Staples of the style magazines, such as the 'straight-up' started to appear in *Vogue*. and, conversely, *i-D* and *The Face* became glossier, in line with the formats of conventional fashion publications (Lynge-Jorlen 2017). The fashion stylist was now a known quantity. The heightened status and cultural capital that magazine work provided led to better paid commercial projects – collaborating with fashion designers, dressing models for advertising projects, and styling celebrities and musicians for promotional videos and performances. Jones had claimed that a stylist could 'literally make or break a person or product', and it seemed that more and more brands or manufacturers were prepared to pay for their expert opinion (1987: 85).

Notes

1 D. Jones (1987), *The i-D Bible: Every Ultimate Victim's Handbook* (London: Levelprint), 85.
2 D. Mason (2017), interview by Philip Clarke, 5 May.
3 S. Miller (2018), interview by Philip Clarke, 23 March.
4 R. Charity (2018), interview by Philip Clarke, 13 February.
5 Laddism being a reassertion of traditional heterosexual values designed to counter new mannism.

Chapter 6

The Rise of the Stylist: Legacy, Status and Hierarchy

This final chapter questions the position and status of the stylist as an occupational role. It explores the job opportunities that have developed for the freelance stylist and reflects on the specific career trajectories of stylists. Building on the question of authorial responsibility and creative hierarchy introduced in previous chapters, I situate the stylist in terms of commerce and artistry. I explore the dynamic between the stylist's role as cultural intermediary – straddling a range of fields of commerce and communication – and as creative director or author of a specific cultural form. In the early 1980s, styling was only very loosely defined as an occupation and many of those who became stylists at this time viewed it as an accidental career move, rather than a decisive one. Their formational experiences varied enormously. Some left school with few qualifications and gained experience by entering the magazine industry directly as an assistant or intern. Some completed a degree in an art or fashion design. Others had previous careers in unrelated fields (waiter, social worker, civil engineer). This chapter asks several questions: Did the increased visibility of the stylist in the 1980s have a positive impact on the status of the stylist as a professional role? Has the remit of the stylist changed since then and in what way? Have the stylists who made a name for themselves at that time retained their status and influence?

There remain many types of styling work for which the stylist is rarely credited. This unacknowledged commercial work is often how they make a living. Freelance fashion stylists engage in consultancy work for designers, production work for events and performances, personal styling for private or celebrity clients such as actors or musicians and collaborate in the dressing of models and construction of sets for advertising photography. In this book, I have focused mainly on editorial styling. By looking at the listings in magazines it was possible to quantify the freelance stylist's contribution. The progressive increase in coverage they received in print during the 1980s suggested that fashion stylists were becoming noticed in an equivalent way to their creative peers. They gained legitimation and prestige in the hierarchy of fashion media roles. Interviewing freelance stylists who started working then has provided a more rounded view of their working life. It has allowed an insight into practices in both editorial and commercial situations.

When I conducted most of the interviews almost forty years had passed since the *The Face*, *i-D* and *Blitz* were first published, magazines which gave many stylists their first opportunities for work. This chapter is largely based on their reflections on their careers, the opportunities they were given as they gained more experience, and their fluctuating attitudes as their own situation and working environment changed. They considered the historical and contemporary position of the stylist within the network of fashion media roles, and explained the hierarchies in this field. Many of the stylists or fashion editors had progressed to other types of work, some leaving the fashion industry completely.

Education and Status

The status of an occupational role is often closely associated with the level and form of education needed to fulfil that role. Defining the practices, status and professional identities of careers in a range of creative industries, Leah Armstrong and Felice McDowell's *Fashioning Professionals* (2018) includes a chapter by Rachel Lifter on the stylist. According to Lifter, styling has graduated from the loosely structured occupation of the 1980s to the status of a professional role (2018). Yet a formal qualification, which one would expect a professional to possess, does not appear to be necessary to achieve success or cultural capital as a stylist.

A common thread among those I interviewed was an interest in art or fashion from an early age, even if they didn't pursue either subject academically. Fashion was traditionally taught within art schools in Britain, as opposed to the business or design focus of fashion education in Italy or many other European counties. Subsequently, fashion design has been viewed as an artistic pursuit in this country, with many fashion designers seeing themselves as artists (McRobbie 1998). By the early 1980s, it was possible to study an art or design subject to the equivalent of degree level. The Coldstream Report, instigated by the National Advisory Board of Arts Education in the early 1960s, was instrumental in legitimating the arts and 'applied arts' as academic subjects and in kick-starting the process of gaining degree status for these subject areas. The first stage of this development was the introduction of a Diploma in Art and Design, proposed in 1960 and rolled out in colleges in 1963. The three-year qualification was equivalent to a first degree. The four main study areas were Fine Art, Graphic Design, Three-Dimensional Design and Textiles/Fashion (Coldstream 1970). In the decade from the early 1960s to the early 1970s the numbers of students in arts subject areas rose by more than 70 per cent. The increase in students undertaking art and design education to a higher level inevitably led to a greater number of graduates, who were seeking ways of utilizing their skills and knowledge in an appropriate career field.

Although many successful stylists have not been art school trained, their perception of their own creative identity has often been modelled on that of the fashion designer. Fashion design has struggled to gain respect as an academic field. It has acquired some credence in conjunction with more critical perspectives on popular culture and the applied arts, but some would argue that it is still not taken as seriously as other art and design disciplines (Steele 1998). The position that the contemporary British fashion designer has created for themself in many ways reflects this need to legitimize their creative practice as an academic field. To have degree status implies that a field of study is 'difficult, abstract and theoretical', so historical and cultural studies are usually taught alongside technical skills on fashion courses at further and higher education level in British colleges and universities (McRobbie 1998: 42). The field of subcultural studies drew attention to youth culture and style as worthy subjects of academic debate and it was also included in curricula to give students an alternative perspective to traditional histories of dress (Breward 1998; McRobbie 1998; Hickman 2005).

As noted at the very beginning of this book, it is now possible to study fashion styling to degree level in some British universities. Like fashion design, the majority of these courses are taught at universities where, even if they are not art colleges, share pedagogical and resourcing models with arts courses. As in the field of fashion design, the study of technical skills is supported with cultural studies and dress history. Emphasis is placed on the visual research process and on the development of a strong concept and narrative, as well as exploration of the audience or market. The educational framework of new styling courses reflects, like fashion design, a need to legitimize the field of fashion styling.

The opportunity for such a specialized form of training did not exist for stylists working in the early 1980s. Caroline Baker started working twenty years before this and witnessed the development of new opportunities for the younger generations, opportunities that she was not given. Having completed her studies in the 1960s (O levels, then secretarial college), she worked her way up through a series of editorial roles. She did not study fashion but many fashion designers at that time had not been formally trained either. Baker claimed that architecture studies were sometimes a starting point for those who went on to work in fashion. Her limited education was common of many women of her generation, but class was also a factor:

> You see, my mother's sister went to university, and that was in the 1930s. She graduated in law, but she couldn't work as a lawyer because you weren't able to. Women going to university probably started with girls ten years older than me. My age group, whenever I read any histories of my age group, we all either wanted to be secretaries, or a nurse, or an air stewardess. Those were the three careers for women. But if I think about women in the media who I've read about – a few of them were, of course, probably more 'upper class money' – they might have gone to university.[1]

By the late 1970s, the educational landscape for aspiring fashion designers had changed. In a very limited way, fashion media was also starting to be seen as a distinct field by some colleges. Although the Fashion Communication pathway of the Fashion course at St Martin's already existed by this point, Simon Foxton and Iain R. Webb studied fashion design. Caryn Franklin and Robin Derrick studied graphic design at the same college. For Foxton, styling had provided an alternative career route, after ultimately realizing that he was not interested in becoming a fashion designer. After graduating, he set up a label, Bazooka, with two friends and worked for a few years as a fashion designer. The realization that a career pathway existed that allowed him to draw on the skills and knowledge he had gained at college but without the laborious production schedules appealed to him, and led to a change of focus:

> I'm quite a lazy person by nature and with designing it's quite an arduous, long process and you have to, apart from the design itself, you've got the production and there's all the deliveries. That's the side of things that I can't be bothered with. Whereas I realized styling was quite immediate, you could just get clothes and put them on people and say what you wanted to say and that was it.[2]

Foxton continues to feel that styling is an innate process, a manifestation of the stylist's tastes and instincts, rather than something that can be taught. On the occasions that he has worked in education (he was a visiting lecturer on the Menswear course at the Royal College of Art), Foxton has felt more comfortable teaching fashion design.

Aside from art and fashion studies, other types of training or experience contributed to the career advancement of the first generations of British stylists. David Bradshaw, who studied as a civil engineer, gained the insights and experience necessary for a career as a stylist through offering to become an agent for a fashion illustrator, then as an advertising salesman for an emerging men's magazine. Sarah Miller gained work experience initially when she was in New York in her late teens and her career path to success included a range of internships and educational opportunities, working with Milton Glaser, the infamous advertising agent, at his company Pushpin Studio and by gaining a substantial amount of editorial experience with Italian *Harper's Bazaar* and *Cosmopolitan*. She was well connected and admits that her mother helped her acquire the internships, as she knew the editor-in-chief of *Cosmopolitan* (2018). Like Bradshaw, Miller had not previously studied in an art- or fashion-related field, so when she returned from her time in New York she first went to Oxford University to study English before finding a position at the British version of *Cosmopolitan* and working her way up the ranks. Of the stylists I interviewed, Zee Shore was the only one who felt that her lack of an arts education had impacted on her confidence and opportunities as a stylist; she felt like an outsider because having originally trained as a social worker she did not have the same educational foundations or, more importantly, the same network as her peers (2017).

Commercial Styling

Styling for editorial photography is the most publicly recognized form of styling work but is only one type of work executed by the fashion stylist. A distinct feature of the stylist's role in British fashion in the 1980s was its freelance status, allowing them to work in both editorial and commercial environments. It gave them more freedom to position themselves as creative trendsetters and visionaries, but also to make money. Status-building and money-making were often mutually exclusive activities. To find enough paid work, freelance stylists had to market themselves to potential employers. As I have noted elsewhere, the multidisciplinary nature of creative work was often motivated by financial considerations – people needed more than one job to live. They were responding to the high levels of unemployment and finding resourceful ways of adapting by inventing jobs that previously didn't exist. As stylists became established, they were able to rely on their reputation to get well-paid, higher-profile work.

The market for freelance workers led to further business opportunities for agents, who represented young creatives and mediated between them and prospective clients. Ziggi Golding formed Z in 1983, and Buffalo also operated as an agency. The agents themselves benefitted from the prestige that a credit in a style press publication would gain for them. For example, Z was named in four different features in the December/January 1985/1986 issue of *i-D*, for models, and make-up and hair. The practice of representation for these types of creative labour was already well established in America. Debbi Mason, when she moved to work in New York in the early 1990s, was represented by the agency Art and Commerce, and they were responsible for liaising with clients and finding all her jobs. Her agents were expected to find both editorial and advertising work but would prioritize better paid advertising jobs. They were paid commission, so would ultimately make more money if they did. Although commercial styling is never credited as explicitly as editorial content, association with high-profile brands can also serve to gain the stylist cultural capital. For example, Zee Shore said that people were 'killing themselves' to work for the clothing catalogue Next, when it was considered highly fashionable in the 1980s (2017).

There are various ways that a stylist can work commercially. Each involves the promotion and sale of some form of product or commodity, but the stylists' remit and working relationship with the manufacturer of that product can vary enormously. Many of these ways of working predate the freelance stylist's involvement in editorial work.

First, a fashion stylist may be hired to style a model for an advertising image, for use on posters, in magazines and increasingly on an online platform. The product they are advertising may be clothing or jewellery. In this setting, they will be expected to select outfits from the manufacturer's current collection or range to create an overall look that reflects the brand's visual identity and the tastes of their customer. They could also be hired to dress models in a scene that includes other types of product. For example, in car advertising, a stylist may be employed to dress the driver and passengers of the car. Again, their choice of clothing should reflect the tastes and lifestyle of the manufacturer's intended market. The late 1970s and early 1980s is seen as a 'boom period' for advertising. Kelly specifically attributes this 'second wave' of advertising (following the previous one in the 1950s) to the 'emphasis on nurturing brand identities as assets', which was encouraged under the neo-liberal, conservative governments in the United

Kingdom and United States. However, this was not solely an Anglo-Saxon phenomenon. In France, for example, investment in advertising grew by 380 per cent under the socialist president Francois Mitterrand, as part of a wider promotion of the visual and applied arts (Templeton 2022). The boom brought with it new opportunities for stylists, coinciding with an increased appreciation of their role as arbiters of fashionable taste. It was possible to make good money. Simon Foxton claimed that offers of advertising work brought about a marked increase in the amount of money he earned towards the end of the 1980s:

> The main leap in my income came, I would have said, more like 1989 or 1990 when I got picked up by Levi's, UK Levi's. Well, I did a couple of shoots with them. A chap called Roy Edmondson was head of marketing at the time and he obviously had heard my name and had seen it in the style press, and he got me in to, I think initially I was styling a look book or a brochure. Anyway, we clicked and then he got me back in on a regular basis as a consultant for the brand. So, I became a kind of consultant for Levi's and stayed with them for about five or six years.[3]

Certain types of work commanded higher rates of pay than others. Zee Shore, in addition to working for Next, also did mail order catalogue work for Marks and Spencer, for which she was paid a fixed rate for the duration of the job. However, she says that her agent could negotiate £200 to £300 a day for other types of commercial work. Despite Ray Petri's status as a one of the most creative, highly respected editorial stylists, Roger Charity recalls working with him on catalogue shoots at the beginning of his career and claims that he himself made the most money working for catalogues like Freemans and Grattan (2018). In this working environment, a stylist would have been employed to dress the models that appear on the pages selling clothing or jewellery. This type of work continues to exist, although e-commerce has replaced the distribution of printed catalogues. Fashion brands selling online will often have an in-house team but also employ freelance stylists. A recent ethnographic study by the commercial stylist Philip Warkander conducted research into the practices of stylists working for the Swedish fast fashion brand H&M (2020). He likens the process of styling for e-commerce to dressing a character for a television series. Warkander explains that prior to dressing the model for each promotional image, the stylist considers the consumer and their tastes. They are given descriptions of the H&M shopper by the buying team, and the stylist is tasked with choosing items from the brands ranges to style an outfit that the shopper would wear. Although catalogue photography has always required the creative team to work quickly and with large amounts of product, the introduction of digital photography has made the production process even more fast-paced. Warkander says that a stylist may be expected to dress thirty-five different looks every day.

Stylists are also called upon to collaborate more closely with fashion designers in the production of promotional shows. In this field, they source and gather accessories, are involved in model casting, and can adopt an organizational role in the coordination of the event. The practice of using live models to demonstrate new ranges of designer clothing predates the photographic representation of fashion. Fashion events generating interest in seasonal collections were introduced in tandem with the evolution of haute couture. Being invitation-only, they also generated exclusivity and elitism around the fashions. Fashion shows have become progressively more accessible, and images of the clothes more widely disseminated, initially through trade publications and specialist magazines, and subsequently via online platforms. The stylist's role in the show production process is again as intermediary, ensuring that every aspect of the message being communicated by the designer or brand aligns with the expectations of the audience. In a freelance capacity, Caroline Baker has worked on the production of shows for Vivienne Westwood, Katharine Hamnett, John Rocha and Jeff Banks. Although it is more commonly used to describe an editorial feature, Baker uses the word 'story' when referring to a live event. She suggests that the process of narrative construction is comparable in both contexts, and even calls the process 'editing' (2017). Nonetheless, Stephen Jones says that designers in the 1980s would not feel that they needed to employ a stylist to collaborate in the production of a live event, 'The fashion designer would have thought "Well what's the point? Why are we fashion designers if we need to have a stylist to style it?"' (2017).

Music work was mentioned by several of my interviewees. This type of work became more common in the 1980s as cable television platforms like MTV demanded video content to fill their schedules. There was an expectation that musicians would produce a short promotional film for each song they released. For these jobs, stylists were called on to dress the acts and any supporting members of the cast (dancers, backing singers, etc.). A fashion stylist could develop a working relationship with a particular band or singer. Linked to her collaboration with Vivienne Westwood, Baker worked with Malcolm McLaren in creating looks for the bands he was managing in the early 1980s. Judy Blame's career success as a stylist occurred towards the end of the period covered by this book. Music styling became a focus for him at the end of the 1980s when, having already worked with Boy George, he became a key influence in the look of the singer and rapper Neneh Cherry when she started to gain success. He later collaborated with Massive Attack and Björk. Jamie Morgan said that the esteem gained from working with a music act started to equal that of editorial work, and was more appealing because it made more money:

> I did a Culture Club album cover with Ray [Petri], we did *Colour by Numbers*, the second one. I did *Soul to Soul* with Mitzi. We did a lot of music. Also, Simple Minds. So, a lot of my money was music, we didn't really make money in fashion, really at that point there wasn't much going. We were starting to do fashion stuff, but music was the thing.[4]

This type of work continues to be carried out by a largely invisible workforce, because the status of the artist they work for is foregrounded. More recently, though, there have been examples of stylists gaining a degree of celebrity status through their association with high-profile music acts. Lifter claims that stylists like Nicola Formichetti (for Lady Gaga) and Mel Ottenberg (for Rihanna) extend the experience and status that they acquire as fashion stylists to the realm of pop styling. She argues that pop styling should be framed 'as a form of fashion work, produced through the mobilisation of fashion skills and knowledge' (2018: 62). Rather than acting as wardrobe assistants or dressers, the stylists bring their own fashion capital, their association with fashion, to elevate the status and identity of the musical act. As an example, the way that Blame dressed Björk for the promotional images on the cover of her 1993 album *Debut* shares many stylistic features with his fashion work of that period. Björk wears a grey mohair sweater, while two small jewels have been placed under her eyes. In the feature 'Headhunters', in the August 1993 issue of *The Face*, the models have been styled almost identically. Blame has used small jewels, haberdasher's snap fasteners and tiny zips under their eyes, and they are dressed in grey fur and deconstructed knitwear.

Stylists are called on to work for celebrities in fields other than music. Caroline Baker feels that contemporary stylists are losing their position as influencers to celebrities (2017). However, celebrity endorsement of fashion is not a twenty-first-century phenomenon. Although the advent of the Hollywood film industry amplified the reach of celebrities, social figures had influence in the promotion of fashions before this. In Chapter 1, I mentioned the relevance of individual tastemakers or critical voices, like Beau Brummell or Oscar Wilde, in the formation of taste in London society. By the beginning of the twentieth century, the lifestyle and fashion choices of personalities, such as the dancer Josephine Baker, or actresses Sarah Bernhardt or Lily Langtry, were referenced by advertisers to sell products to willing consumers (Breward 2003). *Interview* magazine credited stylists from the mid-1970s, for their role in the creation of portrait images of rising stars. Its editor, Andy Warhol, was obsessed with the cult of celebrity. The magazine served as a catalogue of new faces – actors, socialites, pop stars – many of whom would disappear from view as quickly as they emerged. Stylists are now frequently responsible for *all* the clothing that celebrities wear. The increased use of social media platforms giving audiences an insight into the day-to-day activities of celebrities, by regularly publishing photographic images of their lives, has created further opportunity for stylists to consult in this field. This is comparable to the opportunities that the development of MTV brought in the 1980s. In these situations, the stylist devises looks for a broader range of activities than merely onstage events or performances. It is necessary for the celebrity to be dressed consistently, to communicate the same brand message regardless of the situation. For example, Debbi Mason worked regularly with the actress Julia Roberts who, she says, had a reputation for being 'a sort of deluxe hippie'. Mason's role, when selecting clothing for all Roberts' public appearances, was to ensure that the theme of 'deluxe hippie' was maintained at all times.

Art versus Commerce

> I hated advertising. I liked the money. Who wouldn't? You're a young girl making lots of money. I was a teenager and £1,000 a day was my rate, and then in the next

> decade it was £2,000 a day. The next decade it was like £3,000 a day. I mean, it was ridiculous money really. And you'd think that someone would be 'Oh yeah, I'll do that all the time', but I actually wasn't like that. Because I thought the work was really naff and I hated it and I found it a bit soul destroying. I still do. It's a bit 'sell out' really. You know. [There are] very few good advertising jobs. Even the good ones are not good really. What I liked about doing the editorial was that it was about having complete creative control, and in those days, I did have complete creative control.[5]

As exemplified by Mitzi Lorenz's comments, many stylists I spoke to felt frustrated by work that, regardless of how well it was paid, did not fulfil them artistically or did not allow them creative freedom. Despite the willingness of emerging stylists in the early 1980s to align themselves with art practices, there has remained a commercial strand to styling work. It is this inverted economy, undertaking advertising work for financial gain and, often unpaid, editorial work for cultural capital or legitimation, that has become common practice amongst freelance stylists trying to maintain a career (Lynge-Jorlen 2017).

In the fields of art, design and media, a distinction has often been made between those who create performances and texts and those who mediate between production and the audience. Musicians, directors and actors, but also artisans such as film editors or graphic designers, could be classed as the former, while journalists, critics, promoters and advertisers are seen as the latter (Miller 2014). The gatekeepers – those who decide what is culturally relevant and how it is disseminated – are cultural intermediaries. The cultural intermediary is, according to Pierre Bourdieu, a 'popularizer' or influencer. They do not possess the competence or charisma of genuine artistic genius (1990). Regina Lee Blaszczyk's definition of the 'fashion intermediary' provides a useful counterpoint to Bourdieu's. A fashion intermediary works behind the scenes in the space between production and consumption. They follow patterns, interpret trends and facilitate their application in the manufacture of products and their communication to consumers. She uses the term 'tastemaker' to describe those with more charismatic roles, who may influence or define tastes. French haute couturiers and industrial designers are tastemakers. In a fashion context, she classes art directors, retail buyers and magazine editors as intermediaries – and also, stylists (2000: 6). In Chapter 1, I explained how stylists were working with product designers and manufacturers from the beginning of the twentieth century. Blaszczyk says that historically a fashion intermediary would conduct the research into the tastes and buying habits of customers and consider how best to communicate with them. The designers, as the tastemakers, would propose new styles, leaving the stylist and their team to translate the outcomes of their field research into a successful promotional campaign. In most ways, the contemporary fashion stylist's role, as a cultural intermediary, does not differ from that of Blaszczyk's field researcher, or the automobile stylist working for General Motors in the 1950s, or indeed that of the fashion editor working for a mainstream publication. They are employed for their understanding of the relationship between aesthetics and commerciality, between stylistic difference and its interpretation by a defined audience.

The way that stylists presented themselves in the 1980s, in association with certain publications, suggests that they aspired to be artists. In doing so, they were able to raise the profile of the role, at least in certain working environments. In the British education system, there has been – at least since the 1930s when fashion illustration and dressmaking started being taught to diploma level – disagreement between academics who associate fashion design with painting and other fine arts, and those who encouraged stronger links with the manufacturing industries (Breward 2000). Still, the idea that a fashion designer could be an artist existed before it was formally taught in British art colleges. Charles Frederick Worth, who is credited as the originator of haute couture, viewed himself as an artist. So did Paul Poiret, who worked at the House of Worth before setting up his own couture house. Historically, there has been interplay between fashion and art. Poiret, for example, collaborated with the painter Raoul Dufy, who designed textiles for his dresses, and with George Lapape and Paul Iribe, who created illustrations for him. Lapape's catalogue *Les Choses de Paul Poiret Vues Par Georges Lapape* (1911) presented Poiret's designs in 'styled' situations, reflecting contemporary tastes in both fashion and household decoration. It is a precursor to the styled, narrative fashion seen in magazines later in the century. Attempts to situate fashion in a fine art context have often been prompted by the desire to elevate the status of fashion. Arguably, from the 1960s onwards, as the boundaries between fine art and commercial or applied arts became less fixed, fashion has become as much of a reference point for art as vice versa. However, British fashion schools were not accorded equal degrees status with other art disciplines until the late 1960s (Breward 2000; Degen 2023).

Film theory has a rich history of critical discourse around authorship. Like fashion, it was triggered by a desire to legitimate filmmaking as an artistic practice. Accrediting the making of a film to a single artistic genius figure, or 'auteur', was a way of raising the cultural status of film and according filmmaking legitimacy as a cultural practice. Put simply, 'if art is what artists do then, if directors are artists, it follows that film must be art' (McIntyre 2012: 134). Similarly, the tendency to frame the fashion designer as creator or romantic artistic was perpetuated within the emerging field of fashion studies (Skov 2014; McRobbie 1998). Auteur theorists argued that the work of a skilled film director could be compared with that of the author of a work of literature. Indeed, the narrative capability of film as a medium allowed direct comparison with literature, which was considered a 'valid' art form (Sellors 2010). The same argument could be applied to fashion photography. British fashion magazines from the late 1960s onwards started to include images that told stories or communicated meaningful messages. The incorporation of narrative in fashion photography, through the choice of clothing, location, poses and model, could be seen as a means of legitimization, a way of conceptualizing the practice and imbuing it with traits associated with art practice. I have discussed this in more depth in Chapter 4, which explores the stylist's process. The point of contention in defining a single creative visionary is that most fields of cultural production are collaborative. Filmmaking and fashion production, and indeed fashion image-making, are reliant on a complex network of interdependent roles, many of whom make creative decisions. Defining the culture industries in Britain in the first part of the new millennium, McRobbie notes that the 'romance of the scene of artistic labour' continues to influence young creative professionals through their education and as they begin to establish a career (McRobbie 2016: 70). The ratio of cultural and economic capital between artistic and commercial fields had traditionally always been inverse – that is, the more culturally valid a pursuit is, the less money is typically earned (Bourdieu 1990). An anti-fashion, or anti-consumerist, attitude among those contributing to style publishing was also evident in the way that this predominantly freelance workforce perceived itself. Yet they found ways of making money, and ultimately building a career, albeit by more flexible means that their peers in established fashion editorial roles.

The consumerist motivation of fashion publishers was anathema to most of my interviewees. Even in the early 1980s, *The Face* was criticized for embracing commercialism masquerading as rebellion and disruption. Editorial integrity and advertising, says Miller, were never supposed to mix (2018). Ziggi Golding feels that the beginning of a 'corporate buyout' of the magazine industries, including the style magazines, started in the 1980s. It became even more pronounced in the following decade (2017), and Simon Foxton said he is increasingly disinclined to do editorial work for this reason:

> I've said all that I want to with the styling guise, also I think that magazines have changed, and they are not the vehicles of creativity that they once were. I understand why completely; they have far more economic concerns, and they have to get in the advertising, and the advertisers insist that they cover the brands. But they've become almost like shopping brochures. I mean, there are the odd exceptions, but it's hard to be able to do what you want anymore. I prefer to have a freer hand.[6]

Although he spoke from a photographer's perspective, Roger Charity pointed out that a similar shift was experienced in advertising photography, where the creative team started to have less freedom and agency in the decision-making process:

> I used to work with stylists for magazines and for mail order catalogues, a long time ago. That kind of changed too. Catalogues began to take more control. Or wanted more control in terms of what models were being used, hair, make-up and styling, and that changed because of the buyers. It all depended on sales in mail order. If a garment sold 10,000, which was a lot more than any other garment, they'd want to know 'Who's the stylist, who's the photographer, who's the hair and makeup?' and book them, because they'd made a fortune out of that shot. It all changed, and the photographer lost control. They stipulated who they wanted to use. The buyers at the catalogues had massive control over who they were booking. Even down to the photography. Not the art department, the buyers.[7]

The term 'commercial' was used by interviewees to describe advertising work but also, by some, to differentiate a certain type of mainstream editorial job from the more experimental work for niche magazines. Robin Derrick stressed that 'commercial styling is not subordinate' but added that commercial stylists differ from 'createur' stylists in that they select, they do not create (2017). His comments echoed those made by Caroline Baker when describing her role in catwalk production as 'an editor'. However, not all the stylists I interviewed were fully resistant to commercial constraints. David Bradshaw's opinions on the influence of advertisers in fashion publishing were as critical as those of the other stylists, nevertheless he felt that awareness of client requirements and the customer's needs created parameters which actually stimulate creativity:

> I'm not an artist, I'm a creative. The difference being my creativity is applied. I'm not just starting with a blank canvas. I've always known that I've got something to say or achieve with this project, whether that's an editorial project or a show, an advertising campaign. The more I know what that is, the more set those parameters are, the better I perform. I think that goes back to the pragmatist in me being an engineer. Being an engineer requires a certain degree of pragmatism. It's different from being an architect. An architect dreams the dreams, the engineer makes sure it doesn't fall down.[8]

The stylist may view themselves as an artist because of their education, from the way that art, craft and design are typically taught in Britain as academic subjects, and how attitudes to legitimate and non-legitimate forms of cultural production are instilled in these types of education. The level of critical acclaim that the style press had achieved by the mid-1980s meant that freelance stylists, photographers or writers aspired to appear in the publication and would accept the lack of financial recompense because of the cultural capital that having work published in their pages would give them. This cemented the idea among stylists that editorial work was 'art', while commercial work was necessary to earn a living, but somehow less worthy.

Career Longevity and Progression

Towards the end of each interview, those I interviewed generally reflected on the success of their career to date and future plans. Many had given up styling completely. Baker has retired, Debbi Mason works as an artist, Zee Shore moved into interior design and property development, and Paul Frecker now specializes in antique photography. For others, higher-level editorial roles provided an opportunity to further consolidate their reputation through association with a respected publication. For example, Iain R. Webb, having worked as a stylist and fashion editor for more than thirty years, was in 2014 given the role of 'Fashion Features-Editor-at-Large' at *Ponystep Magazine*. Although the hierarchy within styling is not clearly defined, 'creative director' or 'art director' could be seen as senior roles for the stylist. Again, a nod to the hierarchies of the film industry, these directorial titles imply greater levels of creative responsibility or authorship. Interviewed for *SHOWStudio* in 2013, Nicola Formichetti said he preferred to be labelled as 'art director', rather than stylist, despite continuing to be credited for the 'styling' of editorial features, a responsibility which, one would assume, requires him to do the stylist's job. According to Debbi Mason, the progression opportunities available to a stylist are limited:

> I suppose there are two ways. One is to graduate to more executive roles, either on magazines or with designers, or just to say 'That's my lot', and end the career in fashion. But I think there is definitely a time where a stylist has had their day. I do essentially believe it's a youth industry. I think it is. That's when you're really interested in fashion. I mean, I haven't lost my interest completely, I just couldn't see myself functioning in that world anymore.[9]

Like Bradshaw, Foxton also continues to practice as a stylist, although he now only takes editorial work if the project being offered by the magazine really interests him. He prefers the brand consultancy work he also undertakes (with business partner Nick Griffiths, as &Son), for various reasons:

> I guess it's spun off styling but it's much more. I find it a much more enjoyable process because it's not just about the visual image. It means that you can explore all sorts of other areas within a company, you get involved from the absolute start of the process. For instance, for Stone Island we produce documents called pre-creative briefs, which are far-reaching ideas for the design teams to look at and pick and choose from. So, we come up with all sorts of concepts. We get involved in strategy. We get involved in visual merchandising; we get involved in moving image. So, I've found the consultancy side rewarding, and I quite like the fact that it tends to be quite a long-term alliance, or relationship. It's not just that you pop in and style something then you're off again. You're involved in the whole process and if it works, you're there for quite a while, so you can see things through.[10]

Sarah Miller now runs her own brand agency. Her role could be seen as a development of the practices and processes she used when working as a fashion editor. Her company is employed to consult on promotional strategy and brand identity, and her clients include paint manufacturers, hotels, property developers, restaurants and publishers. Teaching was also a career pathway for those I interviewed. Webb is an associate lecturer at Central Saint Martins but is also employed as a 'Professor of Fashion and Design' by Kingston University, a post that indicates that his role has acquired a degree of critical acceptance (2017).

Possibly achieving the greatest recognition beyond the fashion industry of those interviewed for this book, Caryn Franklin quickly made the transition from fashion editorial to working in television, fronting the BBC series *The Clothes Show*. Her first experience of television was producing and presenting a fashion-themed show for Channel 4 called *Swank*. She then collaborated with *i-D* editor Terry Jones on a programme for the short-lived satellite and cable channel *Music Box*, before appearing on MTV in 1984, presenting fashion content and reporting on catwalk shows. Franklin initially appeared on *The Clothes Show* as a representative of *i-D* magazine, as it was felt that the opportunity would provide advertising for the magazine. The show was broadcast twenty-six weeks of the year on a Sunday night and was a popular success, achieving viewing figures of more than nine million at its peak. She acknowledged that, at the time, televised coverage of fashion was limited, and felt that the show provided the opportunity to present fashion in a comparable way to *i-D*, documenting what people were wearing in the clubs and on the streets.

Franklin's interest in presenting issue-based content led to her using her notoriety as a way of drawing attention to important political issues relating to fashion and representation in the media. She co-founded All Walks Beyond the Catwalk, a campaign that addresses the lack of diversity in fashion, and has worked on a range of educational initiatives, including the Centre for Sustainable Fashion at London College of Fashion, and the Diversity Network at Edinburgh College of Art. Franklin has continued to act as a freelance editor and journalist for publications since *i-D* in the early 1980s but no longer works as a stylist.

Those interviewed for this book provide mixed accounts regarding the level of job satisfaction gained from working as a stylist. They acknowledged that there are benefits, but pointed out that aspects of the job are difficult. Beyond a dislike for the realities of the job itself, a lack of respect for the wider fashion industry permeated many of the interviewees' perspectives of their own career. For Caroline Baker there was always, she claimed, a feeling of guilt for being paid by an industry that 'makes people feel inadequate' (2017). Barrie Sharpe said that he specifically tells the students he teaches not to get a career in fashion (2017). It is not surprising that, for those who started their careers fuelled by the anti-fashion sentiment of the style magazines, the industry of fashion continues to disappoint or fails to inspire (Sharpe 2017).

As covered in Chapter 1 of this book, there have been stylists in many spheres of design and promotion since the early part of the twentieth century. They have operated between the processes of design, manufacture and communication. The various fields of commercial styling in which the freelance fashion stylist now operates represent a continuation of these prior roles and responsibilities. However, the status, or cultural capital, that the most successful or well-regarded stylists have achieved has often been based on their prominence in fashion editorial, where they can demonstrate their creativity with fewer commercial constraints, and where their 'artistry' is fully credited.

Notes

1 C. Baker (2017), interview by Philip Clarke, 13 January.
2 S. Foxton (2017), interview by Philip Clarke, 3 February.
3 S. Foxton (2017), interview by Philip Clarke, 3 February.

4 J. Morgan (2020), interview by Philip Clarke, 16 March.
5 M. Lorenz (2017), interview by Philip Clarke, 17 January.
6 S. Foxton (2017), interview by Philip Clarke, 3 February.
7 R. Charity (2018), interview by Philip Clarke, 13 February.
8 D. Bradshaw (2023), interview by Philip Clarke, 11 July.
9 D. Mason (2017), interview by Philip Clarke, 5 May.
10 S. Foxton (2017), interview by Philip Clarke, 3 February.

CONCLUSION

> 'Style' has become a commodity, processed and packaged by advertising agencies and various media from TV to glossy magazines, used to sell everything from 'lifestyles' to lager. The word 'style' is now so debased that it is meaningless and redundant. Yet look along the racks of any newsagents and you'll see a whole range of magazines that didn't exist six years ago, magazines that are perfect bound – not stapled – and full of glossy 'style' pages.[1]

By the end of the 1980s, the style culture that birthed the stylist had been largely subsumed into the mainstream. Nonetheless, British fashion stylists retained their status as key players in the production of both commercial and editorial fashion. In the same way that fashion was said to be unfashionable in the 1970s, style had lost its cachet by the early 1990s (Steele 1998; Beard 2013). The period signalled the end of the very specific, London-centric form of style culture which has been the focus of this book. Certain cultures that emerged from the style press were maintained, as niche publishing became more diffuse and the boundaries between alternative and mainstream less clearly defined. The freelance stylists had been given a platform. Their remit continued to expand. Stylists continued to exist in anonymous, backroom roles, but at the other end of the spectrum, it was possible for stylists to achieve a level of acclaim and celebrity that had not existed before the 1980s. This book asks what factors enabled the stylist to emerge in a new incarnation as an 'artist' and a new kind of social operator. What were the complex cultural, political, local and national contexts that enabled the transformation of this new brand of creative practitioner?

In the first chapter, I introduced three genealogies, histories of style and styling which informed the way that the British fashion stylists worked and the way they were perceived in the 1980s. First, I considered the origins of style, exploring how criticism of the visual arts evolved and how a dialogue developed between artists (those who create) and connoisseurs (those who appreciate and critique). Both played a vital role in the formulation of taste, although artists (as well as architects or designers) have historically been accorded higher status than those other players in the creative economy (also including teachers, consultants and so on). Second, I acknowledged how stylists have worked in the past. It was not a new role in the 1980s. Stylists had operated as design consultants in the promotion of products and the communication of trends since the beginning of the twentieth century. These earlier stylists were considered intermediaries; theirs were mainly unseen, low-profile roles.[2] The aspiration of the 1980s British stylists was to be seen. They wanted to be seen as artists, makers and fashion creators, rather than critics, editors or promoters. The third stem of these genealogies is that of the subcultural stylist, and it this version of the stylist that perhaps contributed the most to the ways in which freelance stylists operated, how they were regarded when their work was first published and how the role evolved and established itself. These young stylists claimed to be anti-fashion, although they were clearly obsessed with clothes.

The young freelance stylists working in London at that time were both culturally and subculturally aware, through their art education, or through the close-knit social scene which enabled art students, post-punk clubbers and entrepreneurs to interact and collaborate. I present this version of the stylist as a product of a certain economic and social situation in London, a situation that evolved through the 1980s, with much of it a consequence of the previous decade's events. The subject matter of their image-making was also often fuelled by political protest, reflecting local resistance to oppressive government policy on immigration and the promotion of homosexuality. Still, the freelance stylist emerged despite negative developments. In fact, the disruption of the publishing industries in the 1980s caused by the Conservative government had an indirectly positive effect on their working environments and job prospects.

This book challenges claims that the stylist was invented in the 1980s by the British independent style press. But there is no doubt that the desire of these magazines to spotlight young stylists, and name them as contributors in the production of fashion images, gave them a platform they had not hitherto experienced. The freelance stylist, rather than the salaried fashion editor – which had existed for decades as a role in fashion magazines – became popularized and recognized as a viable career option. Their freelance status gave stylists the liberty to work across multiple magazines, as they were not beholden to one specific publication, or obliged to work with constraints imposed by that publication's advertisers. The methods of the new breed of stylists were experimental. What the style press did was endorse an alternative version of the stylist as an artist or *auteur*. This was cemented in the way the stylists constructed looks, juxtaposing clothes in a disruptive or abstract manner, reinforcing their position as avant-garde – even if their subject matter was decidedly postmodern.[3]

Peter Wollen suggested parallels between the eighteenth-century dandy Beau Brummell and the contemporary stylist, because they both present an outfit as an art statement (1999: 73). This book frames the stylists' work as bricolage or assemblage. They drew on available materials – both literally and thematically – to create meaning by combining clothing and found objects. Bricolage was prominent in the art, design and music of the 1980s, but had already been a facet of subcultural dress, particularly punk and New Romantic styles.[4] But styling is more than the selection or juxtaposition of clothing items. A stylist also pays attention to *how* clothes are worn – the way the scarf has been tied, the width of the turn-up on a pair of jeans, the angle a hat has been perched on a head. It is for this reason that

Brummell is a point of comparison. He wore items of traditional menswear, but provoked a reaction by wearing them in an unusual way.

The stylist became a decision-maker who directed trends, not just a middleman liaising between manufacturers, designers and their customers. Crucially, it was during the 1980s that new affinities developed between designers and stylists. This manifested both as official working relationships, such as that between Caroline Baker and Vivienne Westwood, or David Bradshaw and Miuccia Prada, or in terms of mutual admiration and respect for creative ideas, as with Ray Petri and Jean-Paul Gaultier. There remains, though, a level of stigma attached to the stylist's role. There is a feeling among stylists that their role is not valued or is seen as inferior to that of the designers or photographers with whom they collaborate. Despite being taught to degree level in several UK universities, styling is still often considered an innate skill. In some ways this is not helped by the stylists themselves; Simon Foxton has said that he doesn't understand how styling can be taught, and Baker has referred to it as 'just getting dressed' (2017).

Although the decision to include Caroline Baker in this book about London's 1980s youth culture may seem misplaced, she represents a starting point. Only known in fashion industry circles, her work went largely unapprised until relatively recently. Her influence in increasing the visibility of the stylist, and in promoting the fashion image as a form of art, has since been given further recognition in academic texts (Beard 2013; Webb 2021). Retrospectively, the work that she produced for *Nova* in the late 1960s and early 1970s, and further editorial features for *Vogue*, *Tatler* and the style magazines is also seen as evidence of the influence of street style. For Baker, the notion of 'styling' in image-making, or in everyday dress, was intrinsically linked to both creative freedom and feminist politics. Her approach to clothing herself or encouraging others how to dress was in equal parts revered and mocked. She was, however, among the first in fashion publishing to perpetuate the idea that fashion could come from the streets, that it could be as influenced by subcultural or countercultural dress as by couturiers or top designers. It is not surprising that she became a go-to collaborator for both street style and mainstream magazines in the 1980s.

Since then, stylists have retained their reputation as cultural influencers, and their affiliation with art and subculture. This is perceptible in the ways in which the stylist has been presented in journalism, in academic writing and in high-profile exhibitions. For example, in his first solo exhibition at the Photographer's Gallery in 2009, Simon Foxton's work was presented as art practice (perhaps unsurprisingly for a gallery setting). It focused less on the commercial aspects of his practice than on his innovation and craftsmanship. Brett Rogers, the gallery's then-director, praised Foxton's 'distinct authorship'. The approach to the construction of the fashion image he developed during the 1980s continued in creative partnerships throughout his career. Included in the exhibition catalogue, the feature 'Hey There, Fancy Pants' from the May 2004 issue of *i-D*, which was photographed by Jason Evans, demonstrated how the assemblage or bricolage that was apparent in earlier styling work was developed in later image-making (see Fig. 16). The scenes were clearly contrived, artificial constructions. The groups of male models, in colour-coordinated outfits of patterned sportswear, were placed in ad hoc sets of white blocks, sheets of paper and suspended shapes. The sense of bricolage was emphasized by the obviousness of the materials and their fixings – the gaffer-taped corners of the wrapping papers, the nylon wires holding the shapes in position. The images were explicitly an art statement. Even the setting the models were placed in resembled a white-wall gallery space, and the men were perched on white plinths, like sculptural forms in an exhibition space.

Judy Blame's exhibition at the ICA, subtitled 'Artistic Differences', presented him as an accessory designer, art director and fashion stylist. It reinforced Blame's art collaborations, with Derek Jarman, the Chapman brothers, or Tim Noble and Sue Webster, but also his commercial, consultancy work with fashion designers, such as John Galliano and Marc Jacobs, or with music artists. Contemporary versions of the role incorporate both. Depending on the situation, the client, or the prominence of the stylists themselves, they collaborate in a range of different ways and have varying levels of creative authority or status. Experimental styling is still being produced, shown in both niche or mainstream fashion publications, or presented in gallery settings, art books or online editorial platforms. However, there remains a commercial strand to styling work and it is this dialogue between commercial and creative, which was so often a bone of contention among young anti-fashion, anti-consumerist stylists in the 1980s, that continues among contemporary freelance stylists. The career profile of the young stylist Ib Kamara demonstrates this point. Six months after the untimely death of Virgil Abloh, it was announced that Kamara would take on the role of 'Art and Image Director' for Abloh's label Off White. The label had become one of the most influential global brands and Kamara's instatement reinforced the status of the stylist as a top-level fashion influencer. In 2016, his collaborations with the photographer Kristin-Lee Moolman were exhibited in London's Somerset House and the Photographers' Gallery. Kamara became senior editor-at-large of *i-D* in 2019 and was awarded the Isabella Blow Fashion Creator award in 2021, the same year he became the Editor-in-Chief of *Dazed* magazine. In addition to editorial styling, he has collaborated on music projects, with singers Beyoncé and Madonna, and has overseen the production of catwalk shows for Louis Vuitton. Having achieved a degree of cultural capital in a relatively short period of time, Kamara's trajectory could be seen as a perfect example of the heightened status of the stylist in contemporary culture. His success also represents the legacy of the stylists working in London in the 1980s: there are clear visual references to the styling of Petri and his peers, which could be considered a direct consequence of the mentoring Kamara received from Barry Kamen, a Buffalo member who had continued to work as a stylist and artist, from assisting Simon Foxton and Judy Blame, or from being taught by Iain R. Webb at Central Saint Martins.

London has a long history of subversive fashion. Figures or groups have, at moments in time, created counterculture with clothing. These subcultures or scenes have often been centred on particular geographical areas, such as the second-hand stores and boutiques of the King's Road in the late 1960s, or the clubs of Soho and Covent Garden in the late 1970s. Although certain social scenes and educational establishments in London have retained their reputation as sites for collaboration and sources of style, the internet has changed how fashion is disseminated and how creatives build networks. Social media has become a useful tool for self-promotion, enabling stylists to represent themselves without the intervention of an agent, and publish their own work without the endorsement of an established editorial platform. The perceived threat to conventional media posed by internet-based influencers in many ways resembles the collective challenging of mainstream fashion media driven by the new wave of stylists in the 1980s. The internet has not removed the need for intermediaries in the field of fashion image production, but merely resulted in the nomination of new intermediaries, who have become the gatekeepers of these new sources of fashion information. The cultural and political contexts that enabled the transformation of the stylist in the 1980s have long since reconfigured. Subcultures, if they even exist, are more likely to communicate shared tastes and lifestyles via social media than in the clubs and on the streets. The environment and media may have changed, but stylists have retained the status they built in the 1980s. They continue to operate as cultural intermediaries and *auteurs*, but they can now do so across print and digital media, and in the production of physical and virtual fashion.

Notes

1 *i-D* (1989), 'Life Beyond Style' 65: 8.

2 I have noted exceptions, e.g., Tobé Coller Davis built a reputation for herself as a trend forecaster and brand consultant; Italian and French ready-to-wear designers – or 'createurs de mode' – were called stylists, and they ultimately became as well-known as their couture counterparts.

3 There are many conflicting opinions on the position of avant-garde in postmodern culture. Some see avant-garde as a typically modern construct, whereas others see it as intrinsic to the postmodern lifestyle which commodifies the identity-forming process and would see any intellectual and artistic countercultures as an available lifestyle choice (McRobbie 1994, 2016; Feathersone 2007).

4 Again, I use New Romantic as a blanket term to describe the scene centred on Billy's, Blitz and subsequent dressed-up club nights.

Appendix: Intervewees and Interviews

I conducted eighteen oral history interviews over a five-year period. This appendix includes a brief biography of each interviewee, not to qualify their inclusion in the project, but to show how each of them offered a differing perspective on the subject matter. It also demonstrates the interconnectedness of professional experiences and personal career trajectories. Some interviewees were found by word-of-mouth recommendations, while other potential interviewees were identified through editorial research. For example, Zee Shore or Sarah Miller were approached because their names appeared in *Cosmopolitan* features, associated with styling and editorial work. Debbi Mason was introduced by a former colleague. In some cases, cross-referencing among peers occurred because they knew who had already been interviewed, so were keen to provide useful anecdotes or further information relating to that person. The recommendations of interviewees broadened the scope of the project. For example, Mitzi Lorenz and Barrie Sharpe were good friends. He was someone who would not have been considered unless Lorenz had suggested him, but he gave an invaluable perspective on both the club scene and independent fashion retail. The comparisons between social life and industry practice in the United States and United Kingdom that Debbi Mason, Sarah Miller and Jeffrey Hinton offered, having worked in New York at various stages in their careers, were helpful when defining the distinct nature of subculture and creative practice in London during the 1980s. The interviewees also suggested further lines of enquiry that could be explored later. The oral history component of this project is ongoing. I have conducted additional interviews, such as David Bradshaw, as I have been writing this book, and the emerging themes from interviewing new stylists has suggested potential approaches to future projects. I have included transcripts of interviews conducted with Caroline Baker, Lorenz and Bradshaw, as each one comments on a different period of the stylist's trajectory and supports the key themes explored throughout the book.

Interviewees

Caroline Baker

Born in Argentina, Baker moved to England at the beginning of the 1960s to find work. Starting in secretarial roles, she took a temporary position at the *Observer* magazine, under editor Shirley Conran, before becoming assistant fashion editor at *Nova*. She was promoted to Fashion Editor and gained a reputation for her fashion features that combined customized designer clothing with second-hand and military items. Baker went on to contribute to British *Vogue*, French *Elle* and *Donna* in the 1970s; assisted the designer Vivienne Westwood; produced features on a freelance basis for *i-D*, *The Face*, *Ritz* and *Deluxe* in the 1980s; and styled the United Colours advertising campaigns for Benetton, with the photographer Oliviero Toscani. She continued to occupy editorial roles until she retired at the age of seventy. Baker developed ways of combining clothing and constructing narrative in fashion images that influenced the next generation of freelance stylists.

David Bradshaw

Having trained as a civil engineer, Bradshaw abandoned his original career plans to first become an agent for a fashion illustrator, then an advertising salesman for a menswear magazine, then finally a stylist and fashion editor. Since the late 1980s, he has maintained a dual focus on editorial and commercial roles, working for a long list of magazines (*Arena*, *GQ*, *V Man*, *Numéro Homme*) and collaborating with a series of influential fashion designers (Katharine Hamnett, Jil Sander, Calvin Klein, Miuccia Prada, Donatella Versace). He recently rejoined the editorial team at *Homme Plus* magazine.

Roger Charity

After completing an Art and Design qualification at Camberwell School of Art, Roger Charity originally worked in a pottery studio before continuing his studies in filmmaking. Older than the other Buffalo members, Charity was already established as a commercial and editorial photographer when he started collaborating with Ray Petri in the early 1980s. He had assisted the fashion photographer Steven Hyatt, before going on to shoot for *Petticoat*, *19* and *Honey* magazines, then *Elle* and *Marie Claire*. Initially working with Ray Petri on mail order catalogue shoots, Charity photographed some of Buffalo's most critically acclaimed stories, including 'The Long Goodbye' for *Arena* in 1989 (see Fig. 15). He provides a comparison between commercial, paid work and the editorial opportunities and recognition afforded by association with the style press. Charity continued working on fashion editorial projects, for *i-D*, *The Face* and *Dazed and Confused*, and has collaborated with many stylists.

Michael Costiff

Refusing to classify himself in one specific occupational role, Costiff has worked as a club host, photographer, interior decorator, fashion designer and filmmaker. His store on Lichfield Street, close to Soho, stocked artefacts that he found on overseas visits, along with clothing and artwork by contemporary designers. Kinky Gerlinky, the club night he co-hosted with his wife Gerlinde, ran from 1989 to 1994 and built on the style culture generated by *Taboo* and *Blitz* by encouraging extreme dressing and operating a similarly exclusive door policy. A compilation of Costiff's photographs and collages was assembled and published in 2013 by Kim Jones, the artistic director of Dior Homme.

Robin Derrick

Born in Bristol, Derrick moved to London in 1980 to become a Graphic Design student at St Martin's School of Art. He produced bitmap graphics for a campaign art-directed by Terry Jones at Fiorucci, going on to contribute to *i-D* while he was still a student. He became Neville Brody's assistant at *The Face* when he graduated, leaving the magazine for the launch of Italian *Elle* in 1987. Derrick started his working life as an ad hoc contributor to style press titles and progressed to high-profile roles, making him a valuable contributor to this study. He worked at British *Vogue* for nineteen years and was Executive Creative Director at Spring Studios until 2018. Derrick now works as a creative director for predominantly commercial clients and has co-founded MyBeautyBrand with his wife, the make-up artist Lisa Eldridge.

Simon Foxton

Born in Berwick-upon-Tweed, on the Scottish border, Foxton moved down to London to study Fashion Design at St Martin's. When he graduated, he started the label Bazooka with Cheryl Easthap, until Caryn Franklin approached him to style for *i-D* magazine. Foxton continues to work as a freelance stylist. His exhibition at The Photographer's Gallery in 2009 was one of the first shows to recognize the creative input of the stylist in the image-making process. He has collaborated regularly with acclaimed fashion photographers, notably Nick Knight and Jason Evans. His focus in recent years has been on the agency &Son, which he formed with fellow stylist Nick Griffiths. Along with Judy Blame and Ray Petri, Foxton is considered fundamental in establishing the stylist as a recognized creative role.

Caryn Franklin

After completing an MA at St Martin's School of Art, Caryn Franklin started working for *i-D* magazine, initially as a photographer and graphic designer, then as Fashion Coordinator, Fashion Editor and Co-Editor. Although she did not consider herself a stylist, she styled for several advertising and television clients. After conducting interviews for shows broadcast on the cable television network MTV, she became a presenter on the popular BBC, Sunday-night fashion series *The Clothes Show*. Franklin now campaigns for diversity and inclusivity in the fashion industry, working with educational initiatives (All Walks Beyond the Catwalk, FACE) and fulfilling a role as Professor of Diverse Selfhood at Kingston University. She has undertaken a range of editorial roles and having worked for print publications, independent and mainstream television and live events, provides an insight into the changing formats of fashion communication from the early 1980s to the present day.

Paul Frecker

Originally a waiter in Soho, Frecker spent a brief time handling PR for a fashion designer before being persuaded to work as a stylist. Despite having several features published in fashion and style publications, both in the UK and Europe, he worked predominantly on promotional, advertising campaigns and television projects. Frecker collaborated regularly with the photographer Carrie Branovan and, later, with the film director Tony Kaye. He gave up styling in 2003 and now collects, archives and distributes antique photographic prints. It is Frecker's perspective on the largely overlooked, behind-the-scenes role of the advertising stylist that makes his inclusion beneficial to this project.

Ziggi Golding

Originally training to become an architect, Golding started modelling in 1977 and gained an insight into the fashion industry. She set up her own agency, K-Z, with another partner, representing models. When she took full control of the business, she expanded the agency's remit to include photographers, make-up artists, stylists and other designers (she represented Tom Dixon at the beginning of his career). Golding's perspective on the network of career roles in the production of fashion image has been useful to this book, as is her opinion on the changes during the 1980s in casting practices, collaboration and the crediting of creative roles. She continues to represent photographers.

Jeffrey Hinton

Hinton works across a range of media and has provided music and visuals for London club nights, including Circus, Cha Cha, Taboo, Anarchy and Daisy Chain. He has created soundtracks for the choreographer Michael Clark, the designers BodyMap, Stephen Jones, Rifat Ozbek, Alexander McQueen and Meadham Kirchhoff, and for the filmmaker John Maybury. Hinton has produced image and sound installations for events and exhibitions at the National Portrait Gallery, the ICA and the Victoria and Albert Museum. He was considered relevant for his insight into the club scene, creative networks and subcultural community. After returning from New York in the 1980s, Hinton squatted in Warren Street with clubbers, artists and designers and collaborated with them on creative projects.

Stephen Jones

Another graduate of St Martin's School of Art, Jones designed a range of hats for the Fiorucci label in 1979 before setting up his own millinery business the following year, a venture funded by the Blitz club host Steve Strange. Living in a squat in Warren Street during the early 1980s, he was part of a community of young artists and designers that helped build the reputation of London as a hub for creative and subcultural activity at that time. He continues to work as a milliner and has developed a worldwide reputation, proving particularly popular in Japan. He curated an exhibition, 'Hats: An Anthology', at the Victoria and Albert Museum in 2009. He was awarded an OBE in 2010. Jones has collaborated with Vivienne Westwood, Claude Montana, Jean-Paul Gaultier, Balenciaga, Thom Browne and Christian Dior, co-authoring a compendium of Dior millinery in 2020. As a peer of the stylists and young creatives living and working in central London in the 1980s, Jones provides an opinion on the evolving London fashion scene and, as a regular contributor to early style press features, a designer's view on the emerging stylist's working life.

Mitzi Lorenz

Born in West London, Lorenz was fourteen years old when she left school to work at *i-D* magazine. A collaborator with the Buffalo collective, she went on to work as a freelance stylist for a range of publications and commercial clients. In 2000, she produced a retrospective publication, reflecting on the work of the stylist Ray Petri and Buffalo's creative contribution to style publishing. Lorenz's insight into London youth culture, her working and personal relationship with Petri, and her further, successful career as a commercial and editorial stylist, make her contribution to this book highly relevant. She has been particularly helpful in suggesting appropriate interviewees and has generously instigated meetings with oral history participants.

Debbi Mason

After studying fashion design for a year at Ravensbourne, Mason started working with the designer Joseph Ettedgui, which provided an in-road into a career in fashion publishing. She started as fashion assistant at the *Evening Standard*, went on to be junior fashion editor at *Harpers & Queen*, then fashion editor at *Miss London*. She was approached by Sally Brampton to join the British version of *Elle* magazine, when it launched in 1985. Moving to New York for several years, Mason was represented by the agency Art and Commerce, and worked for both editorial and commercial clients. She now lives in West Sussex and is a practising fine artist. The launch of *Elle* magazine in Britain is considered significant to this study because it credited stylists from the outset and Mason's part in this, and her perspective on styling work in both the US and UK, make her a meaningful contributor.

Sarah Miller

Raised in London, a period of work experience in New York in the late 1970s led to Miller assisting Lizzette Kattan for *Harper's Bazaar* Italia. After three years of studying English language and Literature at Oxford University, she returned to work in the magazine industry, fulfilling a range of roles at British *Cosmopolitan*. She joined the team of British *Elle* as features editor, along with Debbi Mason and Lucinda Chambers, when it launched in 1985. Shifting focus, Miller then worked at the architectural magazine *Blueprint*, then edited by her husband, Deyan Sudjic. She now runs the marketing agency, Sarah Miller and Partners. Like Mason, she contributes an insight into mainstream publishing, both in this country and overseas, and knowledge of the formative years of British *Elle*.

Jamie Morgan

Responsible for some of the first Buffalo images to appear in print, Morgan worked as a photographer alongside Mitzi Lorenz and Ray Petri, before changing direction to focus on music projects. His prior experience assisting fashion photographers provided him with the technical skills that contributed to his classical approach to lighting and photographing people. Along with editorial work featured in *The Face*, *Vogue*, *Pop* and *Arena Homme Plus* magazines, Morgan has produced promotional imagery for Jean-Paul Gaultier, Burberry, Nike and Puma.

Barrie Sharpe

Sharpe was born in Brick Lane, in East London. In 1984 he co-founded Duffer of St. George, a menswear store in London that evolved from a market stall selling army surplus and second-hand clothing. He started DJ-ing at club nights in central London in 1983 and two years later the Duffer team started their own club night, The Cat in the Hat, at the Comedy Store in Leicester Square. He continues to design and manufacture clothing, sold as Sharpeye. In 2018, Sharpe self-published an autobiography, *This Was Not Part of the Masterplan: Memoirs of a Naughty Boy*, and has since published another, *Outside the Lines* (2021). He was suggested as an interviewee by Mitzi Lorenz, for both his links with the fashion industry and his involvement in the London club scene, which was highly relevant to the development of the stylist's role at that time.

Zee Shore

Zahava Shore, who was known as Zee when she worked as a freelance stylist, was approached as a potential participant after I found a profile feature in a 1982 issue of *Cosmopolitan*, which detailed her roles and responsibilities as a 'photographic stylist'. She collaborated with designers in the production of runway shows, dressed models for clothing mail order catalogues and, although she had work featured in editorial fashion features, mainly provides an insight into the remit and role of the commercial stylist.

Iain R. Webb

An alumnus of St Martin's, Webb initially worked as junior design assistant with Zandra Rhodes. Interested in journalism, he wrote pieces for magazines as a freelance writer, before being invited to work for *Blitz*, a new independent publication. During his career he has been fashion editor of the *Evening Standard*, *Harpers & Queen*, *The Times* and *Elle*, while contributing to various publications, including *New Musical Express*, the *New York Times*, the *Guardian* and *Vogue*. Webb has authored several books, including a biography of the designer Bill Gibb, an anthology of fashion features and interviews with *Blitz* magazine contributors and a retrospective of the work of Caroline Baker (2021). He has worked as a curator, overseeing the production of fashion-themed exhibitions at the Institute of Contemporary Arts, the Fashion Museum Bath and the Paul Smith store in Mayfair. Webb continues to teach, as an associate lecturer at Central Saint Martins and as professor of fashion and design at Kingston University. He was approached to participate in this study for his views on the subcultural community and London social scene, and for his continued involvement in fashion publishing and education.

Interviews

Caroline Baker

13 January 2017, Stamford Brook, London

Philip Clarke (PC): How did you start your career as a stylist?

Caroline Baker (CB): At secretarial college they used to say to me, 'You wear far too much make-up, and you dress too outrageously, you're never going to be a success.' I started off as a secretary then went, as a temp, to work for Shirley Conran, who was the home editor of the *Observer*. I really enjoyed working with her. That was the first time I became aware that there was a whole area of work in fashion journalism. Through the art director of the *Observer*, Ray Hawkey, I was introduced to Molly Parkin, who was the fashion editor at *Nova* magazine. She'd just been appointed and was looking for an assistant. I went to work for Molly Parkin as her assistant and in the fashion team at *Nova* magazine. *Nova* was the first of its kind. In women's magazines at the end of '60s, *Elle* or *Marie Claire* didn't exist in this country; the only options were *Vogue*, *Tatler* or *Queen*. The whole fashion industry was led by the couture end of fashion. There were also some new teenage magazines like *19* and *Honey*, which were very popular because they were beginning to cater for the huge youth market that came out the '60s, what you'd call the 'teenage revolution'.

I was one of the first 'working girls'; I didn't just go and get married and have a family. I was typical of a lot of girls at that time. The '60s were a fantastic time, it was very revolutionary in many aspects. A huge amount of change came from the

'60s. *Nova* was a magazine that was launched for intelligent women. This was the beginning of the women's liberation movement and women were being recognized to be intelligent, to be consumers, to be able to have 'jobs with the boys'; that they might perhaps want to read a magazine that wasn't just about cooking and fashion. The newspaper supplements were huge at this time and if you look at who launched *Nova*, it was a bunch of guys who'd all come from the *Sunday Times* and the *Observer* magazines, things like that. They discovered that they could get the advertisers to back *Nova*. Advertising wasn't quite as crucial then as it became, but it was quite an important part of the whole system. So, when Molly Parkin had a major row with the editor Dennis Hackett, and she walked out or was fired, or whatever, Dennis called me into his office and said 'You look like you love fashion, would you like to try and be the fashion editor?' I couldn't believe it, from being a sort of secretary or assistant to being fashion editor. My brief was to be different, to challenge everything that was already aimed at women in fashion. I started looking at what people were wearing on the streets. Now, the term 'styling' hadn't even come into being at that time. I think styling was born in the 1980s as a term, but it was a recognition of the fact that there was fashion that wasn't just led by *Vogue*, it wasn't led by society women. You didn't have to have money. I was one of those working girls who loved fashion, we were really interested in it, but we didn't have the cash to spend on designer clothing. Now, ready-to-wear had started then, Yves Saint Laurent, Rive Gauche, but it was still jolly expensive stuff. Our salaries were a thousand pounds a year. Would you believe it? Although, at the time, you could do quite a lot with a thousand. Anyway, it was the beginning of the revolution of fashion being more street, more like everyday life, what people were wearing.

PC: Why did you stop working for *Nova*?

CB: The '70s was a total political and economic mess in Britain. There'd been the big Yom Kippur war with the Israelis [in 1974, triggering an oil embargo and economic problems in Western countries], which had a huge influence on the fashion industry. We'd gone from the Labour government into this thing where you only worked three days a week. There were lots of strikes and people were losing their jobs. Things really began to change out there and a victim of all of this was *Nova* magazine, which folded in the mid-1970s. By which time punk had started here. I didn't really fit in anywhere and it was quite difficult. Bea Miller invited me to come and do some stories at *Vogue* but she really couldn't cope with me. The stories I did in *Vogue* were really fun, though. There was Acme Attractions on the King's Road, and they sold all this second-hand American sporting gear, which I really loved. All the baseball t-shirts and stuff. So, I did that in *Vogue*. 'Cheap Chic', that was it, I was cheap chic [laughs]. The stories I did in *Vogue* were really fun, though. I did girls in pyjamas. I think that was the last straw for [*Vogue* editor] Bea Miller. We photographed them in places, rooms with cracks on the walls, she couldn't cope anymore. My career at *Vogue* didn't last very long. I had also started working for British *Cosmopolitan* at that time. British *Cosmopolitan* had opened almost at the time when *Nova* folded. It couldn't really compete because it always tried to be so revolutionary all the time, so it lost all the advertisers.

I got thoroughly into reggae and punk, became a total Rasta girl and went to work for Vivienne Westwood and that was when we did that look with the big skirts. I used to do my hair in rags. That was how I dressed, and Boy George and that lot copied my hairstyle, and Haysi Fantayzee and all those girls. At about that time the fashion world was really beginning to be 'shaken up' and it was becoming much less snobbish. Punk had a real influence in that respect. Then the 1980s were also a huge evolution for gay men. We felt it already with Yves Saint Laurent, who used to be so inspired [by London gay fashion]. He used to come to all the English clubs. He did that very famous look, of the short, chubby fur coats, and that was the way all the boys were wearing them in the clubs. So, in a way, society had started to become, what is now called 'populist'. The idea that we were now *all* accepted. And things like *The Clothes Show* happened, with Jeff [Banks] and Caryn [Franklin], reaching a wider audience with fashion.

PC: What did you do next?

CB: So, styling-wise, I left *Cosmopolitan* because I had my daughter, very late in life. I was forty. I had begun to do Benetton with Olivero Toscani. It was the United Colours of Benetton, which meant the colours of the world, the skin colours of the people. I had a great time with Benetton, I worked with Toscani. We also shot all these massive groups of people and each one was themed: we did a punk theme, and a historical theme and stuff like that. When I did Benetton, my daughter would come with me, and she'd be in the pictures. Then, I guess I ended up at the *Sunday Times*, I did both the newspaper and the magazine. The magazine realized there was a market for a fashion 'extra' [a regular additional supplement], and that idea became what is known as *Style* magazine. So, that brings us up to the end of the 1980s.

PC: Where did your interest in fashion come from?

CB: A lot of people ask me this and I don't really know. My interest in clothes came from newspapers. I was drawn to the fashion pages in my mother's newspapers. [In Argentina, where she grew up] we used to get the *British Herald*, which was an English paper, so I followed that. Then, of course, the films, the '50s films. I loved all of them. James Dean and Natalie Wood. You'd want to wear what the stars were wearing. As a teenager, I did wear jeans. Jeans had become popular because of Hollywood films. People are drawn to someone they think they can identify with, you think, 'Hey, I could be her', you just fall into it. In Argentina we used to have our clothes made at a dressmaker. So, I would find things in magazines and tear them out and take them to the dressmaker. And I remember making this quite racy, 1950s skin-tight dress, with fur cuffs and I never dared wear it. It was only the big circle skirts that you dared to wear. At the time there were so many rules about what you dared to do and what you wouldn't do. You know, you'd never show your underwear to anybody. I think these rules had an effect on how I styled later in my career. That was one of my big stories later on, 'Wear your underwear on the outside', which Gaultier also did with Madonna. The other films that were hugely influential, that I was allowed to go and watch, were Doris Day films. She was wearing the Dior look, which was big skirts and trousers. All of these things fed into the way I worked as a fashion editor and stylist. But I was totally drawn to fashion. I remember going through my mother's wardrobe and finding her 1930s bias-cut frocks, I just loved them.

PC: When we spoke before, you mentioned the link between styling and the evolution of ready-to-wear fashion.

CB: The rag trade was all around Margaret Street, in London. There was the rag trade [ready-to-wear], as opposed to the Paris-led fashion, and then America got important, and then Milan got important. In the 1950s, a store like Wallis would have gone to Dior to buy patterns. That was how you would be allowed to bring it to London and make copies cheaply. That business just grew and grew, as they realized that there were so many women, and later working women with money, who wanted affordable clothes. Mary Quant, you know, Quant was expensive. Biba was hugely influential because we could all afford Biba. Barbara Hulanicki at Biba came up with all these mini dresses, and the great thing about minis is they just takes such a little bit of fabric so they're cheaper to make. She was a big influence on the changes in the fashion scene, and then what became known as styling. I remember shopping in C&A, you know, C&A used to be a hot place to shop. Because they would be ripping the looks off Barbara Hulanicki. We'd all be copying each other and so would the stores. Everybody was copying. But you'd go to Margaret Street, and you would have appointments and see all these people and there would just be companies who were just tuned in to what was happening. It's just interesting because there's always some designer somewhere who captures a vibe that everybody wants to identify with.

PC: Do you follow trends?

CB: Yes, as much as I can. Definitely. I will just do that automatically, even without realizing it. There are obviously sometimes trends that I can't follow, like those really wicked platform shoes, I could never get into. I loved using them in styling, but I just can't wear platforms. When hot pants came in, I'd wear them with leggings. I'd do the layering. I'd just find a way into the trends, how I was going to do it. Because they are obviously shown on the catwalk on beautiful young girls. You have to find a way that it fits with you.

PC: What would you call your style?

CB: The thing is, I did change as I progressed through my styling career, because fashion changes all the time. When I started off, I guess you could say I was a bit revolutionary, bringing new ideas to people about how to dress. Once you've done it, it's done and everybody's wearing it. It's like legwarmers, with Abba wearing them, it just became a bit ordinary. These are the principles of fashion, obviously. But I'm always tuned in to fashion, always picking up on it; I will see someone and think, 'Well that makes sense.' I guess I'm a very sensible person, and that's probably why I've always managed to have a successful career in fashion. I have brought fashion stories to quite a big audience, who have liked my work and I've helped them to get dressed and have changed their attitude to fashion. I've obviously been performing a role that has been successful.

You know, Joe [Corre, Vivienne Westwood's son], the other day, went out and burned all his punk stuff. Punk is now 'high fashion'. That just totally sums fashion up. You start off making an absolute revolutionary statement and then what? I think it used to take ten years for fashion to get to the high street. Then after ten years it would be over. So, there was a sort of twenty-year span, ten years to get people used to it and then ten years later it was gone. It's probably a lot quicker now, with new media.

PC: You mentioned politics a couple of times; are you interested in politics?

CB: Yes, I'm very interested in politics. Looking back, I now see history and how politics and fashion have been so connected. The big political upheaval for me was when *Nova* folded. There was a time when I was really involved in what was happening politically. In the 1960s we were really involved, because the Vietnam War was happening, and we were horrified by it. Then we had the constant threat of atomic bombs and the Cuban [missile crisis]. Because of TV we were seeing it all the time, we were more aware. When I grew up in Argentina in the 1950s it was just the newspaper, or the BBC. My parents would just listen to the radio so there wasn't so much visual information. Whereas now we're constantly bombarded with visual information. But in the 1970s, why it affected fashion so much was because so many people lost their jobs when magazines folded; a huge amount of fashion businesses folded at that time. Then there was a huge change into the 1980s, after the whole punk thing happened. Punk was born out of protest, all these young people with no jobs. An awful lot of us were without work suddenly, so you were aware of what was going on. And then Margaret Thatcher came in; I hated her fashion [laughs].

In the 1960s there was a big feminist movement. There was a big thing going on in America. It was happening at the universities. Here we had [writer and feminist] Germaine Greer. Irma Kurtz was a feminist and one of the journalists at *Nova* magazine. In America there was the 'Burn the Bra' movement. It made you question what you were doing. It was also the same time as this anti-war movement. It was quite a revolutionary thing, the 1960s. The freedom movement wasn't as big here as it was in America, but we were aware of it. I think the British media was rather scared of it, so you didn't really get it as much in newspapers here. It was quite a threatening situation for certain levels of society. The women's liberation group, *of course* it was anti-fashion. I got really involved in that. Seeing women in the 1960s, if you look at David Bailey shoots, the set hair, the make-up. They just looked like objects for men to play with. Women were like dolls, these pretty things. So, that was what the women's liberation movement was against. They were into women being an equal to a man, not the woman as a man's toy, his object, his wife, the mother of his children. I had to go to work when I came to Britain, because I didn't have any money, so I've never felt the need to have a husband to support me. I just felt I belonged to that group of people, women who were more liberated, I suppose. Women who were not doing what we were *supposed* to do. That used to hang over us, what we were *supposed* to do.

I was working with very creative people and the art director at *Nova* was quite an important person. We'd sit down and say, 'What are we going to do to shock and upset everybody?' I'm very known for the army surplus stories, and this was at the same time that *M*A*S*H* [TV series about US soldiers in the Korean war] was very popular, and also there were huge 'Ban the Bomb' protests where everybody was wearing army surplus. Obviously, there was a sort of code at work where you had to dress for work and men wore suits and ties and girls didn't wear trousers, so dressing models in trousers was also a controversy. People now can't believe the kerfuffle in the fashion world about wearing trousers and the fuss that people made. I remember I was sent out when I was at *Nova* to do a talk in the North of England. I had my nails green at the time because there was this lovely stand in Kensington market where you could buy all this really cool stuff. And I remember this woman in the audience standing up and saying, 'Do you think it's alright to go to work with green nails?' And you realized that people were just disgusted! Your nails should be red. You should be wearing a little bit of make-up and nice heels. So, I got into this very anti-make-up, very natural look. I also explored men's clothing for women. I thought that men's clothing was so much more practical and comfortable, with pockets and stuff. So, that was another one of my looks. That was at the beginning of my styling career.

PC: What is styling?

CB: My work is known as styling. Styling is essentially 'putting things together'. You wouldn't just get the whole look turning up from the couturier, from the designer. I would get the pieces of clothing and put them together. I was really into the idea of thick socks and things like legwarmers. This was when designers copied my looks, especially the army looks I shot with Helmut Newton; the next year I went to Paris and the army look became fashionable. And then I was really known for 'piling on', for layering clothes. This was why Benetton hired me. This was 'styling'. And the legwarmers and the gloves and wearing things inside out and tying things on. I really got into wearing things that didn't fit, which then became that whole '80s look with the big shoulders. I loved the idea of enormous shoulders and put huge pads into t-shirts when I was styling. And the huge trousers. I used to just dress models in men's clothing. Of course, men's clothes are enormous on women, so we'd put a huge gold belt on them and wear them with gold high heels. I'd make tiny waists. Whether the thing fitted or not didn't really matter.

That's also styling. So that was the birth of styling, really, working with clothing, manipulating clothing. Because when you work with designer clothing it arrives from the designer and you're not supposed to mix. If you've got a Chanel look, you do not put the high street clothes with it, or you do not put a Calvin Klein t-shirt with it. There are rules. And the designers have very strong power over the magazines because they will just take their advertising out if you don't do what they say. And I think that was where the styling came from; it was when everybody realized 'It's just getting dressed.' There are so many creative people out there doing things with clothing. All these bloggers now, what do they do? They just get dressed.

Mitzi Lorenz

20 February 2020, Hastings, East Sussex

Philip Clarke (PC): What were your first experiences of styling work?

Mitzi Lorenz (ML): I was going out to nightclubs from a very young age, and usually gay nightclubs. My mum allowed me to go because [DJ and music producer] Mark Moore used to drive me and get me home in a taxi. I was only fourteen, but I was allowed to go if I went with him because he'd chaperone me and he was very polite to my mum, so she trusted him. So, I was hanging out with, I guess, the popstars of the day. My friend [Kay Montano] at school wanted to be a make-up artist, go to college and work for the BBC. And I said, 'Oh, fuck all that, come and hang out with me. I'll find you work as a make-up artist', because I knew I had a lot of friends in fashion and music. I got her to do the make-up for [pop group] Haysi Fantayzee and then I asked some photographers to give her work. I felt like I had to be loyal to her because I'd kind of suggested she leave school with me. We went to see Jamie Morgan, a photographer who was working with Haysi Fantayzee. It was just down the road from their studio, where I used to hang out, in Cleveland Street, in the West End. So, I went down there with Kay and met Jamie and we got on really well. I loved the whole environment; I'd been to music studios, and I'd wanted to be a music producer before that, but it was the first time I'd gone into a photographic studio. Even though I'd done a bit of modelling before, I hadn't done it in the studio. I got really excited about the whole set-up, the creative space, the scene, the lighting, the equipment, the make-up room and understanding how you manipulate an image. That was exciting to me. The energy of the place was really cool. Jamie had to go and photograph a band so he asked me to stay and answer the phones. I was just left in control of the studio and really enjoyed it. I was taking calls, deliveries were coming, I was in my element.

Then we arranged to do some test pictures for Kay, and I was living in a squat already by then and [model] Amanda Cazalet lived next door. She was beautiful, but she wasn't modelling yet, she was just a girl in a squat. We did some pictures, and I chose all the models, and I had an idea of the interesting people we should photograph. I was into clothes, so I had lots of things and I brought them to the studio; I just wanted to make the pictures nicer. I was just trying to zhuzh them up a bit. And then Ray [Petri] was living with Jamie in Great Portland Street. He actually lived next door in Jamie's sister's flat, he shared a flat with her. Ray was [the photographer] Roger Charity's agent at the time. So, Ray was also trying to make the pictures more interesting as well, so he was a clothes nerd and had a large collection. So, we used to just go in the studio and try and better the pictures.

That was how the styling started. It was just about interesting looks. That's where we were coming from. It was about image-making rather than just photographing. It was about trying to put a character in and actually say something, express ourselves through the image that was being made. I guess other photographers were doing that, but it wasn't done with clothing, styling, that way of sending a message through the image. A fashion editor's job was to cover designers, or the magazine had to please their advertisers, and what we were doing was nothing about advertising or design. That's really the heart of styling: it's not about clothes, it's not about selling frocks – it's about conveying a message to your audience. And that was the exciting bit for us. When I walked into the studio and that excitement I felt. The *manipulating*. And that's how it developed. We all lived together and moved to a house in Primrose Hill. So, me, Jamie and Ray, we lived together and that meant that our mornings, our evenings, our nights, we would sort of live and breathe image-making. And talk about it. Our social lives were very much about going out to clubs and having a look for the night, and a different look every time we went out. Basically, what we were doing in the nightclubs, what I would be experimenting with in terms of looks and finding interesting, different things to make an outfit, we just started doing in the studio on people.

PC: You were one of the founding members of Buffalo. How did that come about?

ML: It wasn't called Buffalo at the beginning, it was me as Jamie's girlfriend and Ray as Jamie and Roger's agent. Then, very early on I worked with Mark Lebon and Brett Walker and I actually didn't work that much with Jamie even though I was his girlfriend; I had sort of teamed up with other people. There was Eamonn McCabe, Jean-Jacques Castres from Paris and different people in Japan, but the first job we did, that was me, Jamie and Ray was for Levi's and that was very early on. It was a campaign, I think it was called 'We Cut Our Jeans the Way You Cut Your Hair' and it featured Cuts Hairdressers, which at that time was in Kensington High Street. James Lebon [Mark Lebon's brother] was doing the hair. That was at the very beginning when I had first met Jamie. We had just done those tests and he wanted me to be in the pictures, and I refused to do it. He couldn't understand why: it was quite well paid and everything. I wouldn't do it, but I said that I would find the people for him. So, I ended up doing the casting for the girls and Ray did the casting for the men. And the casting was part of the styling, finding people that looked good, that worked, they were like characters. But they had to have the look, it wasn't just the face – it wasn't even to do with personality – it was about the *look*. So, I found all the punky girls and that was my first ever job with Buffalo, as art director, or casting director/stylist.

All the time I worked with Buffalo, but I also worked by myself. So, when I was in Japan, that was nothing to do with Buffalo; in Paris and Germany, it was nothing to do with Buffalo. London was. Buffalo was more than just a label, it was an aesthetic, the feel of it. Buffalo, to me, is inside me. A lot of it came from my childhood. The two stylists were me and Ray, and there was a group of photographers. The photographers didn't have anything to do with the styling, so that would really just be me and Ray. It was based on certain things, it had certain elements that made it Buffalo. It was about being collective, eclectic and gathering certain things. You sort of sourced the best things from each place. It wasn't just about clothes. It had a Jamaican element and that was from my upbringing in Notting Hill. None of the others came from those kinds of backgrounds. My end was the punk; none of others were into that. But Ray's style was classic. He grew up in Scotland and he was Scottish. He understood gentlemen's clothing and loved all those rules around like how many buttonholes you have, and how you leave the last button open, how you tuck things. He really knew that, and he made us do things like shine our shoes and stand straight; he was quite strict. His parents were that way. So, he knew all things classic, and I was this little street, ragga, punk chick. So, it combined those two things, then it also had kind of gangster, hard, tough aspect, which was very Notting Hill. So yeah, it was just a combination of two things really.

When I met Ray, all the things he found exciting, I'd come from those places and grown up with those things. I remember when Mark Lebon said, 'Ray introduced me to reggae music' and I laughed, because I grew up with reggae music. It was kind of funny. Because they'd had a, not a sheltered background, but they were not street kids. They were sent to school somewhere in the country, a vegetarian, kind of hippie boarding school. Quite bohemian backgrounds. I guess they had quite wild parents. Even though I came from nutty Notting Hill, my parents were quite straight and quite formal. Whereas they had formal upbringings but with crazy parents. Not crazy but a bit wild. Mine were really not like that. Ray's family were also super-straight. Like *beyond* straight. That's why he ran away from all that. His family then emigrated to Australia when he was fifteen and that's when he started doing music. He was in a band called the Chelsea Set. He was very influenced by street style and things like that; he was more street than the others, but he was definitely *not* street. He used to have suits sent from London in the 1960s when he was in his band, and they would be [London tailor] Tommy Nutter. He was very clued up. When he was about seventeen his family then moved to Zimbabwe, and he didn't want to. So, him and his girlfriend went to London and his family went to Zimbabwe. Zimbabwe did have an effect on him in terms of African style and he was very attracted to Black guys. He was in a heterosexual relationship then, but he told me his first ever [gay] experience was on that boat on the way out. And the girlfriend didn't mind if he had boyfriends; she minded if he had girlfriends. It was very laid back. He went to London, which I think it was very mod at the time. He was very much aware of what was going on in style but he wasn't a street kid. Buffalo was a mix of classic and street and, I guess, style movements. You've got a little bit of mod in there; you've got a little bit of skinhead in there as well.

PC: What types of jobs were you doing yourself?

ML: Very good ones actually. *L'Uomo Vogue*, that was in Italy. There was a French magazine I did it with a German photographer called Giovani Castel, which was through Caroline Baker. That was like one of my first solo jobs: I went straight in at the deep end. I did that test for the make-up thing [with Kay Montano], but I didn't really do much testing. Most of the things I did were published. One of the first things I did was *i-D* and it got the cover as well. Then there was *Per Lui*, lots of Japanese magazines, and there were some other German magazines, I can't remember their names, but they were quite big German magazines. So, yeah, I did quite a lot then. I did a fashion show in Japan, I did quite a lot of advertising in Japan as well. Japan was good for the money work, and Germany was great for that too. I always felt like I didn't want to compromise my art if you like. So, I felt like the magazines were like my showcase for my art and I got to control it. We'd call up and say 'I've got a ten-page story coming in', and they'd just give us the date. They wouldn't ask what was in it, they didn't get involved in any of that. Nowadays they do, but they left it to us because they didn't feel that they should have any input. They were advertising people, they were magazine people, they didn't have that kind of sense, they just asked us how many pages. That was a nice position to be in and I didn't want to compromise any of that. I would just do what I wanted in the editorials and have advertising from Germany and Japan to give me my bread and butter. I did a lot of music in London, which paid really well.

PC: Who else was styling at that time?

ML: There were people who had been styling for years, but most of them were fashion editors rather than freelance stylists. From my memory, in the early 1980s it was me and Ray, Simon Foxton and Iain Webb. Caroline Baker was definitely around doing it, but she wasn't a stylist in the way we were. So, really all the stylists like us happened after us. Joe McKenna happened later because I remember when he came onto the scene. Caroline Baker and Michael Roberts were early days, but Michael was at *Tatler* as a fashion editor. Sarajane Hoare – she was around but she was also more of a fashion editor, I think she was at *Harper's Bazaar*, one of those high-end ones. Debbi Mason, I think Debbi was at *Tatler*. Amanda Grieve was at *Harper's Bazaar*. Hamish Bowles was also at *Harper's Bazaar*. So that was a very, very different thing to what we were doing, that was like *Vogue* style. Their role was to make nice pictures of the designers that were being advertised in the magazine using just their clothes head to toe, maybe adding a hat or a shoe or a pair of tights that were not by that designer. So, what we were doing was a completely different thing, we were making looks out of everything. A bit more Andy Warhol-style. Eclectic, arty, piecing it together. And creating not just a look but an attitude. Buffalo was an attitude. Even though the pictures were different every time, there was something that held all the way through and that was the attitude.

A fashion editor's role is to make nice pictures of the clothes that are being advertised in the magazine by the designer, and a stylist has got nothing to do with that at all. When we first worked you couldn't even tell the designer what you were doing. It would be annoying if you had to go all the way to Paris to get their clothes, and you just want the trousers, but you have to get the whole thing: the shoes, the socks, the jacket, the shirt, the tie, the overcoat, the hat, the whole thing. If you told them you only wanted the trousers, they wouldn't give it to you. I would make things myself and buy things in markets, funny things that shouldn't even be on clothes. They were like props, just making it visually good, but they had to convey the message, whatever the theme of your picture was. Whatever was cool. 'Cool' is the best word I can think of, but actually within that there was a lot more to it. They had to be attractive and desirable, so maybe cool is the best word to describe that.

PC: You also make clothes. How does that differ from styling?

ML: Well, when I was twelve years old, I went to dress-making school, an adult dress-making school, and I really loved it. So, I'm very good at it, and I did a pattern-cutting course when I had a baby. I just did a couple of evenings a week and then I worked from home. Most of it I taught myself, but I did train with [fashion designer] Matthew Williamson's pattern cutter who was very good. And then I did a few computer courses to learn CAD design. It's a really slow process, but I really enjoy the craft. So, I think of styling and design as art because to me it is all the same thing. My son has just done a Fine Art degree and I watched him do it and it seems like the same process. The pattern cutting, if you're draping on a stand, that's the craft. I really love that. I love having my rulers and my pencils and paper on the floor and I listen to classical music and it's quiet and I can't have anyone else around. I can't be disturbed at all. And that's how I like to work; it's a very different from being a stylist where you're out and about with a million people. Styling is like the kind of end result, the kind of glamorous, exciting, 'let's all go out and be fabulous' part of it. I used to find it often frustrating working with other people because I would have my vision and I wanted it to just be that, or sometimes I felt let down by the final image and the photography, like they weren't really following what I wanted. Or people were unreliable, and I had to wait for them – I used to find it annoying. Whereas, when I design it's just me and my time.

PC: Do you still collaborate with people?

ML: Yeah, but I do most of the work by myself. I did that as a stylist anyway, I used to start off by myself and then when I had everything ready then the photographer would be involved on the day of the shoot. But most of it was prep so that was very much alone. It would start with an image, a vision – for me anyway. I would have a vision of the whole thing. I would see the picture and then it's like working from the outside in. I would see the final result and then I would think who would be the best photographer to do it and then what clothes. It would really be that way round. So, the same way that I used to do the styling as the image first, with the design I actually see a fashion show and I see models walking down the runway, the music, the lighting, the whole show. And then I sort of bring it down to the pieces at the end, so that's how I tend to work. But then other times it can be spontaneous, so styling is exciting because you've done all that prep work and you've got everything ready, and if you're working with someone really good then it goes somewhere completely different to where you intended, somewhere better, if it's a good photographer. So that's exciting, I like that.

Mark Lebon, was probably the person I collaborated with the most, in the early days, definitely. But different times, different people, like Eamonn McCabe, who's become a good friend here [in Hastings]. I've just recently met him again and I hadn't seen him for thirty years. But there was a period where it was me and Eamonn. Then there was Enrique Badulescu in the 1990s, it would've been more him. Then there were some people that I only occasionally worked with, but it went really well, like [Jean-Baptiste] Mondino. Brett Walker was one of my favourites; I worked with him at the very beginning and have more recently as well. There was a period where I only wanted to work with Brett. I did a shoot with Mark not that long ago and it was really lovely. It was of Don Letts for *Jocks and Nerds* magazine. [Mark and I] hadn't worked together for years but it was so nice. Just remembering how well we jelled together, just like being your right arm.

David Bradshaw

11 July 2023, Kings Cross, London

Philip Clarke (PC): When did you become a stylist?

David Bradshaw (DB): I had no idea what a stylist was. I'd studied civil engineering at Brighton but soon realized I didn't have the aptitude, or patience, to make a career of that. While I was studying, I'd been introduced to the fashion illustrator John Babbage. John used to illustrate for *Vogue* – I've got *Vogue*s from the 1980s with his work in – at a time when fashion illustration was more important in the business. He introduced me to a more creative life. I was his agent for a year or so, which is how I first encountered the world of magazines. My appointments with the magazines would always be with the art directors. An art director introduced me to Jonathan Obadia, who was launching a men's magazine called *Unique*, a trade-focused glossy that I soon started selling advertising for. *Unique* was based above the Woodhouse store on Oxford Street, and this job got me out and about in the West End, talking with menswear agents and retailers. If they agreed to buy a page of advertising, I'd take a few pieces of their menswear to a studio, usually at Eamonn McCabe's on Old Street, and he'd shoot the clothes on a model. To me this was simply how I went about my business. It was a hair stylist I regularly worked with that explained to me what was really happening and said 'You should be a stylist.' It sounded like a simple enough thing to do so I naively said, 'Sure, I could do that' and together we went about putting my first portfolio together by tearing out pages from *Unique* we agreed I'd 'styled'. Timing-wise, this coincided with the start of *Arena* magazine. I'd been quite proud of what we were managing to put together with *Unique*, but I knew that *Arena*, with the work of stylists like Simon Foxton, Marcus von Ackerman, Paul Frecker and Ray Petri, was on another level. I think it was particularly seeing Ray Petri's work in *Arena* that made me very determined to become a stylist. I understood that if I wanted to be a 'proper' stylist I had to work for *Arena*.

I'd been used to connecting with magazines via their art director, so I headed to Neville Brody's studio on Tottenham Court Road with my portfolio, and a lot of naïve confidence. I knocked on the door and announced that I'd like to meet Neville. They understandably said, 'Well, who are you?' I introduced myself and said I wanted to be a stylist for *Arena* and was here to show Neville my portfolio. It wasn't possible to see him, but they said I could leave my book and come back for it tomorrow. I returned the following day, and they just gave it back, with no comment whatsoever. I obviously needed to up my game, so I started testing with young photographers and working on stories I thought were perfect for the magazine. Testing, for people who don't know, is where you have an idea for a shoot, you find a team that will do it and you find clothes to do it with. You put together an editorial that you think suits the magazine you are approaching, in this case *Arena*. I'd take them over to Neville's and go through the same procedure: leave it there, come back tomorrow, no comment. This happened a few times, but I never let it deter me as I felt the work was getting better, that I was growing as a stylist.

Sure enough, the day came when I was invited in. So, I went into the space and had been told not to speak. And there were Neville and his team, and they were laying out the next issue of *Arena* on the floor. These huge prints, which I later found out were by Norman Watson, and they were styled by Ray. A tap on the shoulder a few minutes later and I was outside again but energized, realizing this was good, thinking Neville believed in me; I just needed to up my game even more. My next test was my first story published in *Arena* [issue 7]. I'll never forget how great that made me feel.

I then did another test at Repton Boys Club in Bethnal Green. There was a tradition of boxing in my family, and it was one of the venues I'd be taken to as a kid. I think a lot of the men I encountered in these places, as well as my dad, my uncles and older cousins, all influenced the way I styled men back then – sheepskins, heavy boots and baggy jeans or bib 'n' braces and flat caps, from their work as window cleaners and market traders. It was a look I thought was really good, but that you didn't see that much in fashion magazines. I think it made my work a little bit distinctive. I'd like to think it did.

My Repton story coincided with an exhibition of Neville's work at the V&A and last minute he included a few pages from it in the show. I stood next to my work throughout the private view, feeling so incredible, experiencing a rush like no other, and on that same night was introduced to Ray. I remember feeling intimidated by him and his brilliance, but he was incredibly charming and very complimentary about my work, saying 'It's good. You should keep it up.' Ray's work and that whole Buffalo thing was so influential, and still is to this day. I think he's the best stylist ever: he's *the* stylist. That styling didn't really exist before him. He didn't have that long but I think that every single thing he did was amazing. It was all amazing. Who knows what would have happened if he'd continued his career into the 1990s?

I think that even though I was contributing regularly to *Arena*, the next story was my first commissioned one. Dylan Jones called me and said he'd like me to do a shoe story with Jurgen Teller, a young photographer who had just walked into the office. We had a model for one day. I remember one image, in particular, which we shot at the Metropolitan Works, on Kingsland Road, which at the time was a no-man's land. I used a John Moore shoe. I'd just been introduced to John Moore, around the corner at the House of Beauty and Culture. Another place that somebody had to tell me about. The shoes were so extraordinary, I didn't think they belonged on feet. I planned to use them as a hat, but in the end, I tied the laces together to make them long and attached the John Moore shoe to the face of the model, and Jurgen took a picture. That picture was so powerful. It created such a reaction. Back then, *Arena* would have a letters page and so many people wrote in to say how disturbed they were by that image. It gave me a lesson on the power of imagery, which I think is a really important lesson to learn when you're a young stylist.

By 1989 I was a regular contributor to *Arena* and trying my best to get paid work through my agent, Beverley Streeter at Lynne Franks. However, making money styling was tough, so I continued to work with my dad, uncles and cousins cleaning windows and offices in the city, doing whatever I had to do to have a few quid in my pocket. At *Arena* I was working with Norman Watson, whose work with Petri had so inspired me, and he introduced me to his agent, Camilla Lowther, who agreed to represent me, which was a massive step up and I soon began getting regular well-paid styling jobs with Next Directory. Next Directory was big at the time. Those early directories are quite remarkable things. I think, if you find them, they're worth quite a bit of money now. They would be full of proper fashion photographers doing catalogue work. I became a bit of a go-to menswear stylist for Next Directory. Then I began to work for Wrangler at a time when they were trying to keep up with Levi's. They commissioned the same director as the successful Levi's ad – the one with Nick Kamen in the launderette – Roger Lyons, to do a Wrangler ad. Because I'd been doing bits and pieces for Wrangler, I got onto that campaign. It was shot in New York. It was a big project for me, a big job. The first time I'd really experienced a production so huge. And it was a decent payday. My shoots for *Arena* became evermore ambitious and sophisticated. I started representing the magazine at the men's shows in Paris and Milan, standing at the back at Yohji Yamamoto, wondering how I'd ever make it to the front row. I didn't have to wait long because *Arena* was becoming ever more influential, and we were entering the 1990s and the fashion world was about to explode.

PC: Have you worked with fashion designers?

DB: I started working with Katherine Hamnett in 1991, first on her menswear collections and shows and later on her womenswear too. It was my first experience of adapting my styling ideas to a designer collection and I began by doing 'my thing' and introducing her to the style of my South-East London kinfolk: camel coats, 'stay-pressed' and Chelsea boots. I loved working with Katherine because she was both creative and provocative and she encouraged me to be the same. I learned so much from her, particularly about the art and the chaos of a fashion show. We'd have an early morning slot in Milan and the collection inevitably wouldn't arrive until late the night before, which meant us all working fully through the night. She also taught me about the *theatre* of the fashion show and how to wrap looks in a concept that would elevate them. She'd say 'It's an early morning show, let's wake everybody up.' I've always benefited from people, important people, believing in me and my work. I first met Gabriella Forte when she worked in London for Giorgio Armani. She'd tell me she loved my work at *Arena* and wanted to introduce me to Mr Armani. Gabriella moved to New York to work at Calvin Klein and in 1996 I was invited to meet Calvin in New York, which was a career changing moment for me. In his office adorned with pages from magazines, with the work of young photographers like David Sims, Mario Sorrenti and Glen Luchford, we agreed I'd now work on his menswear.

Around the same time, Karla Otto introduced me to Jil Sander, who was at the time the hottest designer on the planet. We agreed I'd help her develop her first ever men's collection. So, I spent a lot of the latter part of 1996 between Jil's showroom at Piazza Castello, Milan, and her menswear factory in Gubbio, in Perugia. We'd be travelling together in the back of a Mercedes and talking about things like the White Garden at Sissinghurst. I learned so much from Jil, particularly about the obsessiveness and rigour of fashion, the meticulous consideration of every single detail. I remember January 1997 being a big month for me. I flew to New York to style my first Calvin Klein show, which was the first time I would work with KCD. They produced the show and showed me methods and mechanics of process I would use in every other fashion show I ever did. I really enjoyed working with Calvin and he made it quite clear the feeling was mutual. The show was a great success. I left for Milan and the Jil Sander show. Piazza Castello 1 is a relatively small space, and everyone wanted to see Jil's first men's show, so there were two shows in quick succession. They were both met with thunderous applause. I was learning how important that moment was, when the designer stepped out at the end of a show. I'd listen for how much noise the audience made and felt a release of energy and emotion backstage. Impossible to control, and totally intoxicating. The next day in Milan I was back to representing *Arena* and also *Arena Homme Plus*, which had been launched in 1994. So, I was doing appointments and going to other shows. One of my first appointments the day after was at Prada. At the time the menswear was the responsibility of Neil Barrett. It was a one-rail presentation in a showroom. Nothing like a show. Just one rail of clothes. I went to that appointment. I met Neil; I'd never met him before. And Neil said, 'Mr Botelli wants to meet you', and I had no idea who he was. Neil told me he was 'the boss'. The three us were soon gathered in a corridor adjacent to the showroom. The first thing Mr Botelli said to me, with Neil translating, was, 'You used to be a boxer,' and I said 'That's right, how do you know?' He said he could tell. The second thing Mr Botelli said to me, through Neil, was 'Next season, you're working for me.' I said something about being flattered but sorry to say I was already committed. As he turned away, he said 'We shall see.' I met Miuccia soon after and worked at Prada for the next thirteen seasons. On the first ever, and all of the following, men's shows. Then on the women's shows too, then on Miu Miu, then we launched Prada Sport and Miu Miu menswear. I worked on all the corresponding campaigns and spent a great deal of time in Milan and elsewhere working for the house, and it was a great, great pleasure. I left Prada in 2005. After Prada I went back to Calvin Klein, this time to work with Italo Zucchelli. I did a season at Alexander McQueen with Lee, and a couple with Tom Ford, before signing a contract with Versace where I helped Donatella with her menswear and a relaunch of Versus. It felt like I could put everything I'd learned through my years working on shows into these shows with Donatella. They were a pure and undiluted celebration of everything wonderful and glorious about the house of Versace.

PC: You've been a freelance stylist and worked as a fashion editor for magazines. What's the difference between the two roles?

DB: There isn't a straightforward definition of what a stylist is but at the heart of it are ideas, attitudes and opinions that all relate to taste. As a stylist you're always challenged to know and to state and be confident about what you like. Miuccia said to me 'We don't always know why we like the things we like', and I took that to mean she wasn't particularly interested in why I liked the things I brought to her attention, vintage samples and books, or the work of a young photographer. But I was convinced somehow that my taste would ensure they would be of interest to her and have a certain relevance to the conversation of the moment. Her attitude gave me great confidence to express myself creatively, and she encouraged a pure uncontained creativity that encompassed everything: art, music, film, theatre, even opera. She'd say 'David, you should learn more about more things so we can put it all into our work together.' As a fashion editor I'd probably attended more than a hundred fashion shows before I worked on my first as a stylist. For the record, I much prefer working on them than attending them, but as a fashion editor of a magazine it's an essential duty to represent your magazine at the shows, in London, New York, Paris, Milan and elsewhere. For years this is what I did, and by doing so I accepted my part within the processes of fashion. Magazines need advertisers and advertisers want editorial. I learnt that in my *Unique* days, and as a fashion editor you need to ensure there's a balance in your work between representing a particular moment of style and sensibilities, against the need to represent the interests of the brands that advertise in the magazine.

There's something fundamental to styling that can't be taught. Something supplementary to its processes and mechanics, to do with taste and experience and how the culmination of so much decision-making sharpens your sensibility. Trying to see and understand the bigger picture and culture of where your styling is taking place – whether that's a magazine environment, in a studio, on location, with a model or a celebrity, for a fashion show, or in a designer studio – is essential and what separates successful stylists from jobbing, journeyman ones. As an engineer I was taught to be thorough and pragmatic and essentially not to take risks; everything was tested and proven by mathematical theory. Releasing myself from my constrictions was a slow and methodical process, a slow-release creativity that I'll admit resulted in some awkward and uptight work during my early days, but I always approached things with the focus and precision and conviction of an engineer. When I first started working at Prada, Miuccia would introduce me to the various teams I'd go to work with by saying 'This is David, he's my engineer.' I'm not an artist, I'm a creative. The difference being my creativity is applied. I'm not just starting with a blank canvas. I've always known that I've got something to say or achieve with a project, whether that's an editorial project or a show, an advertising campaign. The more I know what that is, the more set those parameters are, the better I perform. I think that goes back to the pragmatist in me being an engineer. Being an engineer requires a certain degree of pragmatism. It's different from being an architect. An architect dreams the dreams, the engineer makes sure it doesn't fall down.

PC: Do you still enjoy your job?

DB: I do, yes. I make sure I do by keeping things challenging and exciting. I'm still freelance, and always have creatively interesting projects to do. When I'm not working, I spend time organizing my archive of samples, books and magazines from decades of working in fashion. I'm back on the masthead of *Arena Homme Plus* and I'm proud to have my name on editorials in the magazine alongside a completely new generation of photographers and creative talent, and I still approach each project wanting this one to be the best I've ever done. I feel that's the least I can do for the sake of my creativity, the magazine, the young people I'm working with, and the business I love.

BIBLIOGRAPHY

Adamson, G. and J. Pavitt (2011), *Postmodernism: Style and Subversion 1970–1990*, London: Harry M. Abrams.

Alderson, M. (1986), 'The Stylistics', *Honey* (February): 42–4.

Alpers, S. (1987), 'Style is What You Make it: The Visual Arts Once Again', in B. Lang, *The Concept of Style*, New York: Cornell University Press.

Anscombe, I. (1978), *Not Another Punk Book*, London: Arum Press.

Anyan, J. and P. Clarke (2011), 'The Role of the Stylist in Hypermodern Image-making', in *Fashion Colloquia*, London: Process Arts, http://process.arts.ac.uk/sites/default/files/jennifer-anyan--clarke.pdf

Armour, G. (2010), *Fashion Stylist: A How To Guide*, San Francisco: Creative Space.

Baker, C. (2017), interview by Philip Clarke, 13 January.

Barnard, M. (2002), *Fashion as Communication*, London: Routledge.

Barnard, M (2007), *Fashion Theory: A Reader*, London: Routledge.

Barnes, R. (1979), *Mods!*, London: Plexus Publishing.

Baron, K. (2012), *Stylists: New Fashion Visionaries*, London: Laurence King.

Barr. A and P. York (1982), *The Original Sloane Ranger Handbook*, London: Ebury Press.

Barthes, R. (1967), *The Fashion System*, London: University of California Press.

Barthes, R. (1977), 'The Death of the Author', in *Image Music Text*, London: Fontana Collins.

Barthes, R. (2009), *Mythologies*, London: Vintage Classics.

Bartlett, D., S. Cole and A. Rocamora (2013), *Fashion Media: Past and Present*, London: Bloomsbury.

Bauman, Z. (1992), 'A Sociological Theory of Postmodernity', in M. Drolet (ed.), *The Postmodern Reader*, London: Routledge.

Bauman, Z. (1995), *Life in Fragments: Essays in Postmodern Morality*, Oxford: Blackwell.

Bauman, Z. (1999), *In Search of Politics*, Cambridge: Polity Press.

Bauman, Z. (2004), *Identity: Conversations with Benedetto Vecchi,* Cambridge: Polity Press.

Bauman, Z. (2011), *Culture in a Liquid Modern World*, Cambridge, Polity Press.

Beard, A. (2013), 'Fun with Pins and Rope: How Caroline Baker Styled the 1970s', in D. Bartlett, S. Cole and A. Rocamora, A. (eds), *Fashion Media: Past and Present*, London: Bloomsbury.

Berman M. (2004), 'All That is Solid Melts into Air', in M. Drolet (ed.), *The Postmodern Reader*, 53–66, London Routledge.

Blaetz, R. (2016), 'The Auteur Renaissance, 1968–1980', in A. L. McLean (ed,), *Costume, Make-up and Hair*, New Brunswick, NJ: Rutgers University Press.

Blame, J. (2016), interview by Gregoir Muir, 1 June, https;//archive.ica.art.bulletin/video/judy-blame-conversation-gregoir.muir/.

Blanchard, T. (2002), 'The Style Council', *Observer*, https://www.theguardian.com/theobserver/2002/nov/17/features.magazine47.

Blaszczyk, R. L. (2000), *Imagining Consumers: Design and Innovation from Wedgewood to Corning*, Baltimore, MD: Johns Hopkins University Press.

Blumer, H. (1969), 'Fashion: from class differentiation to collective selection', *Sociological Quarterly* 10: 275–91.

Bourdieu, P. (1990), *Photography: A Middlebrow Art*, Cambridge: Polity Press.

Bourdieu, P. (1993), *The Field of Cultural Production*, Cambridge: Polity Press.

Bourdieu, P. (2010), *Distinction: A Social Critique of the Judgment of Taste*, London: Routledge.

Bradford, J. (2014), *Fashion Journalism*, London: Routledge.

Bradshaw, D. (2023), interview by Philip Clarke, 11 July.

Braham, P. (1997), 'Fashion: Unpacking a Cultural Production', in P. Du Gay, *Production of Cultures/Cultures of Production*, London: Sage.

Braithwaite, B. (1995), *Women's Magazines: The First 300 Years*, London: Peter Owen Publishers.

Braithwaite, B. and J. Barrell (1988), *The Business of Women's Magazines*, 2nd edn, London: Kogan Page.

Breward, C. (1998), 'Cultures, Identities, Histories: Fashioning a Cultural Approach to Dress', *Fashion Theory* 2, no. 4: 301–14.

Breward, C. (2003). *Fashion*, Oxford: Oxford University Press.

Breward, C., Ehrman, E. and C. Evans (2004), *The London Look*, New Haven, CT: Yale University Press.

Breward, C. (2004), 'Fashion in the Age of Imperialism: 1860-90' – 47–60

Brewer, J. (2013), *The Pleasures of the Imagination: English Culture in the Eighteenth Century*, London and New York: Routledge.

Bryman, A. (2012), *Social Research Methods*, Oxford: Oxford University Press.

Buckley, C. and J. McAssey (2011), *Basics Fashion Design 08: Styling*, Worthing: Ava Publishing

Burke, P. (2009), *Cultural Hybridity*, Cambridge: Polity Press.

Burns-Trans, S. (2013), *Stylewise: A Practical Guide to Becoming a Fashion Stylist*, London: Bloomsbury.

Business of Fashion (2013), 'BOF500: The People Shaping the Global Fashion Industry', https://www.businessoffashion.com/community/bof500/search?collections=1.

Butt Magazine (2011), 'Utterly British Fashion Stylist Hates Fashion', *Butt*, http://www.buttmagazine.com/magazine/interviews/simon-foxton.

C., L. (1986), 'An Englishman in New York', *i-D*, March 1986, 65.

Charity, R. (2018). Interview by Philip Clarke, 13 February.

Clancy, D (2014), *Designing Costume for Stage and Screen*, London: Batsford.

Clarke, J. (1976), 'Style', in S. Hall and T. Jefferson, *Resistance Through Rituals: Youth Subcultures in Post-war Britain*, 175–91, London: Unwin Hyman.

Clarke, P. (2014), 'Styling and stigma: Shifting attitudes to the role of the fashion stylist', paper presented to *Crafting the Look: Styling as Creative Process*, Glasgow School of Art, 24–25 April 2014.

Clarke, P. (2015), 'Stylist vs. photographer: Craft, collaboration or creative control?', paper presented to *Fashioning Professionals*, Victoria and Albert Museum, 27 March 2015.

Clarke, P. (2020), 'Stylist: Etymology and History of a Role', in A. Lynge-Jorlen (ed.), *Fashion Stylists: History, Meaning and Practice*, 21–39, London: Bloomsbury.

Coddington, G. (2012), *Grace: A Memoir*, London: Chatto and Windus.

Coldstream, W. (1970), *The Structure of Art and Design Education in the Further Education Sector, Report of a Joint Committee of the National Advisory Council on Art Education and the National Council for Diplomas in Art and Design*, London: HMSO.

Cole, S. (2000), *Don We Now Our Gay Apparel: Gay Men's Dress in the Twentieth Century*, Oxford: Berg Publishers.

Cole, S. (2020), 'Looking Good in a Buffalo Stance: Ray Petri and the Styling of New Masculinities'. In A. Lynge-Jorlen (ed.), *Fashion Stylists: History, Meaning and Practice*, 135–54, London: Bloomsbury.
Coleridge, N. (1988), *The Fashion Conspiracy*, Oxford: Heinemann.
Collins, S. (2008), *The Hunger Games*, New York: Scholastic.
Collins, S. (2009), *Catching Fire*, New York: Scholastic.
Collins, S. (2010), *Mockingjay*, New York: Scholastic.
Costiff, M. (2022), interview by Philip Clarke, 11 March.
Cotton, C. (2000), *Imperfect Beauty: The Making of Contemporary Fashion Photographs*, London: V&A Publications.
Cox, S. L. (2010), *Photo Styling: How to Build Your Career and Succeed*, London Allwork Press.
Crisp, Q. (1975), *How to Have a Lifestyle*, London: Cecil Woolf.
Culture Compass (2009), 'When you're a Boy', *Culture Compass*, http://www.culturecompass.co.uk/2009/08/28/when-you're-a-boy-men's-fashion-styled-by- simon-foxton/.
Dalzell, T. and T. Victor (2015), *The Concise New Partridge Dictionary of Slang and Unconventional English*, Abingdon: Routledge.
Davies, J. (2004), 'The Future of "No Future": Punk Rock and Postmodern Theory, *Journal of Popular Culture* 29, no. 4: 3–25.
Davis, F. (1992), *Fashion, Culture and Identity*, Chicago: University of Chicago Press.
Degen, N. (2023), *Merchants of Style: Art and Fashion after Warhol*, London: Reaktion Books.
Delineator (1937), 'Presenting Tobé', *Delineator* (April): 24.
Derrick, R. (2017), interview by Philip Clarke, 17 February.
Derrida (2014), *L'Ecriture et la Différence*, Paris: Points.
Dingemans, J. (1999), *How to Master Fashion Styling*, Basingstoke: Palgrave Masters.
Durkin, P. (2009), *Oxford Guide to Etymology*, Oxford: Oxford University Press.
Dyer, R. (2007), *Pastiche*, London: Routledge.
Editors of Time Life Books (1974), *Exotic Styling*, New York: Time Life Inc.
Edwards, R. and J. Ribbens (1998), *Feminist Dilemma in Qualitative Research*, London: Sage.
Edwards, T. (2016), *Men in the Mirror: Men's Fashion Masculinity and Consumer Society*, London: Bloomsbury.
Elliott, P. (1977), 'Media Organisations and Occupations: An Overview', in J. Curran, M. Gurevitch and J. Woollacott (eds), *Mass Communication and Society*, 142–74, London: Edward Arnold.
Elms, R. (1980), 'The Cult with no Name', *The Face* 7 (November): 22–3.
Entwistle, J. (2000), *The Fashioned Body: Fashion, Dress and Modern Social Theory*, Cambridge: Polity Press.
Entwistle, J. (2009), *The Aesthetic Economy of Fashion: Markets and Values in Clothing and Modelling*, London: Berg.
Europa (2003), *The International Who's Who 2004*, Hove: Psychology Press.
Evans, C. (2004), 'Post-war Poses: 1955-1975' – 117–38
Evans, C. (2004), 'Cultural Capital: 1976-2000' – 139–60
Evans C. and M. Thornton (1989), *Women and Fashion: A New Look*, London: Quartet.
Evans, C. (2003), *Fashion at the Edge: Spectacle, Modernity and Deathliness*, London: Yale University Press.
Evans, C. and A. Vaccari (2020), *Time in Fashion: Industrial, Antilinear and Uchronic Temporalities*, London: Bloomsbury.

Featherstone, M. (2007), *Consumer Culture and Postmodernism*, London: Sage Publications.
Flick, U. (2015), *Introducing Research Methodology*, London: Sage.
Flügel, J. C. (1950), *The Psychology of Clothes*, London: Hogarth Press.
Formichetti, N. (2013), Interview with Lou Stoppard for *SHOWstudio*, https://www.showstudio.com/projects/in_fashion/nicola_formichetti?autoplay=1.
Foxton, S. (2010), interview with Simon Foxton, for *SHOWstudio*, http://showstudio.com/project/in_fashion/simon_foxton.
Foxton, S. (2017), interview by Philip Clarke, 3 February.
Franklin, C. (2016), interview by Philip Clarke, 14 December.
Frecker, P. (2018), interview by Philip Clarke, 4 January.
Garfinkel, H. (1967), *Studies in Ethnomethodology*, Englewood Cliffs, NJ: Prentice Hall.
Gartman, D. (1994), 'Harley Earl and the Birth of Styling at General Motors', *Design Issues* 10, no. 2: 3–26.
Geczy, A. and V. Karaminas (2013), *Queer Style*. London: Bloomsbury.
General Motors Styling (1955), *Styling the Look of Things*, Detroit: General Motors.
Golding, Z. (2017), interview by Philip Clarke, 6 February.
Gorman, P. (2017), *The Story of The Face*, London: Thames and Hudson.
Gough-Yates, A. (2003), *Understanding Women's Magazines: Publishers, Markets and Readerships*, London: Routledge.
Granata, F. (2021), *Experimental Fashion: Performance Art, Carnival and the Grotesque*, London: Bloomsbury.
Greenhalgh, P. (2011), 'The End of Style', in G. Adamson and J. Pavitt (eds), *Postmodernism: Style and Subversion 1970–1990*, London: Harry M. Abrams.
Griffiths, D. (2016), *Fashion Stylist's Handbook*, London: Lawrence King.
Grumbach, D. (1993), *History of International Fashion*, Northampton, MA: Interlink.
Gunning, T. (1991), *D. W. Griffiths and the Origins of American Narrative Film: The Early Years at Biograph*, Urbana and Chicago: University of Illinois Press.
Gurr, R. H. (1955), *Automobile Design: The Complete Styling Book*, Arcadia, CA: Dan R. Post Publications.
Hall, D. (1982), 'Zee Makes Dreams Come True', *Cosmopolitan* (November): 192–5.
Hall, S. (1982), *Formations of Modernity*, Cambridge: Polity Press.
Hall, S. and T. Jefferson (1976), *Resistance Through Rituals: Youth Subcultures in Post-war Britain*, London: Unwin Hyman.
Hayes, M. (1994), *The New Right in Britain: An Introduction to Theory and Practice*, London: Pluto Press.
Hebdige, D. (1979), *Subculture: The Meaning of Style*, London: Routledge.
Hebdige, D. (1988), *Hiding in the Light: On Images and Things*, London: Routledge.
Hello Kitty: Be a Super Stylist (2010), London: HarperCollins.
Hello Kitty Fashion Stylist (2013), London: HarperCollins.
Hewitt, P. (2000), *The Soul Stylists: Six Decades of Modernism – From Mods to Casuals*, Edinburgh: Mainstream Publishing.
Hinton, J. (2017), interview by Philip Clarke, 23 June.
Interview (1977), 'Grace Jones', *Interview* 7, no. 1: 6–7.
Interview (1977), 'Jodie Foster', *Interview* 7, no. 1: 6–7.
Irwin, J. (1977), *Scenes*, Beverly Hills: Sage Publications.
Jameson, F. (1979), in Lyotard, J.-F., *The Postmodern Condition*, Manchester: Manchester University Press.
Jameson, F. (1991), *Postmodernism, or The Cultural Logic of Late Capitalism*, Durham, NC: Duke University Press.

Jameson, F. (1998), *The Cultural Turn: Selected Writings on the Postmodern, 1983–1998*, London: Verso.

Jenss, H. (2016), *Fashion Studies: Research Methods, Sites and Practices*, London: Bloomsbury Academic.

Jobling, P. (1999), *Fashion Spreads: Word and Image in Fashion Photography Since 1980*, Oxford: Berg.

Johnson, W. (1928), *Gilbert White: Pioneer, Poet, and Stylist*, Grand Rapids, MI: J. Murray.

Jones, D. (1984), 'The Challenge', *i-D* 17 (July/ August): 28–37.

Jones, D. and N. Logan (1989), 'Obituary: Ray Petri', *The Face* (October): 10.

Jones, S. (2017), interview by Philip Clarke, 12 April.

Jones, T. (1987), *The i-D Bible: Every Ultimate Victim's Handbook*, London: Levelprint.

Judy Blame: Never Again (2016), exhibition, ICA, London, 29 June–4 September 2016.

Kawamura, Y. (2006), 'Placing Tokyo on the Fashion Map: From Catwalk to Street Style', in C. Breward and D. Gilbert (eds), *Fashion's World Cities*, London: Berg.

Kawamura, Y. (2012), *Fashioning Japanese Subcultures*, London: Berg.

Kawamura, Y. (2018), *Fashionology*, London: Bloomsbury.

Kawin, B. (2008), 'Authorship, Design and Execution', in B. K. Grant, *Auteurs and Authorship: A Film Reader*, 190–9, London: Wiley Blackwell.

Kelly, A. (2014), 'Advertising', in J. S. Maguire and J. Matthews (eds), *The Cultural Intermediaries Reader*, 67–76, Los Angeles: Sage.

Kelsey, L. (1984), 'Meet Your Cosmo Stylists', *Cosmopolitan* (May): 55–61.

Klein, E. (1967), *Klein's Comprehensive Etymological Dictionary of the English Language*, London: Elsevier.

Kuipers, G. (2014), 'Ethnographic Research and Cultural Intermediaries', in J. S. Maguire and J. Matthews (eds), *The Cultural Intermediaries Reader*, 52–64, Los Angeles: Sage.

Kumar, R. (2014), *Research Methodology: A Step-by-Step Guide for Beginners*, 4th edn, London: Sage.

Kynaston, D. (2012), *City of London: The History*, London: Vintage.

La Motte, R. (2001), *Costume Design 101: The Art and Business of Costume Design for Television and Film*, Los Angeles: Michael Wiese Productions.

Lantz, J. (2016), *The Trendmakers: Behind the Scenes of the Global Fashion Industry*, London: Bloomsbury.

Lash, S. and J. Urry (1987), *The End of Organized Capitalism*, Cambridge: Polity Books.

Lass, R. (2009), *On Explaining Language Change*, Cambridge: Cambridge University Press.

Lee, T. R. (1977), *Race and Residence: The Concentration and Dispersal of Immigrants in London*, Oxford: Clarendon Press.

Levi-Strauss, C. (1994), *The Savage Mind (Nature of Human Society)*, Oxford: Oxford University Press.

Lifter, R. (2018), 'Fashioning Pop: Stylists, fashion work and popular music imagery', in L. Armstrong and F. McDowell (eds), *Fashioning Professionals*, 51–64, London: Bloomsbury.

Lincoln, S. (2013), 'Styling teenage private space: Identity, fashion and consumption in girls' bedrooms', *Film, Fashion and Consumption* 2, no. 2 (1 June): 121–37.

Livingstone, P. (1997), 'Cinematic Authorship', in R. Allen and M. Smith, *Film Theory and Philosophy*, 132–48, Oxford: Oxford University Press.

Llewellyn, N. (2015), *The London Art Schools: Reforming the Art World, 1960 to Now*, London: Tate Publishing.

Lorenz, M. (2000), *Buffalo*, London: Westzone.

Lorenz, M. (2017), interview by Philip Clarke, 17 January.

Lorenz, M. (2020), interview by Philip Clarke, 20 February.

Love, N. (2006), *Language and History: Integrationist Perspectives*, Abingdon: Routledge.

Lurie, A. (1992), *The Language of Clothes*, London: Bloomsbury.

Lynge-Jorlen, A. (2017), *Niche Fashion Magazines: Changing the Shape of Fashion*, London: Bloomsbury.

Lynge-Jorlen, A. (2020), *Fashion Stylists: History, Meaning and Practice*, London: Bloomsbury.

Lynn, V. (1985), 'Summer of the Sari', *Cosmopolitan* (July): 148–55.

Maffesoli, M. (1996), *The Time of Tribes: The Decline of Individualism in Mass Society*, London: Sage.

Maguire, J. S. and J. Matthews (2014), *The Cultural Intermediaries Reader*, Los Angeles: Sage.

Markham, A. (2012), 'Stylist as Mythmaker', paper presented to Oxford University 2nd Global Conference, *Exploring Critical Issues*, September 2012.

Martin, P. (2009), *When You're a Boy: Men's Fashion Styled by Simon Foxton*, London: The Photographer's Gallery.

Mason, D. (2017), interview by Philip Clarke, 5 May.

McCamy, J. C. and J. Presley (1972), *Human Life Styling: Keeping Whole in the Twentieth Century*, New York: Harper & Row.

McCauley Bowstead, J. (2018), *Menswear Revolution: The Transformation of Contemporary Menswear*, London: Bloomsbury.

McGowan, C. (1964), 'Cathy McGowan Takes a Look at the Mod Scene Today', *The Mods Monthly* 7.

McIntyre, P. (2012), *Creativity and Cultural Production: Issues for Media Practice*, London: Palgrave MacMillan.

McLean, L. (2012), *Contemporary Fashion Stylists*, London: Vivays Publishing.

McLellan, J. (1975), *Bodies Beautiful: A History of Car Syling and Craftsmanship*, London: David and Charles.

McRobbie, A. (1994), *Postmodernism and Popular Culture*, London: Routledge.

McRobbie, A. (1998), *British Fashion Industry: Rag Trade or Image Industry?*, London: Routledge.

McRobbie, A. (2007), *Zoot Suits and Second-hand Dresses: An Anthology of Fashion and Music*, London: Macmillan.

McRobbie, A. (2016), *Be Creative*, Cambridge: Polity Press.

Melly, G. (1970), *Revolt into Style: The Pop Arts in Britain*, London: Penguin.

Mercer, K. (1994), *Welcome to the Jungle: New Positions in Black Cultural Studies*, New York: Routledge.

Meyer, L. (1987), 'Toward a Theory of Style', in B. Lang, *The Concept of Style*, New York: Cornell University Press.

Mijovic, N (2013), 'Narrative form and the rhetoric of fashion in the promotional fashion film', *Film, Fashion and Consumption* 2, no. 2 (1 June): 175–86.

Miles, B. (2010), *London Calling*, London: Atlantic Books.

Miller, S. (2018), interview by Philip Clarke, 23 March.

Miller, T. (2014), 'Cultural Work and Creative Industries', in J. S. Maguire and J. Matthews (eds), *The Cultural Intermediaries Reader*, 25–33, Los Angeles: Sage.

Moraru, C. (2011), *Cosmodernism: American Narrative, Late Globalization and the New Cultural Imaginary*, Ann Arbor: University of Michigan Press.

Morgan, J. (2020), interview by Philip Clarke, 16 March.

Mort, F. (1996), *Cultures of Consumption*, London: Routledge.

Mount, H. (2006), 'The Monkey with the Magnifying Glass: Constructions of the Connoisseur in Eighteenth-Century Britain', *Oxford Art Journal* 129, no. 2: 167–84.
Mower, S. (2007), *Stylist*, New York: Rizzoli.
Muggleton, D. (2000), *Inside Subculture*, London: Bloomsbury.
Nadoolman Landis, D. (2012), *Costume Design*, Lewes: Ilex Press.
Nixon, S. (1996), *Hard Looks: Masculinities, Spectatorship and Contemporary Consumption*, London: UCL Press.
O'Byrne, R. (2009), *Style City: How London Became a Fashion Capital*, London: Frances Lincoln.
O'Doherty, B. (1971), 'What is postmodernism?', *Art in America*, https://www.artinamericamagazine.com/news-features/magazines/from-the-archives-what-is- post-modernism/.
Onions, C. T. (1966), *The Oxford Dictionary of English Etymology*, Oxford: Oxford University Press.
O'Reilly, K. (2005), *Ethnographic Methods*, London: Routledge.
Paddison, R. C. (1983), *The New Stylist*, Monk Fryston: Moving Targets.
Panayi, P. (2010), *Immigration History of Britain*, London: Pearson.
Partridge. E. (1958), *Origins: A Short Etymological Dictionary of Modern English*, London: Routledge and Kegan Paul.
Pease, B. (2000), *Recreating Men: Postmodern Masculinity Politics*, London Sage.
Peplow, S. (2019), *Race and Riots in Thatcher's Britain*, Manchester: Manchester University Press.
Petrie, G. (2008), 'Alternatives to Auteurs', in B. K. Grant, *Auteurs and Authorship: A Film Reader*, London: Wiley Blackwell.
Porter, R. (1994), *London: A Social History*, London: Penguin.
Rees, J. and L. German (2012), *A People's History of London*, London: Verso.
Riegels-Melchior, M. (2022), 'In the Changing Room: A Study of the Act of Styling before "Styling" in Danish Fashion, 1900–1965', in A. Lynge-Jorlen, *Fashion Stylists: History, Meaning and Practice*, 41–61, London: Bloomsbury.
Riggle, N. (2015), 'Personal Style and Artistic Style', *Philosophical Quarterly* 65, no. 261: 711–31.
Robinson, D. (1958), 'The Rules of Fashion Cycles', *Harvard Business Review* (November–December).
Rocamora, A. (2009), *Fashioning the City: Paris, Fashion and the Media*, London: IB Tauris.
Rocamora, A. (2011), 'Personal Fashion Blogs: Screens and Mirrors in Digital Self-portraits', *Fashion Theory* 15, no. 4: 407–24.
Rocamora, A. (2016), 'Mediatization and Digital Media in the Field of Fashion', *Fashion Theory* 21, no. 5: 505–22.
Rocamora, A. (2018), 'The Labour of Fashion Blogging', in L. Armstrong and F. McDowell (eds), *Fashioning Professionals*, 65–81, London: Bloomsbury.
Samuel, R. (1994), *Theatre of Memory*, London: Verso.
Samuel, R. (1998), *Island Stories*, London: Verso.
Sardar, Z. (1998), *Postmodernism and the Other*, London: Pluto Press.
Sarris, A. (1985/1962). 'Notes on the Auteur Theory in 1962', in G. Mast and M. Cohen (eds), *Film Theory and Criticism: Introductory Readings*, 3d edn, Oxford: Oxford University Press.
Savage, J. (2005), *England's Dreaming*, London: Faber and Faber.
Sellors, C. P. (2010). *Film Authorship: Auteurs and Other Myths*, New York: Columbia University Press.

Shapiro, D. (2016), *John Vassos: Industrial Design for Modern Life*, London: University of Minnesota Press.
Sharpe, B. (2015), *This Wasn't Part of the Masterplan: Memoirs of a Naughty Boy*, London: Barrie Sharpe.
Sharpe, B. (2017), interview by Philip Clarke, 10 February.
Shore, Z. (2017), interview by Philip Clarke, 16 August.
Silla, C. (2018), *The Rise of Consumer Capitalism in America, 1880–1930*, London: Routledge.
Simmel, G. (1957), 'Fashion', *American Journal of Sociology* 62, no. 6 (May): 541–58.
Skov, L. (2002), 'Hong Kong Fashion Designers as Cultural Intermediaries: Out of Global Garment Production', *Cultural Studies* 16, no. 4: 553–69.
Smedley, E. (2000), 'Escaping to Reality: Fashion Photography in the 1990s', in S. Bruzzi and P. Church Gibson, *Fashion Cultures: Theories, Expectations and Analysis*, 147–56, London: Routledge.
Smith, G. (1983), *Snippets for Saxes: Studies in Dance Band Styling for the Saxophone Section*, London: Studio Music Company.
Smith, G. (2011), *We Can Be Heroes: London Clubland 1976–1984*, London: Unbound.
Smith, G. and W. A. Whitfield (2005), 'The Professional Status of Designers: A National Survey of How Designers are Perceived', *Design Journal* 8, no. 1: 52–60.
Sontag, S. (2018), *Notes on Camp*, London: Penguin Classics.
Spivak, G. C. (2013), *An Aesthetic Education in the Era of Globalisation*. Cambridge, MA: Harvard University Press.
Stanfill, S. (2013), *Club to Catwalk*, London: V&A Publishing.
Steele, V. (1991), 'The F-Word', *Lingua Franca*.
Steiner, H. D (1955), *Crowning Glory*, London: Gerald Duckworth & Co.
Stevens, A. W. (1941), *Highway Safety and Automobile Styling*, Boston: Christopher Publishing.
Stillinger, J. (1991), *Multiple Authorship and the Myth of the Solitary Genius*, Oxford: Oxford University Press.
The Stylist (1905), London: J. J. Keliher & Co
The Stylist (1933), London: The Stylecraft Printing and Publishing Company.
Tasho, E. (1969), *Hair Styling for Women*, Oxford: Pergamon Press.
Taylor, C. (1994), 'The Politics of Recognition', in A. Gutmann (ed.), *Multiculturalism: Examining the Politics of Recognition*, 25–73, Princeton, NJ: Princeton University Press.
Taylor, L. (2002), *The Study of Dress History*, Manchester: Manchester University Press.
Templeton, L. (2022), 'Les Arts Decoratifs Celebrates France's Eclectic '80s in New Exhibition', *WWD*, https://wwd.com/eye/lifestyle/arts-decoratifs-celebrates-frances-eclectic-eighties-exhibition-furniture-fashion-advertising-design-1235388031/.
Thistlewood, D. (2005), 'Curricular Development in Critical Studies', in R. Hickman (ed.), *Critical Studies in Art and Design Education*, Bristol: Intellect.
Tomlinson, J. (2021), 'Deindustrialisation and "Thatcherism": moral economy and unintended consequences', *Contemporary British History* 35, no. 4: 620–42.
Traugott, E. C. and R. Dasher (2002), *Regularity in Semantic Change*, Cambridge Studies in Linguistics 97, Cambridge: Cambridge University Press.
Tulloch, C. (2011), 'Buffalo: Style with Intent', in G. Adamson and J. Pavitt (eds), *Postmodernism: Style and Subversion 1970–1990*, 182–4, London: Harry N. Abrams.
Tulloch, C. (2016), *The Birth of Cool: Style Narratives of the African Diaspora*, London: Bloomsbury, 182–91.

Tunstall, J. (1971), *Journalists at Work: Specialist Correspondents, Their News Organizations, News-sources and Competitor-colleagues*, London: Constable.
Turner, S. (1983), 'A Matter of Style', *Blitz* 16 (November): 24–7.
Van den Akker, R. and T. Vermeulen (2017), 'Periodising the 2000s, or, the Emergence of Metamodernism', In R. van den Akker, A. Gibbons and T. Vermeulen, *Metamodernism: Historicity, Affect and Depth After Postmodernism*, 1–19, London: Rowman and Littlefield.
Vasudevan, A. (2017), *The Autonomous City: Towards a Critical Geography of Cccupation*, London: Verso.
Veblen, T. (2009), *The Theory of the Leisure Class*, Oxford: Oxford University Press.
Volonté, P. (2008), *La vita da stylista: Il ruole sociale del fashion designer*, Milan: Mondadori Bruno.
Volonté, P. (2012), 'Social and Cultural Features of Fashion Design in Milan', *Fashion Theory* 16, no. 4: 339–432.
Volonté, P. (2018), 'The Figure of the Stilista', in M. L. Frisa, *Italiana: Italy Through the Lens of Fashion, 1971–2001*, Venice: Marsilio Editori.
Volonté, P. (2020), 'The Stylist's Trade: Fashion Styling in Milan in an Era of Digitisation', in A. Lynge-Jorlen (ed.), *Fashion Stylists: History, Meaning and Practice*, London: Bloomsbury.
Warkander, P. (2020), 'An Ethnographic Study on Styling Practices at H&M', in A. Lynge-Jorlen (ed.), *Fashion Stylists: History, Meaning and Practice*, London: Bloomsbury.
Wayt, H. C. (2015), 'A Sixties Tour of General Motors Innovative Styling Section', *The Old Moto*, http://theoldmotor.com/?p=147755.
Webb, I. R. (2014), *As Seen in Blitz: Fashioning '80s Style*, London: ACC Editions.
Webb, I. R. (2017), interview by Philip Clarke, 10 May.
Webb. I. R. (2021), *Rebel Stylist: Caroline Baker, The Woman Who Invented Street Style*, London: ACC Art Books.
Weber, M. (1947), *The Theory of Social and Economic Organisation*, Oxford: Oxford University Press.
When You're a Boy: Styled by Simon Foxton (2009), exhibition, The Photographer's Gallery, London, 17 July–4 October 2009.
Wickham, V. (1964), 'Behind the Scenes of the Biggest Mod TV Show Ever! Ready, Steady, Go', *Mod's Monthly* (May): 8.
Wilkinson, D. (2016), *Post-punk, Politics and Pleasure in Britain*, London: Palgrave MacMillan.
Willard Smith, V. (1950), *Nine Lessons in Sewing and Styling*, Durban: Harvey Greenacre & Co.
Williams, V. (1999), *Look at Me: Fashion and Photography in Britain, 1960 to the Present*, London: British Council.
Williams, V. (2004), *When We Were Young: Derek Ridgers – Club and Street Portraits 1978–1987*, London: Photoworks.
Wilson, E. (2009), *Adorned in Dreams: Fashion and Modernity*, London: I.B. Tauris.
Winship, J. (1985), 'A Girl Needs to Get Street-Wise: Magazines for the 1980s', *Feminist Review* 21: 5–46.
Winship, J. (1987), *Inside Women's Magazines*, London: Pandora.
Wollen, P. (1993), *Raiding the Icebox: Reflections on Twentieth Century Culture*, Bloomington: Indiana University Press.
Wollen, P. (1999), *Visual Display: Culture Beyond Appearances*, Berkeley: University of California Press.

Wollheim, R. (1987), 'Pictorial Style: Two Views', in B. Lang, *The Concept of Style*, New York: Cornell University Press.

Yahm, J. J. (1978), *Professional Barber Styling: State Board Exam Review*, Bronx, New York: Milady Publishing Corporation.

York, P. (1980), *Style Wars*, Chichester: Sidgwick and Jackson Ltd.

Zahm, O. (2003), *On the Marked Change in Fashion Photography, in Chic Clicks: Creativity and Commerce in Contemporary Fashion Photography*, Boston: Institute of Contemporary Art.

INDEX